THE FUTURE OF THE FIFTH CHILD

An Overview of Global Child Protection Programs and Policy

Sid Gardner

THE FUTURE OF THE FIFTH CHILD
An Overview of Global Child Protection Programs and Policy

iUniverse books may be ordered through booksellers or by contacting:

iUniverse
1663 Liberty Drive
Bloomington, IN 47403
www.iuniverse.com
1-800-Authors (1-800-288-4677)

ISBN: 978-1-4917-9132-5 (sc)
ISBN: 978-1-4917-9133-2 (e)

Print information available on the last page.

iUniverse rev. date: 03/09/2016

CONTENTS

FOREWORD

This is not a book by a child protection expert or an international policy official. Except for brief periods serving as an intern in the State Department and on a detail from the U.S. Army to USAID, I have worked since 1965 in elected and appointed positions within the U.S. in federal, state, and local government and politics, teaching and staffing a university-based policy center, and as a consultant and advisor to agencies that serve children and families. Our organization, Children and Family Futures, has worked since 1996 with public and private agencies that provide child welfare and substance abuse treatment services to children and families.

Turning from that U.S.-based work to global child protection is based on a conviction, shared by many of the interviewees in this book, that greater progress in global child protection is both urgent and possible. Our organization has approached these issues from outside the arena of global child protection with a growing sense that these issues include important parallels to the work we have done in the U.S. Without in any way underemphasizing the important differences between work in the U.S. and in other nations and cultures, we have come to believe that relative newcomers to this field may offer a detached perspective—one that is informed by our own careers of working across agency boundaries to achieve results for children and families. We have sought to broaden our perspective through interviews with dozens of officials, advocates, and local program operators in several countries, along with an extensive literature review, and travel to China and Turkey.[1]

The conclusions we draw are not intended in any way to diminish the extraordinary efforts of the hundreds of officials of U.S., United Nations, NGO, and other international and civil society agencies who work on child protection issues. Many of these officials have devoted their careers to living and working in developing nations, and their expertise goes far beyond this writer's. In interviewing them and reading their products, I have been greatly impressed with their knowledge, dedication, and perceptiveness. My debt is sizable to each of the officials, advocates, and program staff I interviewed; none of them is responsible for the interpretations I have made of their work or the issues in the child protection field.

The book begins with an introduction that briefly traces the evolution of child maltreatment and protection from prehistoric times to the present, noting the gaps between statements of the exalted status of innocent children who should be protected from harm and the realities of child maltreatment around the world. Chapter Two turns to a definition of the field of child protection, reviewing the challenges in setting clear boundaries around issues that overlap widely with other child-related fields, including child survival, maternal and child health, child development, and child well-being. Chapter Three describes the major players in global child protection, emphasizing the roles of UNICEF, the recently created USAID office on vulnerable children, and the major NGOs and nations that work in this field. Chapter Four describes two very different perspectives on the importance of child protection: its critical impact on children and its relative marginality in the broader arenas of foreign assistance and foreign policy. Chapter Five addresses the difficult questions of the causes of child maltreatment, including poverty, religious and cultural practices, gender inequity and other forms of discrimination, parental addictions, and war and its aftermath. Chapter Six reviews the potential benefits of stronger efforts to coordinate fragmented attempts to improve child protection, In Chapter Seven, eight other proposed remedies for child maltreatment are set forth along with an assessment of their relative effectiveness and potential for impact. Chapter Eight reviews funding options and the prospects of a wider marketing effort for child protection efforts. Chapter Nine is an assessment of the U.S.

governmental role in child protection. Chapter Ten concludes the book with an assessment of the prospects for a global campaign for expanding resources devoted to child protection. An appendix briefly summarizes China's and India's role in child protection.

Throughout the book, the particular issues faced by child protection efforts undertaken by agencies of the U.S. government are at times a focal point, not because of a conviction that the U.S. is necessarily a leader in this field at present, but because the author is more familiar with the U.S. political and administrative landscape. We have also sought to understand and assess other nations' approaches to child protection policy, given the global nature of the problem and its solutions. In addition to the leadership role of the UN, the efforts of the European Union and other international associations of nations are important elements of the global effort to address child protection. Balancing these governmental efforts are the continuing activities of the many NGOs and civil society organizations that make up such a large and critical part of the field of child protection, and we have reviewed their efforts as well.

Each of the problems under the heading of child protection deserves its own book—and many good ones have already been written on these issues, some of which we've cited. This work attempts to bridge across the entire field, and thus seeks breadth rather than depth in any one area. Child protection is fragmented not only in its daily operations, but also in the voluminous material produced by those researching and reporting on it. In a far from exhaustive assessment, we found that the books, reports, and other materials used in researching this book focused on the separate components of child protection—as opposed to the entire field—in a ratio of roughly ten to one. The wealth of materials that address one or two of the many separate problems under the heading of child protection, as defined by UNICEF, appear to dwarf the output that cuts across the entire field.

It may seem an exercise in hubris to undertake such a project without lengthy experience in this field. But alongside whatever hubris may exist, we have acquired a considerable measure of humility as well, recognizing the great challenges of helping hundreds of millions of children to cope with threats to their futures. We hope this product is useful in that critical effort.

Sid Gardner
Lake Forest, California
August 2015

All statements and conclusions, unless specifically attributed to another source, are those of the author and do not necessarily reflect those of any individual interviewee, advisor, sponsor, or the publisher.

INTRODUCTION

In the past decade, considerable progress has been made in spotlighting and responding to the issues of global child protection.[2] Child protection efforts respond to a harsh reality:

One in five of the 2.2 billion children alive has been abused or neglected in ways likely to harm his or her mental, emotional, and physical development and well-being.[3]

In response, the United Nations Children's Fund (UNICEF) and several other United Nations agencies, the U.S. government, many other national governments, non-governmental organizations (NGOs), and thousands of smaller civil society organizations are now working to reduce child maltreatment and improve child protection programs and policy.

The good news includes

- Efforts by the United Nations Children's Fund (UNICEF) to coordinate efforts of UN agencies that address the causes and effects of child maltreatment
- Passage of legislation in the U.S. (PL 109-95) that created a Special Advisor's position responsible for an annual report to Congress on children in adversity and coordination of efforts among U.S. agencies
- Support from U.S.-based and international foundations that expands resources for child protection efforts

- Global surveys that improve data collection on child protection issues, including the annual UNICEF reports on the status of the world's children
- Active involvement by NGOs in operating child protection programs, advocating for greater attention to child protection issues, and working with UN agencies in monitoring national compliance with the UN Convention on the Rights of the Child
- A growing number of programs at the community levels in many nations that rely on local leaders and volunteers, including children and youth, to reduce child maltreatment

But there remain many challenges, some of which undermine the above positive steps, including

- Continuing fragmentation of efforts among national and international agencies which typically operate at the margins of foreign policy with inadequate resources relative to the scale of the problems
- A lack of clarity and consensus about the causes of child maltreatment and how they relate to child survival and poverty reduction efforts
- Few programs that address underlying child protection problems that stem from various forms of addictions and behavioral disorders
- Deep cultural barriers to identifying child abuse, addressing its underlying causes, and treating child protection as a priority
- Inadequate efforts to build the capacity, collect accurate data, and evaluate the impact of grass-roots, village-based prevention efforts targeting child maltreatment
- Weak enforcement by many governments and inadequate transparency of national efforts to comply with the UN Convention on Rights of the Child, including the US failure to ratify the Convention

This book will review these recent efforts and the different approaches used to define and respond to child maltreatment on a global scale.[4] The empirical evidence for progress is assessed, as well as the prospects for reducing barriers to child protection programs and policy and improving outcomes for millions of children and youth.

CHAPTER ONE

Cherishing children: the antecedents and definitions of child protection

> Every culture in the world cherishes its children, yet we
> continue to fail to protect them.[5]

The origins of child protection can be traced deep into history and even pre-history—as can the origins of child maltreatment.

Anthropologists have explored the early signs of the most savage and tragic forms of child maltreatment in rituals of child sacrifice. The Abrahamic religions view Abraham's willingness to sacrifice his son as a critical moment in the history of God's relationship with humans, as James Carroll has described in his recent *Jerusalem, Jerusalem*.[6] Alfred Kahn also discussed infanticide as the ultimate form of child abuse in history.[7] More recently, Steven Pinker, in his book *The Better Angels of Our Nature: Why Violence Has Declined*, seeking to make the case that violence has decreased in human history, included a lengthy section on the decline of infanticide and the rise of children's rights.[8]

Plato, in *The Republic*, argued that children should be removed from their parents and placed in state custody, to be raised in common, less for their protection than as a means of producing the ideal rulers of society without regard for differences in parenting. Rousseau argued that children were

1

born inherently good and are corrupted by the evils of society. However, Rousseau sent all five of his children to orphanages.

Although the first expression of child protection in international law and diplomatic pronouncements came in 1924 with the adoption by the League of Nations of the Declaration on the Rights of the Child,[9] long before this statement, nations, religious organizations, and philosophers had articulated an obligation to care for innocent children who needed protection from harm. Many religions and cultures have valued children as innocents who must be nurtured and protected. But at times, religious motives have also led to treating children as mere property or objects of blind revenge. These texts are reminders of how children have been exalted as the ultimate measures of a society's values—and how far from that standard human history and religious practices have sometimes fallen:

> *Suffer the little children to come unto me, for theirs is the kingdom of heaven.* Mark 10:14

> *At midnight the LORD smote all the first-born in the land of Egypt, from the first-born of Pharaoh who sat on his throne to the first-born of the captive who was in the dungeon.* Exodus. 12:29.

> *A father gives his child nothing better than a good education.* Hadith collected by Tirmidhi and Al-Bayhaqi.

> *If your plan is for one year, plant rice. If your plan is for ten years, plant trees. If your plan is for one hundred years, educate children.* Confucius.

> *A feeling of intimacy toward all other sentient beings, including of course those who would harm us, is generated, which is likened in the literature to the love a mother has for her only child.*[10] His Holiness The Dalai Lama

A literature has emerged that addresses a "theology of childhood," but its emphasis is on children as revelations of divine intention which is unknowable in its ultimate sense. The spiritual life of children is the focus, rather than the need to shelter children from abuse by adults—in some cases in religious institutions.[11] This literature does not appear to address harm to children as a theological concept. A review of a recent book on children and theology, John Berryman's *Children and the Theologians*, states that "in mainstream Christianity, children and childhood, as seen by one of its keenest contemporary historians, were marginal to the point of invisibility."

Later, in Chapter Seven, we discuss the theological basis for the debates about adoption of children and their removal from their own cultural setting.

During the time while this book was being written, the following happened:

- In Israel, an 8-year old girl was called "whore" and verbally abused by ultra-orthodox Jews for the way she dressed when she went to school.
- In Afghanistan, a 10-year old girl was kidnapped and beaten for the misdeeds of her uncle. A 20-year old woman was beheaded by her father for leaving an arranged marriage.
- In the U.S., an ongoing debate about birth control and the morality of sexual behavior was spearheaded by a vastly wealthy religious organization that has for decades shielded pedophile priests from prosecution, while at the same time serving as an articulate and powerful advocate for immigrants and poor children and families.

In its essence, the work of child protection can be viewed as closing the gap between the ideals of nurturing children expressed by many religious and cultural leaders and the continuing realities of harm done to more than one-fifth of all living children. Because some parents, illicit businesses, and others in society are harming children, child protection is needed. And because there are so many different versions of harm being done to children, societies and nations have organized to respond to these different categories of protection, seeking to reconcile our ideals about the lives of children with our practices in raising them.

The gravity of child maltreatment in global settings is deepened by the growing evidence that much of that maltreatment is not only doing deliberate harm to children—it is harm to children that is very often culturally approved and legal, with remedies often blocked by governmental action and inaction. In a 2012 report, a coalition of non-governmental agencies reviewed what were termed "harmful practices based on tradition, culture, religion, or superstition." In a foreword to that report, the head of a UN study on violence against children summed up:

> ...governments in a majority of states across the world are still indulging in justification and compromise... the practices in this depressing but vital report from the international NGO Council is that they are generally perpetrated by parents or others close to children in their communities and they are condoned or actively approved on grounds of tradition, culture, religion, or superstition.[12]

Overcoming the power of those traditions and superstitions is a major part of what the work of child protection seeks to achieve. A portion of that work is highly public, subject to international comparisons, feedback on whether national policies are actually being implemented and enforced, and at times ending up in well-publicized legal action on behalf of children or seeking redress from those who victimize them. But a great portion of that work aims at practices that are virtually invisible, occurring deep within family and clan, involving secrets, stigma, and hidden trauma. Thus child protection has both visible and invisible components, and recognizing the power of both is critical to advancing the cause.

Defining the problem and the field

"Child protection" is a term used very differently in the U.S. and in the rest of the world. In the U.S., *child protective services* is the front end of the *child welfare system*, in which an immediate response is made to a report of child abuse or neglect. "Safety, permanency, and well-being" is how U.S. legislation describes the three primary goals of the child welfare system.

In the U.S., safety is what child protection is most focused upon, for very good reasons.

Internationally, *child protection* has come to mean something different. Best codified by UNICEF, child protection refers to sixteen specific conditions of maltreatment, categorized by type of abuse or neglect in some cases and by the setting of the offense in others, e.g. wartime or humanitarian crises. From UNICEF's website:

> UNICEF uses the term 'child protection' to refer to preventing and responding to violence, exploitation and abuse against children, including commercial sexual exploitation, trafficking, child labour and harmful traditional practices, such as female genital mutilation/cutting and child marriage. Violations of the child's right to protection take place in every country and are massive, under-recognized and under-reported barriers to child survival and development, in addition to being human rights violations.

UNICEF uses sixteen separate categories of child maltreatment to describe the targets of its work of child protection. Some of the most important of those include:

- An estimated 223 million children—10% of the world's children—have been sexually assaulted; this includes 150 million girls and 73 million boys
- More than 115 million children work in hazardous jobs; more than 215 million children aged 5-17 work on a regular basis
- More than 67 million children of elementary school age do not go to school; they are disproportionately girls; the ratio worsens as students enter secondary school[13]
- More than 18 million children had parents who both died; more than 16 million children lost one or both parents due to AIDS
- Only half of the children under 5 years of age in developing nations have their births registered
- Two million children are victims of sex trafficking or pornography[14]

Each of these, combined with the other specific conditions monitored by UNICEF and other organizations, are the focus of programs and funding streams aimed at these conditions.

A thoughtful perspective on child protection as a set of systems was commissioned by UNICEF in 2008. This monograph and a subsequent paper were important correctives to previously fragmented efforts aimed at separate forms of maltreatment which were loosely coordinated under the banner of child protection.[15] As we will see throughout this book, the struggle to link different categorically defined efforts to improve child protection into an integrated system is a continuing challenge.

A somewhat different set of definitions resulted from the legislative initiatives in the U.S. that led to Public Law 109-95, the Assistance for Orphans and Other Vulnerable Children in Developing Countries Act of 2005. The initial impetus for this legislation was concern about children who were left orphans as a result of the HIV/AIDS crisis in Africa, but the definition was widened to include other categories of "highly vulnerable" children, including some but not all of the UNICEF categories. The Action Plan on Children in Adversity issued in 2013 was consistent with the UNICEF framework.

At present, the child protection field is undergoing continuing debates about its boundaries. The most important questions in this debate include

- How does child protection relate to *child survival*; is neglect of basic health and nutritional needs, whether due to poverty, parental, community, or national actions or inactions, a concern that should be included within the boundaries of child protection? At times, this has been framed as the obligation to ensure that children can thrive as well as survive.

- Is *violence prevention* a more effective framing topic than child

> UNICEF uses the term "child protection" to refer to preventing and responding to violence, exploitation and abuse of all children in all contexts. This also includes reaching children who are uniquely vulnerable to these threats, such as those living without family care, in the street or in situations of conflict or natural disaster.

protection, and can it encompass child labor, lack of birth registration, and other components of maltreatment and neglect that do not include violence as such?

- If *child well-being* is used as a broader framework than child protection, how can the organizational effects of this broader topic be handled, since well-being can include prenatal health, child development, child survival, education, and family income? The emphasis in the U.S. PL 109-95 legislation and the subsequent Action Plan on Children in Adversity defined well-being as including early childhood, family care, and child protection. Above all, the question is how can child well-being be framed to ensure that it encompasses family well-being?

- Are children *agents* in child protection? A number of experts and leaders in the field of child protection have described an evolution of the field from a perception of the child as *object* to the child as *subject*, able to act on her own behalf. Dr. Yanghee Lee, Vice-Chair of the UN Committee on the Rights of the Child, describes three stages of this evolution, from a child welfare perspective focused on protecting the child, to child rights with the child as a rights-holder for the first time, and a third stage with children and youth able to act on their own behalf.[16] Gerison Landsown has written a powerful monograph on children's participation "from the village development council at one end of the spectrum to the UN General Assembly at the other."[17]

We discuss this facet of child protection further in Chapter Seven.

As we will see, these uncertain boundaries around child protection create difficulties not only in defining the field, but in raising its priority and expanding its resources.

Definitions and data

A major limitation on child protection efforts is the weakness of many of the data sources on which these statistics rest. Despite a significant expansion of reports on child well-being, UNICEF's annual State of the

Child publications (which began in 1979), and other materials, the data bases for some of the major child protection indicators are scant.[18] As one source indicated, much of what we know about child development and well-being has been collected from research focused on the 10% of the world's children who reside in the developed world.[19] In a 2015 review of the status of the Sustainable Development Goals that are to replace the Millennium Development Goals, a former US official said that "SDGs are what we can measure progress toward, and we can't even define the indicators yet in child protection." Jody Hermann and her colleagues have written a broad assessment of children's futures in a global context, using surveys and interview data from multiple sources. Yet her conclusion, in a book published in 2013, was that while the laws protecting children from violence are a critical facet of children's futures, "We were unable to find systematic global sources of comparable data on this topic."[20]

The good news is that a great deal of progress in filling data gaps has been made in the last decade. An International Society for Child Indicators has been formed, and has published numerous papers on child indicators. The UNICEF Multiple Indicator Cluster Surveys (MICS) have been developed and refined to capture much more extensive data than was available in 1995 when the first cycle of MICS surveys was begun in 60 countries. The MICS 4 cycle took place during 2009-2011 and is now being analyzed.[21] Twenty of the items from the MICS data were used to track the progress toward the Millennium Development Goals end point in 2015. The International Society for the Prevention of Child Abuse and Neglect hosts a Working Group on Child Maltreatment Data Collection that includes academics and practitioners from many countries who are adding to the capacity of their nations and universities to compile and analyze data on maltreatment.[22] The Child Protection Monitoring and Evaluation Reference Group (CP MERG) was launched in 2010 and is co-chaired by UNICEF and Save the Children. Its goal is to "strengthen the quality of monitoring and evaluation, research and data collection, through the development of standards, ethical guidelines, tools and methodologies which are relevant to realities in the field."[23] The Centers for Disease Control and Prevention (CDC) in the US government has sponsored a

Violence against Children Survey that has also improved data collection on this component of child maltreatment.

A significant expansion of child indicators work, led by the International Society of Child Indicators, offers promise that national indices of child well-being could support system-building that rises above the level of isolated projects.[24] When a national office charged with child protection has access to survey and administrative data that can regularly assess the impact of projects on national indicators, there is less risk that disconnected projects, each with their own measures of effectiveness, will simply serve as a buffer to system change at a national level.

A number of NGOs have been actively involved in using survey methods to assess child protection mechanisms at the community level. Relying upon work begun in Sierra Leone, refined in Indonesia, and extended to Uganda, researchers from Save the Children and the Child Protection Network based at Columbia University prepared reports on each of these locations which are justifiably ranked as landmark publications in the child protection field. New emphasis on surveys that focus on the incidence of violence against children has included work begun in Swaziland that has now spread to a total of ten countries with leadership from UNICEF and the CDC.

The development of a "child protection index," as described by some NGOs, has not yet emerged in a definitive form from these beginnings, but these country-specific first approximations are important steps in that direction. Their dissemination will depend upon the external and internal funding to build up trend data over time from the original baseline surveys that have been done. They will also depend significantly on the responses of host governments when both improvements and indicators that are not improving are spotlighted. That political process is still uncertain.

The challenge remains not just collecting this data, but using it to measure impact and making it visible enough to guide policy. Some of the data, such as girl infanticide, is both difficult to collect and loaded with emotional content. Some, such as child labor and trafficking data, must be collected from individuals and firms that know they are technically violating the law if they report accurately. And supporting ongoing data collection and analysis is time-consuming and dependent on an assured source of funding that makes compilation of trend data possible. In Chapter 7 we will explore other innovations in data collection and evaluation that affect child protection efforts.

Three barriers to the collection of accurate data are obvious:

- To compile accurate statistics in rural and conflict-affected areas where government agencies do not operate in ways that permit uniform data collection is very difficult; for one critical item—births not registered—the key data point is how widely the data simply does not exist;
- There are important disincentives for compiling data that has a great deal of stigma attached—both for the parents and caretakers of children and for the host government—in documenting the extent to which children are abused; data collection can also raise challenging issues of privacy;
- To launch studies rather than responding to the urgency of dealing more directly with undeniable needs can be seen as misdirection of scarce resources.

In a detailed review of the status of children's indicators, Asher Ben-Arieh does not focus explicitly on child protection, but notes several trends over the past 20 years that affect the usefulness of this data:

- A greater emphasis on the subjective view of the child herself;
- A wider focus than survival data alone;
- A balanced emphasis on positive as well as negative indicators.[25]

Ben-Arieh summarizes the most important ongoing current efforts:

> The multi-national project on Measuring and Monitoring Children's Well-Being developed a database of indicators including their age appropriateness and data availability (see http://multinational-indicators.chapinhall.org).

UNICEF Innocenti Center is publishing report cards on
children well-being (see www.unicef-irc.org/research/) as
do various other international bodies.

Survey data, while very useful for the majority of children and families,
sometimes omits all children who live outside families—which include
some of the most maltreated children and children at risk of maltreatment.

A final challenge to data is the tendency to rely on aggregate data and the
difficulty of disaggregating data to include excluded groups. Race, caste,
gender, religion—all these are variables that sometimes become invisible in
aggregate data. Yet many nations have large blind spots— "lesser" children
who are not seen as equally deserving of protection or a data spotlight:
the Uighurs, the "backward classes" as they are defined in India, the
Palestinians, the Roma. As in the U.S., once outcomes are disaggregated
by race, geography, national origin, religion, and gender, some abused
children become visible in ways that generalized indicators can conceal.

Is an overview of child protection possible?

To some extent, constructing an overview of the "field" of child protection
systems is a nearly impossible task. Because of the categorical orientation of
much child protection work, in which a single condition such as child labor
or sexual violence is the focus, characterizing progress and setbacks across
all sixteen of the child protection conditions is very difficult. The task is
further complicated by the complexity of monitoring activities aimed at
these separately defined conditions in hundreds of countries as well as
ethnic/geographic subdivisions within them, in many cases. When the
critical role of NGOs is added to the picture, the complications multiply
further. A 1999 study by the UN Development Program estimated that
there were more than 50,000 NGOs active at that time.[26]

And yet the central concept is reducing the harm done to children—and
the reality is that there are many different forms of harm, from which
flow the categories of child protection and the organizations which seek to

respond. Those responses often focus on to a single type of harm, ignoring other types that may be clearly linked and may affect many more children.

A further barrier to defining the field is the difficulty of determining what is being spent on child protection activities. There is no current total or working inventory of child protection activities by NGOs worldwide. A 2006 report on all forms of humanitarian assistance through NGOs, updated in 2008, found that 114 NGOs, including all of the largest ones, spent $4.2 billion compared with $7.3 billion in humanitarian assistance from governmental sources.[27] An assessment in 2011 concluded that

> The USAID website alone lists 671 registered U.S. and international NGOs with total spending of almost $27 billion in 2007; and the top "vendors" (NGOs receiving USAID funding) were allotted a total of $4.9 billion in that same year by the U.S. government.[28]

A report under the auspices of Save the Children sought to track all funding in 2007-09 for child protection projects under the broader heading of humanitarian projects tracked by the Financial Tracking Service (FTS). The FTS, managed by the UN Office for the Coordination of Humanitarian Affairs (OCHA), is a global, online, real-time database of humanitarian funding needs and international contributions. While this tracking effort is a laudable beginning, the overall amount involved in the most recent year covered, 2009, was only $40.8 million across 215 projects.[29]

The categories within these broad funding totals, as estimated by several different sources using different methods, are themselves subject to interpretation. "Humanitarian aid" can mean food assistance, disaster relief, military action to protect civilian populations, or any of several other forms of assistance related to emergencies. From year to year, changes in military conflicts and natural disasters shift the geographic focus of assistance programs, and this can also affect child protection efforts. "Development assistance," another term used in describing foreign assistance, usually means aid intended to promote longer-term, non-emergency projects. And both categories can include child protection activities.

It is not only that there is no inventory *across* agencies and NGOs for child protection efforts overall; it is also that there is little information on the level of resources being devoted to the different components *within* the child protection agenda. "The budget is the policy" is an old public administration adage, but not knowing the aggregate budgets for re-integration of child soldiers vs prevention of trafficking vs birth registration campaigns makes it even harder to get a sense of what the real priorities are, to the extent that those priorities are revealed by spending. Some agencies, including UNICEF, have detailed totals of their own spending on child protection, but others, including many national governments, do not break their budgets out based on this category.

Finally, the challenge of defining the field is also handicapped by tension between efforts defined by the *symptoms* of child maltreatment and those that address deeper *causes*. The lists of causes in this report set forth in Chapter Five are no more definitive than other lists in other sources, but a deeper review of the causes in all these sources would lead, in our view, to better efforts to target resources. If resources are aimed only at symptoms, underlying causes may not be affected in the same way that they might be if efforts were made to change those driving forces.

Child protection as a "wicked problem"

Child protection meets the criteria set forth in recent organizational literature for "wicked problems" arising in complex, open systems that operate in multiple environments.[30] These labels make clear that the multi-problem nature of child protection as a field creates many challenges that do not occur in narrower fields of organizational practice. Calling for greater collaboration in resolving such tangled problems is futile without a clear design for problem definition and consensus-building. Agency and NGO proliferation and the go-it-alone nature of much advocacy for children's programs compounds the problems caused by rhetorical calls for collaboration that collide with the reality of separate initiatives and separate funding.

The use of the term *wicked* can have dual meanings in the child protection field, referring both to the presence of evil in harm done to children and to the factors that make the problem horribly complicated, rooted deeply in culture, addictions, and perversions of religious doctrine. Responses to the problem are also complicated and weakened by narrowed definitions of many different organizations operating primarily within their own spheres of influence, without regard for the widespread overlap of those spheres with those of other organizations.

Weber and Khademian emphasize the mindset of collaborative problem-solvers, as well as the need for government actors to work as equals in governance networks with non-governmental parties.[31] They call for new forms of knowledge-sharing when wicked problems are the focus of networks of public and non-public stakeholders, and suggest that relationships of trust that make up the "soft side" of networking around wicked problems are critical ingredients required for genuine progress.

The coalitions that work under the umbrellas of UNICEF and USAID, as well as those in other developed nations, include stakeholders who are very familiar with each others' programs and purposes. But in the absence of an overview that allows a fuller inventory of those efforts arrayed against the problems of child maltreatment, each organization inevitably works more within its own span of control than outside it. Action is often unilateral rather than multilateral, as the perceived urgency of each organization's own efforts overwhelms the need for consultation, and what consultation exists becomes more *pro forma* than substantive. Agencies do what they do best, and the field becomes that much more fragmented.

The basis for this generalization is not only our interviews with NGOs and other actors in the field of child protection, but also the definite lack of information that cuts across the field to aggregate efforts and holds them up against the magnitude of the problems. Better indicators of progress, as discussed above, are a major step toward improving what is known about the equation between resources and results. But the resources side of that equation is missing an overview in the form of a collaborative effort to inventory total child protection spending. Developing shared priorities in allocating funds to the many components of child protection is impossible without such an overview. That overview is critical to the task of enabling networks of child protection agencies to measure themselves against the wicked problems of child maltreatment.

Some interviewees noted that progress has been made in recent years in countering this fragmentation in two ways: by a stronger emphasis on violence as an over-arching concept in the child protection field and by efforts, especially in humanitarian settings, to work through clusters of child protection agencies and in the efforts of the Child Protection Working Group described in Chapter 6.

A final critical feature of policy affecting child protection is that it attempts to respond to behavior that is often illegal (whether or not the law is enforced) or buried so deeply within family, clan, and tribal roots that outsiders find it very difficult to access. The "hiddenness" of some maltreatment behaviors keeps them protected from outside influence. Thus civil society that functions within a culture is at times the only way in—the only way to access harmful behavior with any hope of changing it. The harm done by hurting, isolating, and selling children will never be as visible as it should be, because of its tangled environment of illegality, guilt and shame. The worst effects of the maltreatment are often located in invisible neurodevelopmental circuits, not in courtrooms or the media. That means that policy, for all its importance, can be weakened by lax enforcement, and enforcement can be undermined by still-powerful norms in the communities in which those children live. We will look further at these connections in discussing the causes of child maltreatment in Chapter 5.

CHAPTER TWO

Who works on child protection problems?

The leadership of worldwide child protection efforts today rests more with UNICEF than any other single agency, although its role is shared widely. Today there are thousands of other public and private organizations in the child protection field, many that are governmentally sponsored, others that are non-governmental in nature, based in civil society down to the village level in thousands of locations on all inhabited continents. As we will see, the laudable efforts to coordinate efforts among all of these agencies and organizations face the obstacles created by widespread fragmentation among them.

UNICEF, other UN agencies, the USAID office directing the Action Plan for Children in Adversity, other nations' programs and governmental units, international NGOs, and thousands of smaller organizations in the civil sector of the world's nations all fund and/or operate programs that are part of the child protection agenda. The field includes service providers, advocates, monitors, evaluators, researchers, and children and parents themselves, acting in their own interests. Selected child protection issues are monitored in depth by the process set in motion by the Child Rights Information Network (CRIN), a private organization based in London which reviews UN actions and nations' compliance with the UN Convention on the Rights of the Child.[32]

UNICEF and other UN agencies

By describing and addressing a wide variety of child maltreatment problems, UNICEF comes nearer to performing the function of providing an overview than any other organization in the field. Collectively, the 11,000 professionals across 190 countries who make up the entire organization and the staff who work in its child protection units in New York, Florence, and in numerous countries can provide a more cohesive review of child protection activities than any other source. UNICEF's leadership in partnership with many other agencies is internationally recognized, and its products are the core reference materials used in the field.

UNICEF's role has changed considerably in its 65 years of history. Sir Richard Jolly has traced the evolution of UNICEF from its earlier crisis-driven, humanitarian orientation to a much broader concern for children as a central component of comprehensive development policies.[33]Its work is based on individual country programs that draw on national resources and seek to facilitate public and private efforts targeted on several distinct categories of children. Its research arm, based in Florence at the Innocenti Research Centre, issues dozens of reports and conducts its own basic and applied research in conjunction with academic institutions, charitable organizations, and national governments.

The adoption by UNICEF's Executive Board in 2008 of a formal Child Protection Strategy was a major landmark in UNICEF's coordination efforts. The Strategy is a 21-page document that sets forth the detailed rationale for child protection as a preventive strategy and links its efforts directly to the achievement of the Millennium Development Goals. It presents five main approaches for building a protective environment:

> (a) strengthening national protection systems, (b) supporting social change; followed by (c) promoting child protection in conflict and natural disasters. The cross-cutting areas are (d) evidence-building and knowledge management, and (e) convening and catalysing agents of change.[34]

Beyond UNICEF, several other components of the UN and other international organizations also work in the area of child protection. Other UN and UN-affiliated agencies that are involved in child protection issues include the Office of the United Nations High Commissioner for Human Rights, the UN High Commissioner for Refugees, the World Health Organization, the UN Office on Drugs and Crime, the UN Population Fund, the UN Development Program, the International Labor Organization, and UNESCO on education issues. A detailed map of all UN agencies that are involved in child rights issues is at http://www. crin.org/Law/map/index.asp. Coordination of these separate entities takes place within the UN, but the lead roles in single problem areas such as trafficking or education often involve agencies other than UNICEF.

Despite the leadership of UNICEF, the fragmentation of international assistance programs as it all affects all foreign assistance efforts is well-documented, in fields ranging far beyond those focused on child protection. A World Bank report in 2010 concluded

> The number of aid agencies has also grown enormously, with about 225 bilateral and 242 multilateral agencies funding more than 35,000 activities each year. A recent OECD survey revealed that in 2007 there were 15,229 donor missions to 54 countries—more than 800 to Vietnam alone. The scope for reducing the number of donors operating in some countries without jeopardizing diversification or overall aid levels is thus considerable.[35]

Some of the most powerful evidence of the fragmentation of child protection efforts comes from recent studies of the broader field of development aid. In a recent Brookings Institution assessment, *Delivering Aid Differently*, a group of authors describe the field of development assistance as a $200 billion industry that is growing larger as the projects funded by its donors grow smaller.[36]

> As the number of donors has increased, the number of new aid projects has skyrocketed, but their average size

has shrunk…The median size of a new activity is now only $67,555, which means that the increase in total ODA [Official Development Assistance] has come about by adding many small new projects rather than by scaling up what works.[37]

Coordination efforts are themselves fragmented, with separate national and international coordinating bodies working on gender equity, school enrollment, child labor, and other child protection issues.

As noted, one of the most important gaps in the field of child protection is the lack of any internationally compiled total of spending on child protection issues. Child protection is only one portion of what UNICEF does, totaling less than a tenth of UNICEF's budget. UNICEF's total budget is $3.7 billion; in their 2011 annual report, $53.1 million was identified as allocated to child protection projects from thematic funds, with a total of $340 million for child protection from all sources. This is projected to increase to an average of $444 million annually over the period from 2014-2017. USAID has compiled a list of $2.7 billion in U.S. spending targeted on highly vulnerable children, which includes categories beyond child protection. Since many of the organizations in this field work on issues beyond child protection, it is difficult to break out spending for child protection purposes separately. In Chapter 6 we attempt to estimate total child protection spending.

NGOs

The NGOs that work on child protection issues include large, multi-billion-dollar global organizations and much smaller, grass-roots, village-based civil society organizations. Some organizations such as the International Justice Mission and The Polaris Project work on a single issue (sex trafficking), while others, such as Save the Children and World Vision, work across many of these issues. The largest and most visible of these organizations that work on child protection issues as well as other development, health, and humanitarian missions include World Vision, Oxfam, Catholic Relief Services, CARE, Plan International, ChildFund

Alliance, Save the Children, International Rescue Commission, Mercy Corps, and Doctors without Borders.[38]

The special role of formally religious NGOs should be noted, since some of the largest organizations such as World Vision and Catholic Relief Services fall into this category. In the latter case, the distinction between relief efforts and support for policy changes becomes important. As noted in the prior chapter, Catholic organizations have at the same time led the efforts to care for detained minors along the U.S.-Mexico border (and many other humanitarian efforts) and have opposed U.S. ratification of the Convention on Rights of the Child—even though the Vatican (acting as a state member of the UN) has ratified the CRC.

Many NGOs based in the U.S. receive one-third or more of their revenue from governmental contracts. These revenues come with important mandates that require reporting on spending and the results of spending, which may at the same time constrain NGOs in two important ways: they require detailed accounting and evaluation staffing, and they make it more difficult for these NGOs to criticize governmental policy. To their credit, some of these NGOs are active advocates and have been able to combine their governmentally funded operations with continuing advocacy. But some in the field have noted the caution taken to ensure that occasional critical comments do not go past the point of endangering funding. This pattern of NGO dependence on governmental funding has a second effect, which is to alter the role of the government. In a recent summary of U.S. foreign assistance programs, one observer commented that "USAID is more of a development contractor than an operational agency."[39]

The careful balancing act which NGOs must follow is at times very difficult. On the issue of child soldiers, for example, some NGOs were very active in securing the passage of the original 2008 legislation that required US military aid to be certified as having no connections with child soldier recruitment. But our interviews indicated that some of these NGOs have deliberately been silent on violations of the legislation and waivers granted by the State Department, out of concern for the safety of their own staff in countries affected by the legislation. For the NGOs most concerned with child protection issues, such caution is sometimes needed in weighing advocacy against safety and credibility with host governments.

U.S. child protection efforts

In the U.S., the passage and signing in 2005 of PL 109-95, the Assistance for Orphans and Other Vulnerable Children in Developing Countries Act, was originally supported by 130 co-sponsors in the House. In its fifth annual report to Congress in 2012, the Secretariat of the PL 109-95 office stated the organizational rationale for creation of the office:

> At present, the U.S. Government's foreign assistance program does not have one administrative home for programming that addresses vulnerable children or child protection, per se. While several programs deal with different aspects of child protection, there is no comprehensive approach to protecting children that runs through all departments and agencies working to improve the lives of children and their families.[40]

The USAID Secretariat for PL 109-95 committed in 2011 to producing a child protection strategy that includes "guiding principles for U.S. Government assistance to affected children." In December 2013 a full Action Plan for Children in Adversity (APAC) was issued, with three major priorities:

- Build Strong Beginnings: Increase percentage of children surviving and reaching full developmental potential.
- Put Family Care First: Reduce percentage of children living outside of family care.
- Protect Children: Reduce percentage of girls and boys exposed to violence and exploitation.

Chapter 9 reviews the Plan in more detail as part of an overview of U.S. policy. The Pl 109-95 Secretariat now operates as the Center of Excellence on Children in Adversity (CECA).

Other U.S. government agencies work with various UN bodies, as discussed in the 2nd Annual report of the 109-95 office:

> Those U.S.G. agencies that have the mandate to coordinate with U.N. agencies already have close working relationships with them: DOS with UNHCR, DOL with the International Labor Organization (ILO), USAID's FFP with the World Food Programme (WFP), as well as its Office of HIV/AIDS with UNICEF. U.S.G. agencies are broadening their efforts to collaborate with international agencies where opportunities present themselves on the ground.[41]

A new initiative, now referred to as the Global Alliance for Children, is being developed by the USAID office as part of its rollout of the National Action Plan. At present, fifteen organizations from eleven nations are involved in its planning efforts.

In our interviews and in the sources we reviewed, numerous explanations have been given to summarize the impact of the U.S. government on global child protection agendas:

- The relatively small portion of official foreign assistance spending that is focused on child protection issues
- The failure of the U.S. to ratify the Convention on the Rights of the Child
- The dominance of some U.S.-based NGOs, foundations, and private contributors to child protection organizations, which reduces the pressure for governmental contributions
- The continuing fragmentation of federal agencies that work separately on child protection issues, despite the recent coordinating efforts of the USAID office
- The mixed record of state and local governments on child welfare issues in the U.S., which in a federal system have major responsibility for many child protection issues

- The political opposition to some parts of the child protection agenda, described above, which weaken the capacity of the federal government to participate actively in international organizations
- Advocacy efforts narrowly focused on adoption, HIV/AIDS, trafficking, and other segments of the child protection agenda rather than the full array of child protection issues
- International reaction to the perceived human rights abuses of U.S. military forces and law enforcement agencies after the 9/11 attacks

Without addressing the merits of these actual and perceived weaknesses, it is clear from the sources we consulted that the U.S., while a significant player in some segments of the child protection agenda, is not at present seen by many international stakeholders in the child protection field as a leading player in addressing child protection issues proportionate to its resources. If there is an exception to this generally low priority given to child protection issues, it is the role played in addressing the issues relating to girls and women under the leadership of then-Secretary Clinton. There are some lessons that can be learned from this important exception, and in later chapters we will assess the potential for improving the priority given to the child protection agenda within the U.S. government. In Chapter 9, we review more fully the history of the new office in USAID and assess the overall role of the U.S. government in global child protection against four criteria: coherence, proportionate resources, effectiveness, and potential.

The Child Rights International Network (CRIN)

The work of the Child Rights International Network (CRIN) is an invaluable resource in monitoring the plethora of UN hearings, reports, and other events and publications that involve the rights of children. An enormous amount of material is available on their website (www.crin.org), including proceedings of committee meetings, reports on each nation that the UN monitors through the Convention on the Rights of the Child, and NGO publications that provide independent assessments of national reports. CRIN was founded in 1995 and is supported by foundations and several national Save the Children affiliates. It currently has 2,100 members in 150 countries. Its 2010 budget was approximately $400,000.

CRIN has organized efforts by its member organizations to review the credentials of the major UN appointees with responsibilities for child protection issues, especially the Committee on the Rights of the Child which functions under the auspices of the Office of the UN High Commissioner for Human Rights. It has encouraged expanded comments by NGOs as part of the ongoing reviews of compliance with the Convention on the Rights of the Child. It is currently reviewing case law and litigation on behalf of children.

The efforts of other nations

In a compilation of articles from 25 nations and the Middle East-North Africa region, a 2010 publication reviewed child protection organizational structures and functions in each of these nations.[42] The variation is wide, from well-developed agencies with strongly enforced legal frameworks to nations that are in the very early stages of setting up small child protection units. Differences are also wide in reporting mandates, cultural barriers to infringing on parents' rights to discipline their children, and legal machinery in support of the Convention on the Rights of the Child. The need for expanded prevention resources and improved data collection was emphasized by the editors of the collection and in many of the articles as well.

On the assistance side, several interviewees noted the proportionately larger contributions from European nations (as well as Japan) and the leadership roles played by several of these nations, especially the Scandinavian countries. Lists of contributors to specific UNICEF reports and projects often include nations based on the scale of their contributions, and European nations frequently lead these listings. The Development Assistance Committee of the Organization for Economic Cooperation and Development collects data on official total development assistance from European nations and six other developed nations (the U.S., Australia, Canada, Japan, Korea, and New Zealand) and reported a total of $134 billion in 2011.[43]Again, no breakout of child protection funding is available.

The European Union is a major partner of UNICEF and other agencies involved in child protection and broader development efforts, as noted in documents prepared for the first 2014 Executive Board session of UNICEF. UNICEF noted that the EU contributes 60% of global development assistance, and the EU contributed $515 million in 2013 to a broad range of UNICEF programs.[44]

The efforts of the Council of Europe have also been impressive, centered around a campaign begun in 2010 called the "One in Five" effort, with sexual violence against children as its focal point.

> The Council of Europe adopted a new strategy to implement fundamental standards to protect and promote children's rights. The strategy will focus on four main objectives: promoting child-friendly services and systems, eliminating all forms of violence against children, guaranteeing the rights of children in vulnerable situations, and promoting child participation. The Congress will continue its efforts towards an effective implementation of the Strategy by local authorities. It contributes in particular to developing local and regional dimensions of the ONE in FIVE Campaign to fight sexual violence against children.[45]

Independent human rights institutions

A recent publication of the UNICEF Innocenti Centre surveyed "independent human rights institutions for children," including more than 200 such institutions in over 70 countries. These children's ombudspersons, children's commissions, and children's advocates were seen by the report's authors as "important actors for the implementation of the Convention on the Rights of the Child."[46] Yet the report also noted that "their recommendations are too often left unattended by the very governments and parliaments responsible for their creation." They are explicitly described as possessing "soft power," able to "demonstrate rights in action by advancing the rights of children through their interventions."[47]

The UN Committee on the Rights of the Child, a body formed under the Convention, sets forth guidance on the functioning of these independent institutions. Emphasis is placed on the best interests of the child as a guiding concept and on child participation. These institutions are seen as complementary to other measures that implement the Convention, including "law reform, resource allocation, governmental bodies and strategies, data monitoring systems, awareness-raising, and the role of civil society."[48]The European Network of Ombudspersons for Children included 39 institutions from 31 countries by mid-2012.

An example of the role of these institutions which has been copied by other nations is the methodology developed by Scotland's Commissioner for Children and Young People for carrying out "child rights impact assessments of proposed policy." In playing this role, it is important to note that these institutions often work outside the boundaries of child protection, addressing family income assistance, education, and monitoring child care providers and detention centers. The study found that one-third of these institutions worked with a mandate to assess the conditions of the most excluded groups of children. Many of them also represent individual children in cases brought before legal institutions, including issues of sexual abuse and child labor. In some cases, these complaints originate with children's online and telephone "helplines" that are publicized and provide another form of voice for children themselves.

The report noted the inherent tensions between these institutions' roles as public bodies that are intended to monitor and evaluate public policy and at the same time work cooperatively with public policymakers.[49] Support from a legislative body is seen as more protective of an institution's independence than creation under an executive order. Half of the countries responding to the survey indicated that their existence was prescribed by the national constitution. Yet some are required to consult with or clear their activities with executive agencies. The report notes that

> The Committee on the Rights of the Child has consistently noted in its concluding observations to state party reports

that efforts to provide reasonable and secure funds to child-related institutions are insufficient.[50]

In a section titled "Practical question: How can institutions withstand threats?" the report notes the dismantling of some of these institutions, and threats to their existence in other cases. Links with the media, with NGOs, and with civil society organizations are seen as helpful in protecting the autonomy of these institutions.[51]

The mixed record of these institutions should be compared with their proliferation over the decades since the enactment of the Convention on the Rights of the Child. These are not institutions of significant power, in most cases, but their existence provides important evidence of the growing willingness of many nations to develop centers of influence over policies affecting children in need of protection. Tracking the trends in the ability of these institutions to change policy and to maintain their independence will be a significant benchmark of the standing given to children's rights.

The human rights movement and children's rights

To a surprising extent, most of the human rights organizations that address violations of human rights around the world do not yet encompass children's rights or child protection issues. While the overlapping issues of women's rights have made it onto the agenda of some of these NGOs and advocacy organizations, children are not yet a major focus of their work. The most recent, definitive history of international human rights by one of its leading spokesmen, Aryeh Neier, does not mention children's rights at all, while discussing "marginalized groups," disabilities, the effects of HIV-AIDS, landmines, and other conditions that overlap with the global child protection agenda.[52] In fact, it is striking how often the literature of human rights almost completely ignores any reference to the rights of children while using the examples of girls' schooling and female mutilation—archetypical examples of child maltreatment—to make their points about human rights and culture.[53]

Yet the lessons of the evolution of global human rights in recent decades offer considerable relevance for children's rights. Neier is not optimistic about governments in general; his downplaying of the U.S. role is consistent with his judgments about other governments as well. He describes international civil society organizations as the most likely foundation for major achievements in human rights, in mobilizing their members, securing no-strings (or fewer-strings) contributions, and documenting abuses with objectivity and balance that gains media attention and international respect. He praises the improvements in the U.S. government's annual certification of foreign governments' human rights records, noting how much leverage is provided by these procedural requirements which enable observers to add their voices to the catalogues of abuses. And he notes the tentative use of "responsibility to protect" language adopted by the UN in 2005 (based on an original draft by Canada in 2001) and the movement of some human rights groups toward more concern for economic and social issues that involve discrimination against specific groups—without mentioning children as one of those groups.

What this framework ignores is that if the "responsibility to protect" doctrine can be seen as combining humanitarian goals with potential military means, the extension of that doctrine to protect the world's most vulnerable children requires humanitarian goals to be carried out by economic investments in the tools and structures needed to reduce harm to those children. As discussed above, the crucial interaction between results and resources is what is often lacking in strategic discussion of child protection, and the responsibility to protect doctrine could provide a framework for improving that discussion. But our interviews and research found few examples of such an extension of the doctrine.

Michael Ignatieff, a human rights advocate and author who has served as Chairman of Canada's Liberal Party, frames the issue quite differently, and offers a framework in which human rights advocates can view rights of children as integral:

> Human rights is the only universally available moral
> vernacular that validates the claims of women and children

> against the oppression they experience in patriarchal
> and tribal societies; it is the only vernacular that enables
> dependent persons to perceive themselves as moral agents
> and to act against practices—arranged marriages, purdah,
> civic disenfranchisement, genital mutilation, domestic
> slavery, and so on—that are ratified by the weight and
> authority of their cultures.[54]

And yet, it must be added, at the practical level, distinctions between children's rights and human rights blur far more than they seem to among those who write about these issues. Tostan, the Africa-based social entrepreneur group that has led thousands of village-based dialogues that brought about the steep reductions in female mutilation in some regions, begins its work with a focus on human dignity—not rights-talk, but dignity, which it grounds in common religious and cultural traditions. Molly Melching, the founder of Tostan, does not use rights language when she refers to mutilation; she says their work seeks "a new, socially accepted option to not cut girls."[55] And so human rights and child protection are one, at least in this important arena.

Governments and NGOs alike will continue to sort through these claims about the relevance of human rights to the rights of children, but Ignatieff's comments and Tostan's work remind us of the power of culture to affect the lives and the perceived rights of children. We will return to that issue in Chapter 5 when we review the causes of maltreatment.

CHAPTER THREE

The components of child protection: a brief overview of specific child protection issues

This section briefly reviews recent developments in each of the sixteen areas listed as the components of child maltreatment by UNICEF. They are listed in the alphabetical order that they are found on the UNICEF website. It should be noted that this is not a comprehensive list of all forms of child abuse and neglect; it is based on the categories used by UNICEF, not the full range of child protection measures and problems.

Armed violence reduction

In 2012, UNICEF stated that "programming for Armed Violence Reduction is at a relatively nascent stage compared to many other sectors." Yet armed conflict has so clearly involved children in deadly cross-fires in so many parts of the world in the last several years that this category has necessarily received more attention, including a 2015 UNICEF report on the effects of the conflict in and around Syria as it affected hundreds of thousands of children.

UNICEF works with several other UN agencies on this issue, including UNDP, UNODC, WHO, UNODA and UN-Habitat, in developing an "Armed Violence Prevention Programme."[56] The OECD's Development Assistance Council published reports in 2009 and 2011 on armed violence as it affects children and families, pointing out its strong gender equity impact, the use of sexual abuse as an instrument of war, and the impact of armed violence on the growing population of youth.[57]

Several NGOs and research organizations have contributed to this work, including the Quaker United Nations Office (QUNO), the Danish Demining Group, Saferworld, and the Clingendael Institute Conflict Research Unit. In 2011, a conference on Geneva with over 500 participants focused on armed violence programs under the umbrella of the 2006 Geneva Declaration on Armed Violence and Development. From 2004 to 2007 UNDP and WHO operated an Armed Violence Prevention Programme in Latin America; at present "best practices seminars" on AVP are being held in several countries to disseminate program strategies.[58]

Birth registration

An estimated 70% of births in the "least developed nations" are not registered, and 50% are not registered in developing nations. This data is annually updated by nation in UNICEF's State of the Child indicators table. The most recent data from early 2014 indicate that an estimated average of 65% of all births are registered, with rates in those countries classified as "least developed" estimated at 38% registered.[59] This goal is based on Article 7 of the Convention on the Rights of the Child which states that every child has the right to be registered at birth without any discrimination. UNICEF reports that

> in less developed countries...only half of the children under five years of age have their births registered. Countries dealing with armed conflict or civil war make up the majority of the countries with the lowest birth registration.[60]

UNICEF has published reports on case studies of developing nations that have improved these indicators.[61] Reviews of this issue make clear that it is rural, lower-caste, lowest-income groups whose children are least likely to be registered at birth, underscoring the extent to which this issue is one of discrimination as well as accessibility. The 2014 UNICEF report *Every Child Counts* points out that

> Groups commonly undercounted or overlooked include children living in institutions or temporary housing, children in detention, children living and working on the street, children with disabilities, trafficked children, migrant children, internally displaced and refugee children, and children from ethnic minorities living in remote areas or following a nomadic or pastoralist way of life.

UNICEF currently supports 62 country-based offices involved in improving birth registrations.

Child labour

UNICEF works closely with the International Labor Organization on child labor issues. Data in this area is uneven; UNICEF's 2014 summary states that

> Fifteen per cent of the world's children engage in child labour that compromises their right to protection from economic exploitation and infringes on their right to learn and play.[62]

An interagency effort has developed a "Roadmap for achieving the elimination of the worst forms of child labour by 2016,"[63] which was developed at the Hague Global Child Labour Conference in 2010. The "roadmap" refers to actions aimed at corporate and multinational employers, as well as social norms that support child labor. Progress in this area has been marked by what ILO terms "modest" declines of 3% in the 2004-2008 period, and a 10% decline in the 2000-2004 period.[64] The 2010 ILO report, "Accelerating Action Against Child Labour," points out that the current rate of progress calls into question achieving the 2016 goals in the "roadmap." An annual World Child Labour Report is being published by a coalition consisting of ILO, UNICEF, and the World Bank, as part of the "Understanding Children's Work Programme." The most recent report estimates that 168 million children aged 5-17 are engaged in child labour. In 2015 UNICEF and Save the Children published a report on the expansion of child labour in Syria as a result of widespread displacement of families.[65]

Child marriage

UNICEF defines child marriage as a formal marriage or informal union before age 18. The most recent UNICEF summary of the problem states that "eleven percent of girls are married before they turn 15, jeopardizing their rights to health, education, and protection." [66] An earlier report summarized in more detail:

> About a third of women aged 20-24 years old in the developing world were married as children. Child marriage is most common in South Asia and Sub-Saharan Africa, but there are big differences in prevalence among countries of the same region. While data from 47 countries show that, overall, the median age at first marriage is gradually increasing, this improvement has been limited primarily to girls of families with higher incomes. Overall, the pace of change remains slow. While 48 per cent of women 45-49 years old were married before the age of 18, the proportion has only dropped to 35 per cent of women 20-24 years old.[67]

The prospects for improvement in this area are evident in the geographic concentration of the problem. Half of the world's child brides live in South Asia and one-third live in India.[68]

This problem is so closely linked to other child maltreatment and child survival issues that it can be seen as a very high-leverage issue. UNICEF materials note the lower survival rate of births to younger mothers, the higher incidence of sexual and other violence against women who married young, and lower school attendance. UNICEF was involved in organizing the International Day of the Girl Child, which raised awareness using the theme of child marriage.

A position paper published by the Council on Foreign Relations in 2013 reviewed the status of child marriage and links the issue to U.S. foreign policy goals.[69]

Children Affected by Armed Conflict

This issue, which has received greater attention since the outbreak of hostilities in Syria and adjacent countries, falls under the Optional Protocol to the Convention on the Rights of the Child on the Involvement of Children in Armed Conflict, issued in 2000. This Protocol was based on a landmark study by Graca Machel, an advocate from Mozambique who made the original report on the effects of armed conflict on children to the General Assembly in 1996 and then updated it with a ten-year strategic review issued in 2009.

UNICEF works with several other UN agencies on this issue, as well as with USAID and other nations. The UN agencies include the Special Representative of the Secretary-General for Children and Armed Conflict, the Special Representative of the Secretary-General on Violence against Children, the Office of the High Commissioner for Human Rights, the Committee on the Rights of the Child, and the Special Rapporteur on the Sale of Children, Child Prostitution and Child Pornography. These agencies are currently seeking universal ratification of the Optional Protocols to the Convention of the Rights of the Child. The 25th anniversary of the adoption of the Convention in 2014 led to UNICEF encouraging adoption of the third protocol to the Convention, which emphasizes children's rights to means of communications and grievance procedures.

One estimate presented to the Security Council put the number of children associated with armed groups or armed forces at more than 250,000.[70] In 2010, UNICEF supported the reintegration of some 11,400 children formerly associated with armed forces and armed groups, along with 28,000 other vulnerable children affected by conflict.

Child trafficking

Under the Protocol to Prevent, Suppress and Punish Trafficking in Persons, Especially Women and Children (2000), child trafficking is defined as "the recruitment, transportation, transfer, harbouring or receipt of children for the purpose of exploitation."[71] Data on the prevalence of this problem is not widespread; the International Labor Organization's 2002 estimation of 1.2 million children being trafficked each year is the reference used in most documents.

In 2009, the UN Office on Drugs and Crime issued "An International Framework for Action to Implement the Trafficking in Persons Protocol." Because of the legal issues encountered in prosecuting and enforcing anti-trafficking laws, a wide array of UN and international agencies are involved with this issue. Numerous NGOs and research agencies track the issue, including the International Justice Commission, Polaris, Anti-Slavery International, and The Protection Project at Johns Hopkins University.

The U.S. government is also very actively involved in this issue, through the Department of Justice's Child Exploitation and Obscenity section and the State Department's Office to Combat and Monitor Trafficking in Persons, which issues an annual report ranking countries' support of anti-trafficking measures in three tiers of effectiveness, in response to the 2000 Trafficking Victims Protection Act. Both the Department of Health and Human Services and the Department of Homeland Security also have units on anti-trafficking programs. Secretary Kerry chairs the President's Interagency Task Force to Monitor and Combat Trafficking in Persons. Legislative action in 2014 emphasized the links between domestic trafficking and child welfare programs that serve older children in foster care.

In his overview of the 2011 report, the State Department's lead professional on trafficking issues, Ambassador Luis CdeBaca, said

...unlike a decade ago, the language of abolition has reached the upper echelons of government. The fact that a form of slavery still exists in the modern era and that it must be confronted is now spoken of by heads of state and CEOs, at shareholder meetings, in church groups, and around the blogosphere.

And yet modern slavery continues to be a reality for millions of people, rather than for an isolated few. And the only solution to it is for governments to step up.[72]

The 2009 UNODC report concluded that

the majority of States Parties to the Protocol have adopted at least a minimal legislative and institutional framework to ensure such implementation. However, in view of the varying capacity of Member States to fully implement existing or future measures in the areas under discussion,... more concerted efforts have to be made to help Member States in need to develop effective and multidisciplinary anti-trafficking strategies and build dedicated and sustainable resources to implement such strategies.[73]

Children without parental care

UNICEF endorses the Guidelines for the Alternative Care of Children adopted by the UN General Assembly in 2009. UNICEF uses an estimate of 2 million children living in institutional care, noting that many institutions are unregistered and many countries do not collect this data, so the estimate is "likely to be severely underestimated due to under-reporting and a lack of reliable data."[74]

This issue overlaps with the family separation issue described below, and the Inter-Agency Guiding Principles on Unaccompanied and Separated

Children, issued in 2004, are intended to apply during emergency situations.

Because of the major concern of U.S. agencies, legislators, and advocacy groups with orphans affected by their parents' AIDS/HIV status, USAID has devoted considerable attention to this issue. As noted above, the legislation creating the new USAID office in 2005 was titled The Assistance for Orphans and Other Vulnerable Children in Developing Countries Act. The USAID-sponsored Evidence Summit on Protecting Children Outside of Family Care held in 2011 spotlighted this issue, which is also one of the three objectives of the Action Plan for Children in Adversity described in Chapter 9.

Children with disabilities

The issue of children with disabilities overlaps with several other problems, including violence and sexual violence, school attendance, and other forms of discrimination in receiving services. Data on disabilities is very uneven, with country estimates ranging from 3% in Uzbekistan to 48% in the Central African Republic.[75] UNICEF has launched new disability surveys in several countries; eighteen are referenced in the 2011 Thematic Report.[76]

UNICEF's 2013 State of the World's Children annual report was focused on children with disabilities; it noted that girls with disabilities can be doubly disabled due to gender bias that reduces treatment. A current estimate cited in the 2013 report found that 93 million children live with a moderate or severe disability of some kind.[77] UNICEF materials point out that some disabilities are caused or worsened by maltreatment; the reality that fetal alcohol exposure is a leading cause of intellectual disability, however, is not featured in most discussions of disability in international documents.

Family separation in emergencies

UNICEF estimates that in 2006, 18.1 million children were living with the effects of displacement, including 5.8 million refugees. The context for this data is that over 1 billion children live in countries or territories affected by armed conflict. This category clearly overlaps with the issue of children without parental care.

To quote from UNICEF materials,

> Save the Children, the International Rescue Committee (IRC) and UNICEF have been working together since 2005 to promote the use of a standard inter-agency child protection information management system for the child protection sector. The information management system is a practical, field-level tool that supports effective case management. It is comprised of database software and accompanying 'tools', such as template paper forms and data protection protocols.
>
> The original demand for this system came from Family Tracing and reunification programs in emergencies. The system is also being used to facilitate case management in Release and Reintegration programs, and programs supporting children with specific vulnerabilities in camp settings. The system has been used in 16 countries by a range of child protection actors.[78]

Female genital mutilation/cutting

Some of the most effective efforts of UNICEF and its partners have been evident in the area of FGM/C. In few other areas have international organizations been as clear about the power of social norms to affect child maltreatment. Estimates of FGM/C are subject to under-reporting, but UNICEF estimates that 70 million girls and women have undergone this practice in Africa alone (plus Yemen). Forty percent of the girls and women who are affected live in the Middle East and North Africa. Overall, UNICEF reports, "the prevalence of FGM/C has declined slowly during the past decades. UNICEF reported a 30% increase in the number of communities abandoning the practice from 2010 to 2011."[79] In 2013, UNICEF published a report analyzing data from the 29 countries where the practice is most prevalent, and presenting new data on girls younger than 15.

Yet "millions of girls remain exposed to the risk of genital cutting in the future." UNICEF reports note that in some regions the level of support among women for the practice is lower than the actual prevalence of the practice, suggesting that changing attitudes among community members does not always result in changing practice. As summarized in a 2009 UNICEF report,

> ...large scale abandonment requires that members of practising communities not only change their individual attitudes about the practice—which is insufficient for behavioural change—but also explicitly and collectively agree to abandon it.[80]

UNICEF and its major partner, the UN Fund for Population Activity (UNFPA), have commissioned work at the University of California at San Diego and at Penn on changing social norms that is based in part on this continuing effort to reduce genital cutting. Radio dramas and soap operas, animated videos, posters, and comic books have all been used to communicate the case for changing social norms.

UNICEF states

> As of 2014, nearly 12,000 communities in 15 countries, representing about 10 million people, have renounced the practice, of which over 2,000 communities declared in 2013.

Gender based violence in emergencies

"Conflict and natural disaster increase the vulnerability of children, and women to all forms of violence and exploitation."[81] Unwanted pregnancies, sexually transmitted diseases, and exclusion from their communities can result from gender violence during emergencies. In response to the Haiti earthquake, UNICEF developed a handbook for addressing gender-based violence in humanitarian responses. Teams were sent to Chad, Pakistan, and South Sudan to assess these issues in those emergencies. This issue has also increased in urgency due to conflict in the Middle East, as well as refugee movements towards Europe from North Africa.

Although few references to climate change have yet found their way into child protection documents, to the extent that some observers of environmental change predict more serious natural disasters as a result of the impact of climate change on low-lying regions, children may be affected by climate change that worsens the severity of damage and dislocation in these emergencies.

Justice for children

This category is concerned with the more than one million children estimated to be detained in justice systems at any one time, as well as children in contact with the law who may need access to justice. In violation of the Convention on the Rights of the Child, detention in many nations is used as a sanction rather than assuming innocence until proven guilty. For nations where data is available, 59% of children in detention had not been tried and sentenced.[82] This category also deals with the legal rights and needs of children who are witnesses and victims; UNICEF and the UN Office on Drugs and Crime have developed a toolkit for professionals working with child witnesses and victims.[83]

A new spotlight on these issues has resulted from the publication of *The Locust Effect* in 2014 by International Justice Mission CEO Gary Haugen.[84] The book compiled a great deal of material on the effects of lawlessness, weak court systems, and corruption in developing nations as they affect the widespread violence that constrains economic growth. In many of the examples cited by Haugen and his co-author, children are the most affected parties.

Landmines and explosive weapons

UNICEF estimates that 78 countries are still contaminated by anti-personnel mines and 85 are still affected by other explosive remnants of war. In 2007, 72 countries reported new victims of explosives, with children nearly a third of the total. The 1997 Mine Ban Treaty and a newer international convention in 2008 banning cluster munitions signed by 96 nations provide legal justification for action against explosives, but implementation of these treaties has proven very challenging.[85]

The United States is the world's single largest financial supporter of efforts to clear landmines and unexploded ordnance. Since 1993, the United States has invested more than $2.1 billion in more than 90 countries through more than 60 NGO partners around the world to reduce the harmful worldwide effects of at-risk, illicitly proliferated, and indiscriminately used conventional weapons of war.[86]

Monitoring and Reporting Mechanism (MRM) on grave violations of children's rights in situations of armed conflict

In 2004, the Security Council passed a resolution requiring the Secretary-General to develop a monitoring and reporting mechanism to track six specific violations of children's rights: killing or maiming, recruiting or using children in armed conflict, attacks against schools or hospitals, rape or other sexual violence, abduction, and denial of humanitarian access. The MRM had been extended to 14 countries as of 2009. The Office of the Special Representative of the Secretary-General for Children and Armed Conflict monitors this reporting process and UNICEF's engagement with national organizations that are part of the process.[87]

In a June 2015 panel discussion sponsored by the Center on Children in Adversity/Displaced Children and Orphans Fund with the Child Protection in Crisis Network, a senior U.S. official estimated that only 1/10 to 1/20 of all incidents were actually covered by the MRM data.

Mental health and psychosocial support

This category overlaps with children without parental care as well as the other categories that relate to emergencies. In 2011, a major initiative in this area, Strengthening the Child-Friendly Spaces, used comprehensive psychosocial programs for children whose lives had been disrupted in settings such as the Libya-Tunisia border, Egypt, and Yemen. Working with an inter-agency standing committee on mental health and psychosocial support reference group, UNICEF has endorsed a set of "Guidelines on mental health and psychosocial support in emergency settings" developed in 2007.

Sexual violence against children

This category, which clearly overlaps with the trafficking problem, is very weakly documented due to the legal risks and stigma attached to the issue. A 2002 WHO study estimated that 150 million girls and 73 million boys under 18 years experienced forced sexual intercourse or other forms of sexual violence involving physical contact.[88] But as UNICEF notes

> Yet the true magnitude of sexual violence is hidden because of its sensitive and illegal nature. Most children and families do not report cases of abuse and exploitation because of stigma, fear, and lack of trust in the authorities. Social tolerance and lack of awareness also contribute to under-reporting.[89]

More than 130 countries have ratified the Optional Protocol on the Rights of the Child on the Sale of Children, Child Prostitution, and Pornography, which criminalizes all forms of sexual exploitation of children. UNICEF's Innocenti Research Centre has published materials on the online threats to children that contribute to sexual violence. In November 2008, the World

Congress III against Sexual Exploitation of Children and Adolescents took place in Rio de Janeiro, Brazil. The Congress, which was organized by the Brazilian Government, UNICEF, ECPAT International and the NGO Group for the Convention on the Rights of the Child, gathered more than 3,000 participants from 137 governments, civil society, the private sector, academic institutions and 300 adolescents and youth. The resulting *Rio de Janeiro Declaration and Call for Action to Prevent and Stop Sexual Exploitation of Children and Adolescents* called for the creation of holistic national protection systems to deal with sexual exploitation and a direct attack on social norms that reinforce exploitation and violence.[90]

This is an area with very active NGO participation, as exemplified by the Together for Girls initiative launched at the annual meeting of the Clinton Global Initiative in September 2009. It brings together 10 public and private sector organizations focused on the goal of halting sexual violence against girls, as well as boys. Participating organizations include the United States Department of State-President's Emergency Plan for AIDS Relief (PEPFAR), the Office of Global Women's Health Issues, CDC, UNICEF, United Nations Population Fund, Joint United Nations Programme on HIV/AIDS (UNAIDS), United Nations Development Fund For Women, Becton, Dickinson, and Company, the CDC Foundation, Grupo ABC, and the Nduna Foundation.[91] CDC's Violence against Children surveys have improved tracking of progress on these issues.

A 2014 UNICEF study entitled, *Hidden in Plain Sight,* estimated that about 120 million females under the age of 20, equating to about one in ten girls, were subjected to forced sexual acts or intercourse at some point in their life. Boys' reports of sexual violence experiences are less prevalent compared to girls.[92]

At an international meeting of the International Society for the Prevention of Child Abuse and Neglect, held in Istanbul in September 2012, a significant portion of the workshops and papers presented dealt with sexual violence.

Beyond the 16 issues

In addition to these 16 issues listed on the UNICEF website, there are other problems affecting children that are recognized to be closely linked to child maltreatment, and still others that are less often connected—but should be. These include:

- School attendance
- Environmental issues affecting children
- War- and disaster-related (other than child soldier recruitment)
- Early childhood

School attendance

While there is no explicit goal under the UNICEF child protection umbrella for children attending school, the child labor, child marriage, and family separation goals all mention decreased school attendance as a critical effect of these forms of child maltreatment. These efforts also note the positive effects of increasing attendance in reducing these other closely related problems. UNICEF's education sector works closely with UNESCO and with ILO on this issue. The 2011 data show that in the least developed countries, 81% of children are enrolled in primary schools—an improvement from 53% in 1990.

Environmental abuse

Environmental abuse is not listed as one of the conditions under the UNICEF child protection categories. UNICEF has worked, however, in India and Uzbekistan, as well as other countries, on the protection of children in the agricultural industries who may be affected by pesticides and other chemicals. Two recent developments have turned a spotlight onto the special effects on children of pollution and climate change as a result of carbon emissions. Chemical spills in China and severe air pollution in Beijing led to widespread comments on the increasingly active blogs in China, including speculation about the "cancer villages" that have been identified as high-incidence locations for cancer.[93] At the same time, efforts by environmental groups in Houston have pointed to air pollution near petrochemical plants in Texas as having a severe effect on children's health.[94]

The normalcy of emergency

A fundamental reality of child protection is that planning must include what cannot be planned for in site-specific frameworks: the emergency needs of children who are affected by war and natural disasters. While some of these resources come from the refugee and humanitarian assistance categories of the UN and other agencies, child protection issues are nearly always present as well. Children who have been separated from their parents, whose parents have been killed, or who are at risk of being preyed upon in the chaotic daily life of temporary shelter—all these are child protection problems.

The key point is that the resources needed to respond rapidly to these emergencies inevitably come at the expense of longer-term strategic goals. One of the reasons that inventorying child protection spending is so difficult is that it becomes impossible to distinguish between short-term spending for child protection and spending that happens because "temporary" shelter has become, in effect, permanent. Children who cannot return to their homes are, by definition, in need of protection.

Early childhood

The critical developmental tasks of the first five years make these especially important years for the related goals of child survival, development, and protection. Positive influences during these years have been widely shown to yield positive returns in cognitive and social-emotional growth of younger children. Negative influences reduce the prospects for these children becoming learners and contributors to their communities and their nations. As we point out in the next chapter, neurodevelopmental science has contributed to a new sense of urgency on these issues.

Yet data on these younger children in developing nations, while much improved, remains difficult to assemble in disaggregated form as part of the child protection agenda. WHO has begun to develop population-based assessments on early childhood development, and UNICEF's MICS data system has added early childhood indicators. A recent review of early childhood issues in 28 developing countries using the framework of the Convention on the Rights of the Child assessed ongoing programs and policies in the areas of child survival, development, and protection, finding that what is needed is

> A common metric to assess how different health, education, and child protection interventions can be delivered in an integrated manner so as to synergistically effect a holistic and sustainable caring environment for young children.[95]

The data from these countries provide both positive and troubling signs of the status of younger children. In particular, the survey data on discipline in the home indicates that many of these parents have a long way to go to understand the long-term effects of violent discipline. Only 18% of surveyed caregivers said that "no one in their household has used any violent form of discipline in the past month," with respondents from different countries varying from 0% to 49%. Overall, the authors concluded that CRC "Rights to Survival, Development and Protection could potentially be at risk for one fourth to one third of young children."[96] Given the strong presumption in most of these countries that younger children were the responsibility of the family alone, these findings are a strong indication that public policies do not typically focus on these children.

Issues of younger children also intersect with the concerns expressed above about addiction and culture, which are addressed further in Chapter Five. The combined effects of prenatal substance exposure and early exposure to trauma suggest that these surveys should address parents' substance use as well as violence in the home—especially given the correlation of the two issues.

Overlap with Millennium Development Goals (MDGs)

The conditions defined by UNICEF as child protection only overlap in part with the UN's Millennium Development Goals. The 2010 UNICEF report "Achieving MDGs with Equity", includes a table listing two of the child protection-related goals under the eight MDG categories: Birth registration and child marriage.[97]

Substantial efforts are under way within the child protection community to ensure closer links among their agenda and the revision of the MDGs. Encouraging signs in the planning toward the revisions of the MDGs in 2015 include a greater emphasis on measurable goals, strengthened data collection, child and youth participation, and closer links between development and survival goals with child protection efforts." Real-time monitoring" and an emphasis on excluded groups are also referenced in planning documents such as the "UNICEF Key Messages on the Post-2015 Development Agenda."[98] Yet a USAID official in June 2015 described the final draft of the Sustainable

---

The Millennium Development Goals:

The original eight MDGs adopted by the UN overlap with those reported on by UNICEF. UNICEF includes seven and an eighth, separate category of child protection. These are listed as

MDG 1: Eradicate extreme poverty and hunger
Underweight; Stunting; Breastfeeding and micronutrients.

MDG 2: Achieve universal primary education
Primary and secondary education

MDG 3: Promote gender equality and empower women
Gender parity in primary and secondary education

MDG 4: Reduce child mortality
Under-five mortality; Immunization

MDG 5: Improve maternal health
Interventions related to maternal mortality; Interventions related to reproductive and antenatal health

MDG 6: Combat HIV/AIDS, malaria and other diseases
HIV prevalence; Comprehensive, correct knowledge of HIV and AIDS; Condom use during last higher-risk sex
Protection and support for children affected by AIDS; Pediatric HIV treatment; Malaria prevention through insecticide-treated nets; Other key malaria interventions; Malaria: Achieving coverage with equity

MDG 7: Ensure environmental sustainability
Improved drinking water sources; Improved sanitation facilities
Child Protection

Development Goals that will replace the MDGs as having "a massive hole in terms of child protection." We will return to the relationship between the components of child protection and the broader SDGs in Chapter Ten.

Each of these sixteen components of child protection deserves its own book—and several excellent ones have been written on most of them. But very few publications, other than those produced by each organization as reviews of their own efforts, range across all of these issues of child protection and attempt to be specific about how they can and should fit together more effectively to achieve more impact as a coordinated package of policy and programs.

CHAPTER FOUR

The marginality problem: How important is global child maltreatment?

Any abuse of children who cannot protect themselves has self-evident moral and ethical content, in that it represents harm done to an innocent person. But it is important to update that ethical judgment with recent science that documents the neurodevelopmental damage done by trauma and what has been labeled "toxic stress" by the American Academy of Pediatrics.[99] The brain of a child changes as a result of trauma, and it does so in ways that can diminish the lifelong potential of that child. To have that kind of damage done to the brains of hundreds of millions of children has both ethical and economic content, in increasing the unfairness of what happens to those children as well as diminishing the contributions those children can make to their economy and their society.

In 1842, Charles Dickens anticipated the findings of brain science in writing about imprisonment:

"I hold this slow and daily tampering with the mysteries of the brain to be immeasurably worse than any torture of the body; and because its ghastly signs and tokens are not so palpable to the eye and sense of touch as scars upon the flesh; because its wounds are not upon the surface and it extorts few cries that human ears can hear; therefore I the more denounce it, as a secret punishment which slumbering humanity is not roused up to stay."

Child protection is the other side of the coin of child development and well-being. If children are stimulated by quality parenting, health

51

care, and early education, they will flourish. And if they are harmed by early trauma and continuing abuse, powerful barriers may prevent them from flourishing.[100, 101]

The scale of child maltreatment and its impact on hundreds of millions of children argue for these issues being treated as crucial to the human future. But separate from the question of the inherent importance of these issues to children is the question of the importance of child protection issues in the broad scope of public policy. Unfortunately, children's issues are, for the most part, a side issue at the margins

> For some children, child protection *is* child development, in providing early care and education to orphaned or abandoned children. A 2008 report sponsored by the van Leer Foundation made that equation concrete in reviewing the prospects for early care for orphaned children in sub-Saharan Africa.

of international policy. The only issues touching even peripherally on children that might make it onto the agenda of a G-8 or G-20 meeting are the Millennium Development Goals, set by the UN, which provide a partially overlapping framework for some of the child protection indicators. UNICEF uses the phrase "child survival, development, and protection" to encompass the full range of child-specific efforts to achieve the MDGs. But in reviewing resources allocated to child protection compared with other goals, child protection issues do not emerge as priorities.

In four recent books taking an overview of U.S. foreign policy, there were barely passing references to the issues of global poverty, and none about children's issues.[102] A recent review by a former federal official of the history of foreign aid programs in five nations did not address child protection efforts at all, with the exception of a passing reference to education for girls. The book reviews the tradeoffs between diplomacy and development goals of foreign aid, tracing the critical role of domestic political interests in making those tradeoffs. The book does note the "unexpected coalition of the Christian right and the secular left…possibly leading to higher aid levels over time."[103]

Clearly, progress has been made in recent years. In a 2011 summary of the field of child protection a decade and a half ago, the then-Director of the USAID Center on Children in Adversity, Neil Boothby, declared that

> 15 years ago, UNICEF was just beginning to develop its division of child protection, and NGOs had to "beg, borrow or steal" humanitarian funds to address gender-based violence or child soldiers. Today, dedicated child protection staff and child care and protection programs are standard features of humanitarian, peace-keeping and human rights operations.[104]

Yet within the categories of children's issues, child protection remains a relatively small segment of overall children's policy, with child survival and child poverty receiving considerably more attention.[105] In the U.S., the passage of PL 109-95 and its emphasis on vulnerable children is positive, along with the creation of a new office in USAID as a focal point for these efforts. But it was set up without giving the function any discrete funding.[106] And its new efforts aim at child survival, child development, and child protection goals.

Global child protection issues are a subset of foreign assistance issues, which are in turn a subset of foreign policy. Thus they are marginal by definition within the U.S. government. For the most part, with the exception of occasional media spotlights that turn on and off quickly, these issues are perceived to have far less urgency than the other problems of foreign policy.

This marginality is perhaps the largest single barrier to increasing U.S. and other governments' resources and focus on child protection issues. Responses typically take the form of projects and programs rather than policy. Once a program is announced, the political need to deal with this issue may be satisfied, however token the scale of the program. Very few announcements of programs and few evaluations measure the effects of the program against the scale of the problem. This contributes further to the marginality of child protection policy, since projects take the place of policy when their aggregate impact is not in focus.

A contrasting example may make this clear: in U.S. nuclear proliferation policy, to announce an international agreement to scrap 500 warheads immediately leads to the obvious question: out of how many? How many are left? The purpose of this policy is to solve or at least significantly reduce the scale of the problem, and so *both the program and the baseline are on the table.*

This rarely happens in child protection policymaking. As the rollout of the new Global Alliance for Children suggests, programs and projects are typically in the spotlight, rather than the scale of the remaining problem. While indicators are tracked, these results are largely divorced from the resources devoted to given problems. This lack of total information on resources is a diagnostic of the analytical gap between resources and results. UNICEF's annual State of the World's Children reports provide some of those baselines, but it is still rare that projects' results are aggregated against national baselines. The new US Action Plan for Children in Adversity intends to improve results in its three priority areas, using baseline measures that are not yet established in each of the recipient countries (described in more detail in Chapter 9).

NGOs and advocacy groups can confront this marginality with their efforts to change policy, but their choices in doing so reveal the second barrier: each NGO tends to take on "its own" issues in making the case for child protection investments, rather than the whole of child maltreatment as a complex mixture of enduring problems affecting millions of children. Fragmentation at the project level contributes to the marginality problem, forming a major obstacle to mobilizing a higher level of resources for child protection programs and olicy.

The risk of the marginality of child protection is that success also becomes marginalized, and gets defined as launching (or re-labeling) projects and

> A fragmented new box on the organization chart labeled "child protection" is no guarantee of impact on the myriad of child protection issues.

organizational units, rather than changing policy with the leverage of new resources. If child protection necessarily involves health, education, child development, disabilities, family services, legal issues, and family income supports, then a fragmented new box on the organization chart labeled child protection is no guarantee of impact on these other arenas. Projects without critical mass or any viable hope of replication at scale may not "move the needle" on key national and global indicators, however laudable their individual efforts.

In the U.S., the PL 109-95 legislation calls for new coordination efforts, and the publications of the new USAID office are very clear in adopting a "whole-of-government" approach. The breadth of representation from agencies throughout the government is another positive signal. In Chapter 6, we will review the sizable literature on the barriers to coordination in governmental agencies as they affect functions with much higher priority than child protection has been given thus far. The Action Plan issued in December 2012 addressed some of these barriers, but not comprehensively, as discussed in Chapter 9.

The issue of the relative importance of child protection in the larger context of foreign assistance and foreign policy remains a critical part of the policy environment for these activities. In Chapter Ten we discuss the prospects of heightening the visibility and importance given to these issues.

CHAPTER FIVE

What causes child maltreatment?

The idea of universal human rights underlies the UN Convention on the Rights of the Child, and the monitoring efforts focused on the Convention are based on those rights enumerated in the Convention. In some cases, the language of the Convention addresses the underlying causes that may undermine those rights. But if the causes differ based on culture, biases against race, ethnicity, religion, caste, gender, or sexual orientation—those driving factors are critical barriers to achieving human rights.

Poverty

> Poverty and gender exclusion often intersect with protection risks, further undermining children's rights. The most marginalized children are often deprived of their rights in multiple ways. There is evidence…of disparities within disparities – for example, gender disparities within the poorest communities and in rural areas.[107]

The distinctions are not precise between children whose futures are diminished by poverty and malnutrition and those who are maltreated. A child who is severely underweight or malnourished may be labeled "neglected," and that neglect may be seen as maltreatment. Research exists on the extent to which parents' poverty is a root cause of neglect or maltreatment. But what is "the parents' fault" and what is beyond parents' control is a difficult line to draw, especially when many of those parents are among the "bottom billion" of the world's population who live below $1.25 a day. It remains a fact, however, that most of those parents do not mistreat their children, and many make valiant sacrifices to ensure that their children will escape poverty through education.

So there is an important question about non-poverty-related causes of maltreatment. A growing body of evidence suggests that a combination of *cultural norms* and *multiple forms of addiction* must be distinguished from poverty itself as three sets of reinforcing ingredients of the underlying causes of maltreatment.

Child survival and poverty reduction strategies clearly have the potential to affect child maltreatment. Families under less financial stress will be able to make better long-term decisions about sending their children to school, keeping them from working too soon, delaying children's marrying and having babies, and giving them the healthier food that will enable brain development. Yet some poverty reduction has been accompanied by increases in child maltreatment, as when urban migration leaves some children behind in rural areas, separated from parents working in cities, and when growing urban concentrations increase the demand for alcohol and drugs and sex-related employment.[108]

However much causation can be determined, most who work in this field see a need for a very close link between distinctive child protection initiatives and those aimed at child survival and poverty. Within an overall Division of Programmes, UNICEF has separate units for Child Protection and for Child Survival and Development. Save the Children, the largest NGO that works on children's issues, includes child protection as one of five areas of its work.

Strengthening these links among different priorities in children's services and protection is one of the major challenges facing all governmental agencies and NGOs, as they seek to avoid isolated, fragmented efforts that may drift to the margins of policy and thus receive grossly inadequate resources. In some cases, such as maternal and child health—a specific target of foreign assistance mentioned, appropriately, in the U.S. *National Security Strategy* document of 2010—child survival and anti-poverty goals are inextricably connected. UNICEF has succeeded in explicitly linking child labor issues to the Millennium Development Goals on poverty and education, although the antipoverty goals and child survival clearly dominate the agenda.[109] In other forums and publications, however, the child protection agenda is separated from anti-poverty initiatives in ways that may lead to fragmentation.

As noted above, a critical unifying tool across problems affecting children is the expanding use of social indicators drawn from survey and other data. UNICEF's annual updating of its indicators combines risk factors that are primarily about maltreatment with those that are primarily about poverty and preventable diseases.[110] UNICEF has also undertaken some sophisticated analyses of the connections between several anti-poverty policies and child protection goals. Recent reports review the connections between social protection and child protection, legal reform and child protection, and the challenges of defining and measuring equity for children.[111] UNICEF has also framed these issues at times as "poverty plus," noting that gender bias and poverty can both affect a girl, along with disabilities and poverty, caste and poverty, and so forth.

So, to summarize: Poverty matters to child protection, but it is not the only thing that matters. And tragically, in some cases, improvements in family income increase pressures on children and the potential for maltreatment, such as parents' consumption of alcohol, children forced to work for added income, and migration of parents away from children to urban employment centers.

Cultural and religious practices

Many forms of violence against children are tacitly or explicitly condoned by society—these include child marriage, female genital mutilation/cutting, corporal punishment, and domestic violence.[112]

In addressing maltreatment in a global framework, it is important to ask whether cultural and other norms that differ across nations have any influence over the effects of developmental harm done to children. Very simply, if everyone does it, is it harmful? Do brain changes happen similarly to all children independent of culture? Obviously, it depends on what the specific harm is. But if a community accepts certain forms of maltreatment as a norm that may be viewed as harmful by external observers in a different place and time, it is important to be clear about what is universal and what is culturally and socially determined.[113] Universal statements of human rights do not easily affect cultural norms, as the monitoring reports on the UN Convention make painfully clear.

Cultural practices can have child protection consequences—both positive and negative. Cultural sensitivity in therapy for child maltreatment can have highly positive effects, ensuring that therapists have an in-depth understanding of the cultural boundaries around families and child-rearing. For some abused children, healing that takes place within their culture can soften the pain of separation from their families, ensuring that food, setting, and language helps them orient themselves in familiar surroundings. Cultural practices that emphasize the importance of community can help a child or youth understand that they have ready access to people who care about them, whatever the harm done to them by abusive parents or traffickers.

But culture can also cause maltreatment, through a variety of mechanisms:

- Discrimination against out-groups in a dominant culture, defined by ethnicity, caste, tribal origins, or gender
- Acceptance of forms of corporal punishment and family violence at home and in school that meet the definition of maltreatment
- Fear of community rejection of a family or a child for bringing sexual practices within the family into public view in communities where these are regarded as private family matters to be settled within the family

- Placing rigid boundaries around what is possible for girls and women in ways that limit their participation in school and community life
- Adaptation to separation as an economic necessity, subordinating children's needs to family practices in which children are left with relatives while parents seek employment by migrating to urban areas or other countries.

There are numerous statements of this cultural outlook; one that captures its pervasiveness well was contained in the NGO response to the September 2012 UNHCR review of the Philippines' compliance with the Optional Protocol on the Sale of Children, Child Prostitution and Child Pornography (OPSC)

> A general lack of understanding around children's rights still exists within the Filipino society. This is a strong contributing factor in the commercial sexual exploitation of children (CSEC). Children are considered 'parental property' and are taught to be submissive and obedient to adults at all times. This may compromise their ability to defend themselves when being sexually exploited in the home or community. Also, families may be reluctant to bring charges related to child sexual abuse for fear that it might tarnish the image and reputation of the family and cause them to be ostracised within the community. The stigma and persistent cultural attitudes surrounding child sexual exploitation hinder adequate service provision to children who are affected by prostitution and sexual exploitation.[114]

The interplay between gender inequity, culture, and poverty is pervasive. When women are denied any role in earning or allocating family income, poverty can worsen by subtracting their earnings and their influence from decisions about a family's investment in its children. To take one example, dowries for girls' marriages can represent a great economic setback for a family struggling to escape poverty. The World Bank team that studied poverty in India cited a woman who told of having to save money for her daughter's dowry since the child was born:

> I was happy on her birth because she was my first child. But I was also sad because the birth of a girl in a poor family is equivalent to death.

The study found that nearly a third of the families that moved into poverty in West Bengal did so because of "social shocks," including the cost of dowries.[115]

In a very thoughtful essay in an edited collection on *Young Children and Trauma*, Marva Lewis and Chandra Ghosh Ippen developed a typology of "distinct forms of trauma experienced by young children and their cultural groups."[116] Of the 25 forms of trauma listed, however, only two had gender content. Another article in the collection addressed neurodevelopmental effects of trauma in younger children, but without any links to cultural practices that may cause trauma.[117]

In an analysis written in 1996 for UNICEF, Philip Alston and Bridget Gilmour-Walsh sought to set forth a "synthesis of children's rights and cultural values."[118] Their focus was on the "best interests of the child" references in the UN Convention on the Rights of the Child and how to reconcile that principle with cultural practices.

> ...the central importance of the best interests principle within the CRC framework does not mean that its interpretation or application is in any way straightforward or uncontroversial. Paradoxically, the stronger the agreement as to its centrality, the greater the diversity of approaches advocated in its applications.

The word 'trauma' does not appear in this article, which was written prior to much—but not all—of the recent research on childhood trauma. In addressing female circumcision in the context of the best interests of the child, the article's initial conclusions are very different from the tone of more recent UNICEF documents:

> If the test of the child's best interests were the only consideration, and if other substantive provisions of the CRC did not preclude the practice, the outcome would depend upon the value placed on the relevant concerns such as the child's integration into society and the child's health.[119]

But later in the article, the authors cite the end of female mutilation in Burkina Faso after discussions among community members as an example of how concern for the best interests of the child—in this case viewing the child's health as the critical factor—can reverse prior norms.[120] They call for dialogue between those seeking to uphold international norms and those defending what another author calls "folk models" of treatment of children.

In one of the few studies located that assessed the effects of physical punishment in a context of social norms, a study of mothers and children in China, India, Italy, Kenya, the Philippines, and Thailand, found that "although more frequent physical punishment was related to more child aggression and anxiety in all six countries, these links were weaker in countries in which the use of physical punishment was more normative."[121]

While those with a comfortable, Western perspective need a considerable measure of humility in attempting to understand cultural values and culture-based practices in other parts of the world, if human rights have any universal content, it is essential to weigh these cultural factors against harm done to children. And if the science on the long-term effects of trauma is taken seriously, then there are additional grounds for weighing brain damage against cultural practices that allow that damage to continue. Mutilating girls is one form of child maltreatment that can have profound physical and mental consequences; damaging brains as a result of physical forms of trauma is no less important for being less visible.

Kwame Anthony Appiah has written about global ethics as demanding a "conversation" among different cultures that may need to precede discussion of values: a conversation that "helps people get used to one another."[122] But one should not lose sight of the fact that in discussing child protection, *there is a third party to such a conversation*—an innocent child whose life and prospects may be greatly affected by the lack of agreement on values across cultures. It is indisputable that changing social norms requires gradualism, but the harm done while awaiting gradual change is also indisputable—and tragic. Weighing the virtues of patience in changing cultural norms against the urgency of reducing trauma and long-term damage is one of the most difficult challenges of working in the arenas of child protection. The good news is that social and cultural norms do change over time, but if the interests of children are a priority that goes beyond lofty rhetoric and pilot projects, that change will need to be accelerated in some parts of the world.

If, in fact, there are no neurodevelopmental grounds for concluding that culture mediates the damages of trauma in any significant way, then the arguments for universal values of children's rights are strengthened. If human children are all affected by maltreatment in ways that can cause neurodevelopmental damage, then explaining differences in how children are treated based on cultural and religious differences is not a valid defense of that harm.

The neurodevelopmental perspective also strengthens the case for closer links between human rights and child rights. If medical experiments were being conducted on the brains of 400 million children that impaired their cognitive and emotional capabilities, it would be impossible to argue that this is not a human rights issue. But 400 million children *are* being harmed, with undeniable neurodevelopmental consequences. Whatever foundational concepts are held to be the underpinnings of human rights doctrine, systematic harm to children cannot be excluded simply because most human rights organizations essentially overlook these forms of maltreatment and their effects.

Issues of human rights, like issues of children's rights, can be debated on philosophical and ethical grounds. But it is difficult to find a case for children's rights that has been put forth and defended on neurodevelopmental grounds. Only recently, as evidence builds up on the effects of trauma and toxic levels of stress, has it become possible to frame the rights of children in terms of their right to develop their cognitive, emotional and physical potential without being stunted by violence or neglect.

Human dignity is an abstract term, although we can easily recognize what denial of dignity looks like in its extreme forms. But the operations of the human brain, while far from fully understood, have become comprehensible at levels unimaginable a few decades ago. Once we know about the flow of cortisol in a traumatized brain, and the emotional and cognitive effects of that flow in later life, we cannot ignore what that does to either a developing child or a former combat soldier. Trauma is a reality in the lives of both of them, and it can have dangerous consequences for both. Whatever human dignity is, it must involve an effort to reduce that harm to human brains and those affected by that harm.

Does brain science trump cultural pluralism? We may not yet know enough to answer this conclusively. But surely we know enough to recognize that the question matters, and that culture is a weak defense for the worst forms of maltreatment when the result is lifelong neurodevelopmental damage. Our review of the available literature and our interviews with experts in the field of neurodevelopmental growth found far less attention to the intersection of culture and neuroscience than seems necessary, given the numbers of children affected. Determining how much that damage may or may not be affected by cultural norms would seem to be one of the most important targets for research in both the child protection and neurodevelopmental fields in the future.

Western values and the sources of activism

The issue for children's rights as it relates to cultural relativism is whether the exceptions in national "ratifications" are so great and the enforcement tactics such as naming and shaming so weak as to make the original standards mere rhetoric. The reality test, then, becomes whether states and cultural/religious leaders have worked to change their practices as a result of internationally prescribed standards of child protection.

The large, historic expansions of human rights are for the most part not helpful guides; slavery and apartheid ended as public policy. It is today's hard cases such as female mutilation and schooling for girls—cases affecting millions of children—that test the relevance of children's rights to cultural norms most directly. Progress made by some nations is noteworthy, but the sources of that progress must be reviewed carefully to see what works in changing social norms.

On most of these issues, leadership from the West and the Western traditions remain suspect in much of the developing world; many of those knowledgeable about children's rights believe it is leadership from the South that will make the difference. Controversies over the composition of the Human Rights Council, including as it does representatives from theocratic, repressive regimes, may be resolved if the sustained behavior of these representatives can be analyzed against standards of the CRC. Are these representatives consistently defensive about the worst practices that most clearly violate the CRC, or have they spoken up on behalf of *any* of the changes proposed by UN rapporteurs and NGO critiques? If such analysis exists, it should be used as a key piece of evidence answering the question of the utility of the Council in monitoring compliance with the CRC. And again, it should be noted that as a non-ratifier, the U.S. is handicapped in its role in this arena.

But we should not tilt so far toward politically correct perspectives that we ignore the fundamental motivations of activists. It was not Western values that led 15-year-old Malala Yousafzai to advocate schooling for girls before the Taliban shot her in Pakistan in the summer of 2012, any more than it was Western values that placed that lone, iconic figure in front of the tank in Tiananmen Square in 1989. Labeling brave activists as subversive does not make them subversive, "Westernized," or any less brave.

Michael Ignatieff has bluntly framed the issue:

> Human rights are a political set of claims that seek to enhance and defend the powerless against the powerful.

By definition, patriarchal, theocratic authoritarians are not going to sign up.[123]

Religion and culture

The discussion of culture and trauma should not ignore the significant overlap between religious and cultural practices. The literature on cultural practices and trauma often calls for professionals to be sensitive to cultural issues in responding to trauma.[124] But the trauma is typically treated as an aberration—not an inherent part of the child's and family's culture. That is not always the case in a global setting, in which the subordination of women and early marriage are in some settings deeply embedded in the culture and justified by well-defended interpretations of religious teaching.

If there is an element of child protection that is more emotionally charged than cultural effects on trauma, it is the effects of religious beliefs and practices on trauma.[125] In the U.S., media attention to the practices of a few religious cults that have been charged with child abuse has brought these issues into intermittent visibility. "Spare the rod and spoil the child" is a much wider folk saying supposedly derived from the Bible that is invoked at times to justify corporal punishment. And the high visibility of court cases concerning priests' abuse of children and youth (as well as by athletic coaches and youth group leaders), both in the U.S. and other nations, has also been framed in terms of trauma and its lifelong effects.

The entire arena of gender equity is, of course, also affected by the overlap between culture and religion in many countries. Interpretations of scripture are used to justify subordination of women in many parts of the world. But the sensitivity of these issues is perhaps illustrated by the fact that the word 'religion' is used only once in the U.S. National Action Plan on Women, Peace, and Security, and then only to refer in passing to freedom of religion. Working with religious leaders is mentioned once.

This caution in references to religious grounds for children's rights is an understandable response to the intensity of recent objections in the U.S. to the Convention on Rights of the Child and what is described by some conservative religious groups as the "anti-family bias" of the U.N. Linda McClain and others have traced the recent history of these objections to the CRC and the U.N.'s work on gender equality, though without explicitly linking these to a broader international movement to defend family and religious choices against government or international agencies' interventions.[126]

These issues boiled over in early 2013 in the debates over a U.N. Declaration on Violence against Girls and Women. Language was finally approved declaring that violence against women could not be justified by "any custom, tradition or religious consideration." Initially, delegates from Iran, Libya, Sudan and other Muslim nations, as well as the Vatican, threatened to block adoption of the Declaration, which led to removal of references to sexual orientation and abortion rights.[127]

As noted in the set of religious quotes in Chapter 1, religion can exalt the role of the innocent child—and it can justify unspeakable harm to children in the name of filial piety and other values claimed to have a religious foundation. The double-edged sword of religious practices as they affect childhood trauma makes religious beliefs an inescapable part of the discussion of the underlying causes of child maltreatment. That discussion must seek the difficult balance between judgmental Western attitudes toward other religions and cultures and an effort to uphold standards of child protection that are truly universal. That balance must include recognition that there are scholars and practitioners of Islam who have made a powerful case against the subordination of women as being at odds with the core tenets of Islam and the economic future of the Middle East and North Africa.[128] But the divisions among different religious perspectives on the rights of children to be free from harm within their own families and community remain important barriers to universal standards. They also weaken enforcement of those standards in areas where they are most ignored.

Addictions and culture

The interplay between culture and addiction is fraught with difficult, inevitably subjective interpretations of human behavior. In substance abuse, a loosely described "culture of addiction" is one way of describing lifestyle differences that characterize some persons with addictions in some settings.

But extending the concept of addiction beyond substance use disorders to other behaviors is itself controversial, and adding cultural issues complicates the problem further. Yet in our view it is impossible to understand child abuse or neglect as something that only bad parents or bad people do, without probing for the underlying factors that make some forms of child maltreatment culturally acceptable—or make it acceptable to essentially ignore them as behavior that happens within the family, in a place where public policy should not intrude. And that is where cultural norms and addiction collide.

When "everyone" smokes pot, or chews qat, or binge drinks on Fridays– then that form of addiction has become normalized. And when "everyone" visits prostitutes regularly, beats their children as a form of discipline, or keeps their girls home to work in the household rather than attending school, then it becomes important to ask what cultural norms underlie that behavior, and whether some form of addictive behavior is part of the motivation underlying it as well.

A cultural tradition is not an addiction. But part of the definition of addiction is that even though what you are doing harms you, *or someone else*, you keep doing it. If you take that definition seriously, then not only substance abuse, but sex with younger children is also a form of addiction. And insisting on male power over all decisions made by women can also be seen as a form of addiction to power, if a neutral observer can see the harm done by depriving women of a measure of autonomy and movement toward an equal role in society.[129]

Addictions are a significant, underlying, correlated condition of child maltreatment.[130] Those addictions and the underlying brain disease that drives addiction must be addressed directly by treatment, incentives, sanctions, law enforcement, and social marketing. Some addictions are culturally reinforced and maintained, and responses to maltreatment correlated with addictions must be based in culture without accepting child maltreatment as a norm. But the literature on child protection is almost completely devoid of any discussion of addiction, preferring to address social norms without the added complications of chemical dependency or behavioral disorders. This seems a major omission, if a public health perspective on these forms of addiction is included in policy and programs, including the need for prevention and treatment of addiction.

The line between "bad" parenting and parents living under great economic and mental stress is a difficult one to draw. Drug and alcohol issues can complicate these distinctions. Substance use disorders are diseases of the brain, and like diabetes and hypertension, the diseases can be managed by following a regimen of treatment and aftercare. But for vast numbers of parents, such treatment is inconceivable, for the reasons that Paul Farmer and others have described in assessing disparities in health care. Yet the critical link remains: addictions can contribute to child maltreatment. Because of the economic effects and the behavioral effects of substance use disorders, many parents harm and neglect their children. When treatment is inconceivable because resources are not available to these parents, harm can become irreversible.

It should be clear that the importance of addiction to legal and illegal substances is not because it directly causes child maltreatment, but that substance abuse is highly correlated with family instability and violence that can add to child maltreatment. A family whose working members spend excessive amounts of their small income on their addictions can feel greater pressure to divert their children from school to work. And a family who has difficulty keeping appointments because their substance abuse affects their daily schedules can fail to use the resources already available for their children such as immunizations and health checkups.

In reviewing the worldwide literature on alcohol research, a group of researchers concluded that

> The consumption of alcohol is globally one of the main social and public health problems. The World Health Organization estimates that 4% of world mortality is directly attributable to alcohol. There is a causal relationship between alcohol consumption and more than 60 different types of illness, besides the fact that alcohol consumption is frequently related with numerous problems such as traffic accidents, antisocial behavior, low performance at work, *abuse in the family*, suicides, violence, crimes, homicides, and delinquency.[131]

A joint effort by WHO and ISPCAN to address child maltreatment in 2006 concluded

> Alcohol misuse by adults is strongly associated with fetal alcohol syndrome and increased risk of child physical and sexual abuse by parents and other family members. Reducing access to alcohol can thus be expected to have a preventive effect, and there is some evidence to suggest that increasing the tax on alcohol can be effective in reducing child maltreatment.[132]

In the U.S., 11% of children—8.3 million children—live with a parent who is alcoholic or chemically dependent on an illegal drug. There is no statistic that serves as a global counterpart, and drugs are more widely available in the U.S. than in many parts of the world—though not in those regions where drug cultivation and distribution are major economic activities.

The 2012 World Drug Report by the United Nations Office of Drugs and Crime cited an increase in synthetic drug production worldwide, "including significant increases in the production and consumptions of psychoactive substances that are not under international control." Overall, use of illegal drugs remained stable during the past five years, at between

3.4 and 6.6 percent of the world's adult population. Marijuana was the most widely used drug.[133] The report concluded that drug abuse kills approximately 200,000 people annually; treatment for global drug abuse would cost $250 billion a year, according to the study.

This categorization, however, ignores the effects of the legal drugs— alcohol and tobacco—which have a much greater impact on global public health. Recent work by the International Center for Research on Women has underscored the links between masculine stereotypes about drinking and sexual abuse.[134] Another study reviewing alcohol patterns in 26 countries found that lower national income correlated with higher social consequences as a result of drinking alcohol.[135] Another study published in 2015 found that "An estimated 4.9% of the world's adult population (240 million people) suffer from alcohol use disorder (7.8% of men and 1.5% of women)…"[136]

Two recent assessments of child protection systems in developed nations almost completely ignored the impact of substance abuse on child maltreatment.[137] While brief references were made to high rates of addiction and fetal alcohol syndrome among aboriginal populations, there was no discussion of drug and alcohol treatment as a component of child welfare services in either book.

Yet other studies have linked alcohol to violence and gender equality.

> Alcohol consumption will predictably rise with personal incomes, so an effective long-term view of development must incorporate effective measures to prevent alcohol-related harm. While throughout the world men do the bulk of the drinking, women bear the consequences disproportionately in the form of interpersonal violence, its impact on family budgets, and other secondary effects of others' drinking. Thus addressing harmful use of alcohol is critical to resolving issues of gender equity as well as maternal and child health.

A systematic review of alcohol use and sexual risks for HIV/AIDS in Sub-Saharan Africa identified four factors that are most closely related: drinking venues and alcohol serving establishments, sexual coercion and poverty. A review and meta-analysis of 20 studies from Africa found that drinkers have a 70% greater chance of being HIV positive when compared to non-drinkers in the bivariate case, and a 57% increased risk of HIV infection when potential confounders were controlled in multivariate analysis.[138]

These connections between HIV/AIDS and alcohol suggest that the origins of the USAID emphasis on vulnerable children in concerns about HIV/AIDS argues for closer scrutiny of alcohol as it affects HIV/AIDS transmission and adherence to medication regimes.[139] To be committed to reducing the effects of HIV/AIDS on children without taking alcohol into account overlooks this critical link.

There are several reasons that addiction has been under-emphasized in most reviews of child maltreatment. The first is that in many cultures, especially those under Islamic law and tradition, alcohol is prohibited. This does not mean that addictions are automatically minimized, but it clearly reduces the use of alcohol, especially when these prohibitions are reinforced by overall repression and punishment. Other factors leading to neglect of this issue include

- The disease theory of addiction as a brain disorder has not been accepted in many nations
- Fetal alcohol data is very limited
- Alcohol in some cultures is heavily gender-related, as an accepted practice of males and a rite of passage for young males
- Alcohol is perceived as a problem in aboriginal cultures, but not majority cultures

The issue of addiction is also affected by the fact that addictions policy confronts multinational corporate policy if it is serious about reducing alcohol abuse that affects families. As noted in the NGO coalition comments on the WHO non-communicable diseases (NCDs) policy from the Global Alcohol Policy Alliance,

> The evidence base for the most effective, cost-effective and sustainable interventions to address nutrition and alcohol as risk factors for NCDs points to fiscal (tax based), regulatory and other market based measures. In line with measures required for harmful tobacco products, these include measures on price, marketing, labeling and claims, composition and promotion. These measures are affordable, cost effective and cost-saving, and can also help to raise revenue for governments and public health.[140]

Corruption and non-enforcement of laws

Another issue affecting child protection policies that combines both cultural and economic factors is corruption, to the extent that the rule of law and compliance with child rights are undermined by corruption that compromises law enforcement regarding child protection. As stated bluntly by one interviewee for this book, who is very familiar with community realities through decades of work in Central Asia, "The laws don't make any difference; they aren't enforced."

Jeffrey Sachs, summarizing a study on levels of adequate governance (which he equates with efforts to eliminate corruption) and economic growth, concludes that "...the focus on corruption and governance is exaggerated, and seriously overstates the causal role of corruption and poor governance in Africa's laggard growth performance."[141] The other side of the debate is briefly summarized by William Easterly and others who argue that corruption and multiple other barriers make assistance programs ineffective.[142]

Working through host governments is essential in foreign assistance programs, but too many NGOs have complained publicly and privately about corruption to dismiss it as easily as Sachs does. Recent corruption headlines in China and India make clear that this is far from an African issue; if anything, the scale appears to vary with the size of the economy.[143] And it should be acknowledged that the role of money in politics as a corrupting influence has Western variations on a scale far more vast than a brothel owner's bribe to the local policemen.

For child protection, corruption has two undermining effects: its overall damage to the credibility of foreign assistance in general, and its weakening of the enforcement of child protection at the local level when law enforcement and judicial operations are compromised. In an extraordinary statement on the continuing relevance of corruption, Kofi Annan in May 2013 published an opinion editorial titled "Stop the Plunder of Africa," that cited the findings of the annual Africa Progress Report strongly criticizing "the hemorrhage of revenues associated with tax evasion, secret deals, and illicit financial transfers." Adding that "corruption remains endemic," Annan called for a crackdown on illicit financial transfers, referring to the U.S. Dodd-Frank legislation as an encouraging recent development.[144]

The World Bank's reviews of the relationship between foreign assistance and corruption are particularly blunt.

> Given the lack of effectiveness and potentially harmful effects of aid in poor governance environments with high levels of corruption, less aid should be given to countries with high levels of corruption, and more aid to reward countries with good governance, where aid is more effective. However, there is no empirical evidence that this in fact is the case... aid in fact went in equal amounts to countries with poor as well as good governance. This is because the allocation of bilateral aid is mostly influenced by the strategic interests of donors... At the same time, multilateral aid has been largely uninfluenced by political or strategic interest. Here, aid allocation has been targeted towards lower income countries with good management,

which received 30% more than poorly managed countries in the same income and population group...[145]

Wars and the aftermath of wars

War is also an obvious and fundamental cause of global child maltreatment, as revealed by the sixteen UNICEF categories of child protection, of which at least six relate to war and its dislocations. Both boys and girls are swept up in wars, civil wars, and bandit groups operating in dozens of nations. Accessing these children is very difficult because of the conflicts, and thus armed conflict must be understood as one of the underlying causes of child maltreatment. Children without homes, children in refugee status because of armed conflict, and the other risks to children in time of war can suddenly absorb resources that greatly exceed the available child protection funding, creating a drain on longer-term activities intended to benefit children at risk.

Prior to taking up her current role with the National Security Council, Susan Rice and colleagues at the Brookings Institution edited a volume on the connections between poverty and national security. It noted

> ...global poverty is not just a humanitarian concern. Over the long term, it can threaten U.S. national security. Poverty erodes a state's capacity to prevent the spread of disease and protect forests and watersheds...Poverty can also give rise to tensions that can erupt into full-scale civil conflict, further taxing the state and allowing transnational predators greater freedom of action.[146]

The volume pointed out how civil war within and among weak states endangers the most vulnerable citizens of such states; although the effects on children were not a focus, the connection between warfare and its aftermath in national and international chaos clearly affects children in precarious situations.

Ironically, some of the most effective interagency coordination and collaboration among NGOs and governments have come in response to the dislocations of children by war. Because it is seen as temporary, perhaps, some barriers to working across agency lines are lowered in the interests of getting resources to children and their families.

In some senses, "war" is too simplistic a concept in framing threats to the safety of children. The full range of threats to public safety—non-state armed conflict, urban gangs, drug cartels—these are not war as we understand it, a conflict between armies or even between armies and insurgents, but rather a disintegration of safety due to the collapse of government and the rise of what some have called "feral cities."[147] When a city is unsafe, its children are especially unsafe, and child protection activities as such are inadequate to the much larger and more complex tasks of restoring order and predictability in urban communities that contain many children.

UNICEF's 2011 annual report focused on cities as the dangerous arenas for children that many urban areas have become.[148] Urban conflict endangers children, whether due to conventional war or to other forms of violent non-state disruption to stability. Understanding these arenas is critical to responding effectively to the conditions that threaten children.

David Kilcullen's recent book *Out of the Mountains*, describes this collapse as it increasingly occurs in coastal mega-cities as what he regards as the newest frontier of conflict. Using examples drawn from throughout the urban world, he describes the likelihood of increasing devastation in urban areas that have exploded as the poverty of rural life is replaced by vast flows of urban migration. He calls for a post-counter-insurgency strategy that relies on *co-design* by credible insiders and expert outsiders who can map the sites and sources of conflict using a combination of technology and grass-roots civil society organizations.[149] Some of his prescriptions, drawn from the world of counter-insurgency, can be interpreted as preventive strategies in the arena of child protection, if one takes seriously the threats to children in urban areas as a definable segment of the overall threat.

Resettlement as a cause of child maltreatment and neglect

Displacement affects children in many ways, whether caused by war, natural disaster, or more supposedly benign economic forces. Sometimes those economic effects are justified as economic development. But dislocating thousands of families in the face of construction of major dams, highways, or new housing developments still leaves the children in those families with fewer roots to their communities, fewer opportunities for stable education, and threats to their safety in unstable, temporary communities, whatever the overall economic effects of the development.

Refugee resettlement across borders is subject to international oversight, though enforcement of the guidelines for resettlement is very difficult. Internal resettlement, however, has fewer appeal points, since decisions by a national government, a development authority, or multinational corporation may not be subject to any external review. NGOs have sought to address this gap, including the International Accountability Project and the Internal Displacement Monitoring Centre, as well as the World Bank's efforts to develop an Involuntary Resettlement Source book.[150]

Well-intended development projects are widely recognized to have caused dislocation as a result of resettlement planning that has been inadequate to consider the full impact of uprooting entire villages and moving them to a new location. With support from the Oak and Van Leer Foundations, a group of researchers with the Bank Information Center (BIC) documented the effects on children of their families' relocation from a dam site in Uganda that was funded by the World Bank. They used the CRC framework to assess the harm done, which in their analysis was substantial. BIC researchers estimate that as many as 15 million people are displaced annually as a result of development projects, and have developed remedial policies that BIC has urged the World Bank to consider.[151]

Energy policy and shortages can also affect this kind of displacement of children and families, since hydropower remains the fastest growing "renewable" energy source. The enormous dams that result from such policy may be less environmentally damaging than use of fossil fuels, but their dislocation impact can be severe. This becomes another area where corporate policy has indirect but powerful effects on the well-being of children, especially in developing nations.

Structural violence as a cause

Finally, Paul Farmer has framed the issues of public health disparities as "structural violence," drawing upon other literature and research.[152] The issues of child survival and maternal and child health are, from this perspective, ultimately child protection issues in the sense that protecting children from structural violence is a logical extension of the concept of child maltreatment and neglect.

By structural violence, Farmer means that institutional norms—the way resources are allocated and the priorities given to different forms of health care—result in harm done to the poorest and most often excluded citizens of many nations as a result of disparities in health care. Those structural patterns deny life-saving medicine and medical care to the poorest children and families that are readily available to the rest of the world. Farmer rightly equates this denial of care with violence.

Here is where the boundaries between child protection, child survival, and poverty reduction completely collapse. For those child protection issues where gender disparities underlie denial of care, it is easier to see how child survival for female infants and children is a child protection issue. Simply keeping female newborns alive is still a challenge in many nations. But child protection as a whole, as several writers have noted, is appropriately viewed as a public health issue. Farmer repeatedly makes the point that human rights advocates have not seen public health as a human rights issue, and when children's rights are added to the equation, the point becomes even clearer.

When structures become central in focusing on child maltreatment, two separate sets of structures must be spotlighted. The first are those structures that preserve male dominance over girls and women and the second is those structures that discriminate against lower caste, minority groups defined by ethnicity, national origin, religious identity, or tribe. It is these children who are disproportionately violated, kept out of school, and unregistered at birth. The child protection issue here is clear-cut: the right to be free from harm and to have access to benefits that are supposedly universal. The closely related public health issue is the right to good health care. Farmer points out that epidemics are often caused by human rights violations. The epidemic of sexual violence targeted on children and youth, although Farmer does not mention it explicitly, is an example of his point.[153]

Finally, it should be pointed out that these categories are not universally accepted as the most important causes of child maltreatment. UNICEF cites five separate causes of child maltreatment in its 2011 report on child protection:

- Current trends of urbanisation
- Mobility of populations
- Changing demographics (with the success of child survival efforts leading to an increase in proportions of children in middle and late childhood)
- A rise in countries moving toward middle income status. where violence against children remains a core concern, and
- An increase in the scale and severity of conflict situations and natural disasters.[154]

Each of these is a valid explanation of the causes of maltreatment, but a deeper set of causes, including those listed in this section, can be seen as drivers as well. Omitting cultural bases for discrimination seems especially troubling when reviewing recent events and the extraordinary efforts required to elevate gender equity to the status of a priority issue.

Four easy answers

To sum up our review of the causes of child maltreatment, child protection issues are often distilled into a few cross-cutting problems. The risk is that important components of child maltreatment get boiled out of the distillation. There are at least four forms of this distillation that risk oversimplification of the policy responses to child protection:

1. *It's gender bias*

As noted above, at least half of the UNICEF list of child protection indicators can be linked to gender equality. It seems safe to say after a review of U.S. and UN documents over the past five years that gender equality commands more resources and leadership from both networks than do the full gamut of child protection issues.

But a careful review of the data on several of the child protection indicators makes it difficult to equate child protection and gender equity. With tens of millions of young boys affected by sexual violence, non-registration of rural births, and child labor, and with boys the primary victims of military coercion, such an equation ignores lasting harm done to males. And if the lifelong effects of trauma are a major reason to elevate the entire child protection agenda, gender equality does not encompass all of that trauma by any means. Abused boys become angry young men, and angry young men are some of the most dangerous.—and most tragic—victims of the failures and omissions of child protection programs and policies.

2. *It's child survival*

As noted above, the lines are very unclear between neglect in the form of malnutrition and neglect that denies children with disabilities or girls their fair share of developmental supports. The extraordinary work done by public health advocates and health providers has spotlighted ways in which children are profoundly neglected by failures to provide the right antibiotics in the right amounts at the right time.[155] Farmer's framing of

> The college student returned to her home village and visited her old classroom. She noticed that one child was sitting in the back of the room and not participating as much as the rest of the students. When she asked the teacher why, the teacher explained that he was one of the students whose parents were not living in the village any longer because their work was in another city. These "left-behind" students are getting more attention in China, as their numbers increase along with the evidence that they are having serious problems.

structural violence adds to our understanding of these links. Yet proper immunization or malaria nets are no guarantee that girls or lower-caste or minority children will be allowed to attend school once they have survived some of the worst childhood diseases. Survival rates with significant gender and minority disparities are another signal of child maltreatment based on bias and exclusion.

3. It's poverty

Child protection and poverty reduction overlap, as pointed out throughout this review. But children are abused in families that are on the way out of poverty, as well as among those who have escaped poverty completely—and among those who are the poorest families. Poverty can reinforce some, but not all of the underlying causes of child maltreatment. So equating the two conditions misses the areas where they are not correlated, as well as those where increasing family income may increase the risk of maltreatment. One of the clearest examples of the latter issue is the abandonment of children in the interior rural areas of China whose parents have had to move to urban areas nearer the coastal economic regions to find jobs.[156] As family income has risen, so has child dislocation and, in some cases, virtual abandonment.

4. It's human rights

Because the Convention on Rights of the Child is monitored through the Human Rights Council, there is a significant overlap between the sixteen UNICEF indicators and the work of the Council. Some of the thematic topics monitored by the Council's special rapporteurs who conduct site visits include child maltreatment indicators, including prostitution and pornography involving children, sale of children, trafficking, rights to education, and violence against women.[157] Advocates and staff working on children's rights repeatedly point out that children's rights are human rights, but the human rights agenda as defined by the Human Rights Council and the (institutionally separate) UN Commissioner on Human Rights do not include the full range of the UNICEF definitions, and site visits do not address these with any unified framework separate from the thematic areas. As noted above, this gap remains a challenge to both fields, in excluding the rights of children from a significant portion of human rights monitoring.

These "easy answers" are not wrong; it is that they are not complete that is the problem. Each explains a portion of what child protection policies seek to address, but none is adequate to encompass the full range of child maltreatment.

CHAPTER SIX

Would better coordination make a difference?

What strategies and policy tools can make a difference in child protection?

The categories of present action to influence child protection outcomes[158] include

1. Direct assistance by governments and consortia of governments
    a. programs specifically aimed at child protection issues, as well as
    b. efforts to influence and coordinate other major funding streams and initiatives that affect child protection directly or indirectly, including early childhood education, maternal and child health, economic development, and teacher training.
2. Direct assistance and project operations by NGOs, CSOs and private donors
    a. Advocacy and services programs at the level of civil society and individual communities and regions, both those that are staffed professionally and those based on voluntary efforts and the role of children and youth themselves
3. Monitoring progress and problems by UNICEF, CRIN, and other agencies, including
    a. tracking improvements in indicators of child maltreatment

    a.   assessing national compliance with the Convention on the Rights of the Child and enforcement of laws on the books but not uniformly implemented

4.   Law enforcement and prosecution in the U.S. and other nations aimed at child protection offenses and offenders, including use of technology and cybersecurity techniques

5.   Efforts to influence multinational corporate behavior that affects child labor and other child protection-related issues

6.   Media and social marketing campaigns to spotlight the issues, engage in advocacy, seek increased donations and public aid, and mobilize action by religious and other civic organizations

Separate from assistance programs aimed at child protection problems, but affecting them indirectly, to the extent that family poverty and economic development influence maltreatment, are

7.   Trade expansion[159]

8.   Foreign investment

Examples of tactics and strategies that fall into these strategies are summarized in the following two chapters. First we turn to the issue of strengthened coordination and its potential impact.

The coordination problem: What would coordination achieve that is worth the effort?

In management and public administration studies, a predictable comment points out that specialized agencies operating in the same general area are often ill-coordinated. But coordination is not always a value-added process. At times, it is clear that coordinative efforts can be a weak substitute for efforts to make individual programs more effective. Meetings of a collaborative group are sometimes merely time-costly show-and-tell reviews of what separate agencies are doing to operate separate programs and projects, rather than a genuine effort to link programs more fully in achieving shared outcomes. In our work, we use a diagnostic of asking whether collaborative meetings are about what agencies do or about whether children and families are doing better.

A comment from a coalition of NGOs on the first annual USAID report on vulnerable children issued in 2006 underscored these issues: "There is often a disconnect between the higher-level theoretical discussions on the need for cooperation between the major NGO actors and the reality at the field level, which is unfortunately often dominated by competition and a lack of collaboration."[160]

The ultimate tests of coordination are straightforward: *resources and results*.

- Does coordination mobilize more *resources*, beyond levels of token funding for isolated projects?
- Does coordination achieve better and broader *results*, drawing upon multiple sources of support for the good of children and their families, rather than relying on a single agency, funding source, or project?

If neither of these is happening, coordination may be marginally helpful, but it is at risk of becoming a drain on scarce resources without a significant improvement in results.

The nature of child protection as a multi-faceted set of problems, as outlined in the systems paper developed for UNICEF by the Chapin Hall team cited previously, underscores the need for greater coordination and the costs of fragmented efforts. But talking about it and doing it are two very different things. One expert on child protection issues who has worked at both global and village levels, Gerald Mackie, summarized the coordination tasks as follows: "We have all learned to talk about holistic programming, but talking about it and doing it are two very different tasks."[161]

To be specific, if child labor efforts are not coordinated with school attendance efforts, it is possible that both will be less effective than if the effort to increase school attendance is based on a recognition that a combination of factors and underlying causes, including gender bias and family income pressures, drive both conditions and worsen both sets of outcomes.

A second example is the degree to which trafficking of young girls and sexual violence, while classified as separate conditions with distinct indicators, overlap substantially. Similarly, if a human rights rapporteur from the Human Rights Council who is part of the thematic group working to monitor violence against women is not closely linked to the country team or headquarters representatives from UNICEF, UNESCO, and UNODC—and to the NGOs that work on these issues as well—he or she is unlikely to have access to the full information base on those issues. Ted Piccone's recent review of the role of the human rights rapporteurs (known as "special procedures" in UN parlance) refers to frequent lack of contact among country team and rapporteur roles within the UN's several agencies concerned with these issues.[162]

Jody Heymann uses numerous examples of the need for coordinated policies in her recent book on measuring progress in global children's well-being:

> Child labor, marriage, and education policies are fundamentally intertwined. When children marry young, they are less likely to continue going to school; when they are prohibited from working, they can stay in school longer. When the laws targeting each of these areas are complementary, their power increases exponentially; when they are contradictory, their impact is severely limited.[163]

Heymann terms these "critical complementarities."

Coordination is also essential when progress in one area of the development agenda can worsen conditions in other arenas. In the initial years of HIV-AIDS preventive work, it became clear to researchers closest to communities in sub-Saharan Africa that improved roads can enable faster transmission of AIDS as roadside businesses and liaisons expanded contact among more infected persons. In U.S. agencies dealing with child welfare, parents are often affected by what some refer to as "the triad" of co-occurring disorders: substance use disorders, family violence, and trauma-related mental illness. To deal with any one of these in isolation can border on malpractice if the treatment ignores the co-occurring problems. Treating drug addiction and sending a parent back into a violent home may make relapse more likely and may endanger the children involved.

Coordination is not just an issue across different program areas such as child labor and school attendance; it is also an internal challenge that faces agencies such as UNICEF and USAID. Thirty agencies participate in the interagency discussions convened by USAID under PL 109-95. Within the UN, at least eight separate offices and appointees have roles in the sixteen child protection conditions set forth by UNICEF, in an alphabet soup of overlapping agencies. The positive side of that overlapping is widespread involvement by UN and UN-affiliated agencies in child protection work. But the challenge comes in seeking to pull those agendas together in a comprehensive child protection strategy rather than sixteen separate problems addressed by at least eight separate agencies.[164]

For an outsider, there appear to be multiple, bewildering networks of agencies and organizations working in the child protection field, overlapping with those that work on child development, child survival, and global health issues. While the benefits of working on many fronts are obvious, the questions that are unavoidable are how much these venues duplicate their efforts and whether they achieve critical mass or simply fragment further the scarce energy and resources available to child protection tasks.

In one recent report on events during a single year, references were made to the Washington Network on Children in Armed Conflict (WNCAC), USAID's Displaced Children and Orphans Fund, The Forum on Investing in Young Children Globally of the U.S. National Academy of Sciences, the Children in Adversity Policy Partnership (CAPP), The Global Partnership for Children and Youth in Peacebuilding, the Child Protection in Crisis (CPC) Network, ISPCAN, and the Keeping Children Safe Coalition, And these were only a list of meetings held in the US, which would be expanded several times over if the lens were widened to a global focus.

Because of all this fragmentation, there are multiple attempts to improve coordination, which at times create a further challenge to reducing fragmentation among the coordination efforts themselves:

- Interaction, a consortium of NGOs in the U.S., operates a Protection Working Group[165]
- The Child Rights Information Network (CRIN), as mentioned, is a clearinghouse of extraordinary information resources on children's rights
- The biennial meetings of the International Society for the Prevention of Child Abuse and Neglect (ISPCAN) bring together a larger number of practitioners in the child protection arena than any other convening effort.
- The Child Protection in Crisis (CPC) Learning Network based at Columbia University in New York includes "over 150 agencies working in 32 countries on the development of an evidence base for efficacious child health and protection programming." The Network includes the International Rescue Committee (IRC), Save the Children, the Women's Refugee Commission, UNICEF, ChildFund International, and local agencies.[166] Its work was recently summarized as follows:

The CPC Network has become a central global hub for cutting-edge research and learning in the child protection sector and includes agencies working on child protection learning, research, policy advocacy and training initiatives in more than a dozen countries. Local learning networks are active in Burkina Faso, Colombia, Indonesia, Liberia, Sri Lanka and Uganda. In these countries, the CPC Network brings together policymakers and practitioners to determine learning priorities and ensure the results of these endeavors are incorporated into government and civil society policy and practice.[167]

- The Child Protection Working Group brings together NGOs, UN agencies, and other international partners in humanitarian, emergency settings. These agencies are described as

    working in line with the 'Principles of Partnership', endorsed by the Global Humanitarian Platform. In the humanitarian system, the CPWG constitutes an 'Area of Responsibility' within the Global Protection Cluster. At the global level, UNICEF leads on the coordination of the CPWG and is also the 'provider of last resort'. All group members then lead on the implementation of CPWG initiatives and drive the development of the work-plan. Many of the strong inter-agency relationships within the global CPWG are also reflected in field-level child protection coordination groups."[168]

These and the other coordinating efforts (including the State Department's Task Force on Children in Adversity that has been meeting since early 2013) are laudable attempts to bring together the many public agencies, NGOs and other national and international stakeholders in child protection. But the overlapping memberships among these coordinating efforts make clear that some of the major players devote considerable time meeting with other agencies in these multiple arenas of coordination—none of which has yet produced either an inventory of child protection spending or a consensus on priorities and resources gaps across the multiple components of child protection.

The structural approach to coordination is perhaps best illustrated within the UN. A report in October 2013 included a section on "Mechanisms of collaboration among United Nations child protection actors."[169] This section referred to four different coordinating mechanisms for child protection issues within the UN: The Child Protection Working Group of the Global Protection Cluster, the Task Force on Children and Armed

Conflict, the Monitoring and Reporting Mechanism Technical Reference Group and the Inter-Agency Working Group on Violence against Children. Separate structures exist for coordinating child protection in humanitarian settings, in settings of war and civil conflict, in gender equity issues, and in issues of violence against children. Since it is possible for all four of these to take place in a single setting, this structural approach to coordination would seem likely to raise some challenging issues. New coordinating bodies may not be the best approach to coordination, compared with wider exchange of information and deliberate planning that sets priorities backed up by resources and measures of results. Resources and results remain the most highly valued currency of coordination.

Many of the same issues affect larger NGOs in coordinating their "front end" with the "tail" of their organizations, i.e. the support systems that ultimately back up direct services workers in the field. The reality of coordination in a large NGO is that it is a multi-layered process, with international headquarters at the top, regional offices in major parts of the world such as South Asia and sub-Saharan Africa, country offices, local teams, and the indigenous workers and translators who either directly provide or assist those providing services who are face-to-face with clients. Back at the headquarters offices, units that focus on fund-raising are separate from those that handle human resources, program evaluation, and liaison with other NGOs, the UN, and national governments. Many NGOs fund and some operate direct services programs, while others play facilitative roles, providing evaluation, training, and technical assistance services at least one or two steps removed from direct services. The largest are multi-billion dollar organizations, with all the complications of running an organization of that scale with locations throughout the world.

Advocacy groups compound the problem with their single issue focus, mirroring domestic politics and policy. In earlier work, we have drawn on the work of several students of coordination to note a peculiarly American blend of pragmatism, specialization, and media-based interest group politics to explain the strengths and weaknesses of the categorical programs that make up much of U.S. efforts to address the problems of children and families.[170] But it would appear that this narrowing disorder is either contagious or universal, as revealed by the tendency of many international advocacy groups and service providers to concentrate on their own issues, often avoiding in-depth consideration of underlying causes, overlapping programs, and children who are victims of more than one form of maltreatment at the same time.

There is nothing wrong with focusing an organization's efforts on a single problem, using a clear picture of the harm done by that problem, in order to attract resources, talent, and media attention. The tension between single-issue advocacy and a broader perspective on human problems is a constant theme in the writings of many academics and others who study the workings of governmental and non-governmental assistance programs. But ignoring connections across programs and agencies can be fatal to their effectiveness, if a programmatic effort focuses so narrowly upon one facet of a set of related causes and effects that it neglects the potential power of links to other problems to have a greater effect on outcomes. Fixing a car's engine by changing its spark plugs and ignoring the rest of the parts simply won't work; a more detailed diagnosis and treatment is often needed. And when the targets are not machinery but humans, their communities and norms of behavior, it is rare that a single problem has a single solution unrelated to the rest of the person's life or community.

The benefits of fragmentation as pluralism

Yet fragmentation is good, sometimes. Pluralism can test multiple ideas, some top-down, some bottom-up, adapting different strategies and tactics to different cultures, rather than conforming to a single prescribed model of how to do child protection. Coordination would be a step backward if it brought increased bureaucracy, time-wasting clearance processes, or fruitless, endless meetings for the purpose of having a meeting.

Fragmentation also builds on the natural inclination of advocates to press hardest for "their own thing," the cause that motivates them most. There are far fewer advocates for the field of child protection as such, compared with hundreds of advocates for portions of the agenda that aim at specific conditions and forces that harm children. Diluting that passion would also be a step backward, and we do not recommend that—as if narrow advocacy would ever disappear in a world made up of categorical programs and governmental units based on categorical thinking.

The categories of child protection used by UNICEF, and variations and expansions of this list of harmful conditions, are important ways of keeping track of what is getting better and what isn't. As data multiplies and its quality improves, data must be sorted into logical categories to make sense; grouping land mine demobilization with birth registration obscures the critical importance of each of these and the other child protection issues. Accountability for results depends upon clear indicators of results, and tracking each set of conditions separately increases the spotlight on specific outcomes. So it is not eliminating categorical programs that is the challenge; it is linking them effectively.

Coordination and collaboration: history and lessons

The question of coordination of governmental efforts is one with a long pedigree—if not many "best of show" awards. If a personal comment may be permitted, it is a question to which I have devoted much of my career. Those roles began with work in community action and Model Cities programs in the mid-1960's and assessment of the even earlier efforts to integrate the military services that began with the establishment of the Department of Defense in 1947. The experience base deepened with more recent work across multiple federal agencies, states, and localities concerned with substance abuse and child welfare.

In this work, I have long been fascinated by the many efforts to put the scattered pieces of government agencies together to produce better results for citizens, clients, and taxpayers. The title of my 1998 book *Beyond Collaboration to Results* expresses my skepticism about coordination for its own sake, as well as my belief that sometimes children and families do better when the programs that try to help them aren't working at cross-purposes. There is a wonderful acronym, attributed to the State Department, which expresses this institutional skepticism about coordination for its own sake: BOGSAT—a bunch of guys sitting around a table. No meeting by itself ever helped a child; it is what happens after and as a result of the meeting that matters.

Drawing on original work by Eugene Bardach and our experience in more than 200 sites in the U.S., we have framed coordination issues as having both subjective and objective dimensions:[171]

- Relationships of trust among professionals and stakeholders in different organizations who need to work together to achieve outcomes they cannot achieve by themselves, and
- Data-driven accountability for results across agencies with overlapping tasks.[172]

The value of trust as a separate ingredient in collaboration efforts emerges clearly from recent work looking at the factors in scaling up successful smaller-scale programs. In a recent set of studies of scaling up compiled by the Brookings Institution, trust was described as a key prerequisite to establishing both customer satisfaction and partner cooperation.[173]

Trust also means that if my agency acknowledges that your agency's goals and mine overlap, mine won't be submerged or subsumed by yours. If we agree to share

> Data-driven accountability and relationships of trust are the two sides of the collaboration coin, including both objective and subjective ingredients. One without the other cannot be effective.

resources to help more children and families, or to follow up initial services with continuing care, your agency will honor my referrals and handoffs. And when your agency seeks external resources, you will sometimes recognize overlap in our missions and not retreat from collaborative efforts with narrowed, single-agency proposals.

Naïve? Perhaps. But then let's admit that competition for resources and narrowed agendas in the nonprofit sector can have results just as pernicious as it sometimes has among multinationals.

Applying these two constructs of trust and accountability to international collaboration leads to an emphasis on effective working relationships among professionals and citizens who must achieve closer connections in their collaborative efforts, combined with indicators that measure child protection outcomes achieved by those efforts. Many NGOs, working with governments and grass-roots civil society organizations, have been able to achieve elements of these two goals at the project level. Much rarer are linkages that achieve them at scale. And within national governments, the initial "whole-of-government" efforts at USAID and in other nations suggest that the challenges are far greater at the interagency level in governments with foreign assistance budgets in the billions.

In searching the literature on global child protection efforts, we did not find any examples of an operational definition of coordination in this setting. Some attempts have been made to describe host government or NGO "capacity" to provide child protection programs, but these refer to coordination as a self-evident element of capacity without much of a functional definition. The closest definition that we could assemble combines the following components of coordinative capacity in child protection:

- An inventory of child protection programs that enables an oversight body to know what programs are operating, what scale they operate at, how they are funded, and how their effectiveness is measured, recognizing that you can't coordinate what you can't count;
- A regular review of outcomes that goes beyond head count to impact, recognizing all the challenges to solid evaluation discussed elsewhere in this report, but acknowledging that you can't coordinate what you can't monitor;
- Clarity about how "handoffs" are supposed to work: how a child or family gets from one agency to another, when followup by one agency is critical to lasting results from the work of another agency (termed *aftercare* in the substance abuse treatment world and other medical settings), and what is supposed to happen when the handoff succeeds;
- A periodic review of priorities measured by resources applied to specific problems against the scale of the problem.

The question of priorities makes clearer that coordination is at best, as Bardach and others have noted, a craft rather than a science. There is a growing literature on "implementation science" that usefully addresses the elements of program implementation, fidelity to a given program model, and other important implementation issues.[174] But the majority of this literature appears to take values and priorities as given and rarely addresses the costs of innovation. It would be remarkable if this were true—if resources were allocated by some invisible hand that knew where to put funding and for what reasons.

But priorities are much more political than that, influenced by media spotlights, election cycles, external budget constraints, and sustained personal leadership. Few of these can be easily programmed into an implementation model or a coordination template.

To be specific, no purely scientific or managerial criteria can decide the right scale of allocations that aim at the harm done to the two million children who are estimated to be trafficked compared with the 220 million children who have been sexually abused. Those decisions are either explicitly or implicitly about values, as well as what works to reduce harm and trauma. Again, what is needed is a subjective and an objective dimension to priority-setting. The question is whether relationships of trust are strong enough to enable separate agencies to agree how they will be held accountable for what they can do together that they cannot achieve separately.

And so coordination across multiple programs must address the questions of *shared outcomes* among funders, providers, and advocates that can affect priorities among allocations to different programs and problems. Otherwise, each problem receives a semi-random allocation made up of little more than the aggregate of fragmented decisions made in isolated processes. This is not a recipe for success.

The focus on coordination needs to be designed so that coordination happens at both policy and practice levels. Agencies' narrow vision of their mandates can affect what front-line staff do when they are face-to-face with children and parents needing help. These separate, fragmented responses to distinct kinds of child maltreatment mirror a similar phenomenon in U.S. domestic policy, in which each discipline demands its own screening and assessment tools as the gateway to treatment. As mentioned above, in work with parents in the child welfare system who have co-occurring mental illness, substance use disorders, and family histories of trauma due to sexual abuse and domestic violence, many agencies will require that these women be screened by each of these agencies separately, forcing them to "tell their story" over and over, ignoring the effects on trauma. In response, a few exemplary agencies have developed composite screening tools that address all three of these conditions in a single instrument.

Many global child maltreatment issues are also co-occurring, with sexual violence, non-school attendance, and child labor all affecting the same child at times. With separate projects that address only one of these at a time, each project will focus on only one facet of the child's trauma or neglect. A single-problem focus may be functional for the agency, operating "in the best interests of the system." But it may not help the child as much as if the overlapping conditions were dealt with together. Unified assessment, closer working relationships in which referrals are made among agencies familiar with each other's practices, and continuing dialogue about shared cases can improve these links at the level of individual children and families.

Coordination assessment tools: some options

As evidence that a more unified approach is possible, Save the Children U.S.A, one of 29 national STC operations in the NGO's worldwide network, has developed a more detailed approach to making strategic choices in allocating its resources. The factors taken into account included severity and magnitude of need, STC's status as leaders in the particular field, and funding potential. This calculus led to choice of four strategic areas, allocating a percentage of overall resources to each area.[175]

Following the issuance of the UN Secretary General's Study on Violence against Children in 2006, Save the Children UK issued its own response to the study, saying that nations should establish "national child protection systems based on a child rights framework." The six points in this document form a basis for a more detailed assessment system that could yield ratings of each nation's child protection systems.[176] As suggested above, further research on such an assessment, which could be designed similarly to other self-assessment tools used in the U.S. and other nations could produce a tool that would enable nations and NGOs to track progress over time in specific areas that make up the components of coordination detailed in concrete terms.[177] The use of a global gender gap analysis by the World Economic Forum is another example of a tool that ranks this dimension of gender equity by country, using four sets of factors: access to healthcare, access to education, political participation and economic equality.[178]

It may be possible, as has been done in rating and ranking nations on anti-corruption and transparency efforts, to develop a composite scale that could be used to assess child protection efforts at the national level. This tool would include the indicators of child well-being and maltreatment and add at least four other systemic factors:

- Governmental structures and processes at national and local levels, such as child protection committees, enforcement, prosecution, and convictions for child maltreatment
- Governmental leadership—the champions of child protection efforts combined with the relative allocations for explicitly child protection activities
- The extent of civil society activities at local levels and the support given to it at national levels
- A review of the CRIN material summarizing nations' assessments by UN human rights reporters and NGOs, combined with the corrective action taken by nations in response to these reports

The Child Protection System Mapping and Assessment Toolkit developed for UNICEF and issued in 2010 as a product of the background papers on child protection systems also offers criteria for assessing national systems, including seven components of a child protection system and questions about "optimizing coordination in child protection." The toolkit is described as having been tested in seven nations, but the available materials do not include an example of a nation that has actually filled out the categories in the spread sheets provided. As with any assessment tool, whether it is filled out as a self-assessment or by external observers will affect its objectivity.

A series of papers have been developed by the CPC Network at Columbia, based on work in Africa, which assess community-based child protection efforts. While the specific questions listed in an appendix to these papers are helpful, the materials do not yet indicate how national governments have reacted to these models or what changes have resulted.[179]

System-building at the national level

Coordination ultimately requires strong national leadership, as well as international links among the external players who are funding projects within a given nation. As our estimates of total child protection spending make clear, far more funding is available for national efforts than comes from external assistance, although this is skewed by the much larger expenditures in developed nations. Some international aid efforts have focused on this reality in working with national governments to build up their child protection systems. A recent report by UNICEF and its partners on case studies of child protection reviewed national child protection system-building efforts in Indonesia and Malawi, concluding that "Indonesia is beginning to formulate a systematic approach to child protection" and "Malawi used revision of the Malawi Growth and Development Strategy (2011-2016) as an opportunity to raise the profile of child protection and influence the structure of the strategy to incorporate the issue."[180] The latter example is an instructive one, as it contrasts "riding other tides" in national planning that can link child protection to parallel initiatives, rather than creating a separate "child protection plan" that may more easily be set aside or implemented with isolated pilot projects. The Malawi case study also refers to a commitment to evaluate the implementation of the new system, which is another ingredient that distinguishes a paper plan from one with accountability for results.

International comparative studies have emphasized the importance of culture, resources, and recent history in determining what structure and processes are adopted by child protection systems in different nations and in dealing with tribal and aboriginal populations within nations. Where a nation has significant ethnic variations within its population, child protection policies run the risk of perpetuating existing disparities. In the U.S., Canada, and Australia, variations in policy responding to aboriginal and tribal populations have delegated some portions of child protection enforcement and services to these community groups.[181]

Continuing efforts to assess the impact of these national system-building efforts are important, but remain challenged by the scarcity of independent assessments of such planning. Periodic reports on international models of child protection plans tend to be written by the authors of these plans or consultants involved in their preparation, resulting at times in lofty abstractions about what is intended rather than a realistic assessment of how well it is working. The time lag in the U.N. processes for periodic reviews and the tendency of NGO advocates to view only their own slice of the larger child protection picture are further barriers to effective ongoing assessment. An important exception is a recent report by UNICEF on Sub-Saharan Africa that assessed 24 nations on seven criteria for strengthening child protection systems, using a matrix rating of each nation on three levels of implementation for each of the seven indicators.[182]

Coordination at the delivery point: joint staffing

Staffing child protection is an enormous challenge in developing nations. It is unlikely that separate, specialized child protection staffing will be implemented other than in small pilots. But links to community-based health staffing offers the potential for multiple roles for such workers, including child protection. The gaps in health professionals and paraprofessionals affect not only health outcomes, but also child protection outcomes, because health systems are often the first level of prevention and detection of child maltreatment. Health staffs can also support prevention efforts through basic health and nutrition initiatives that reinforce school attendance.

Efforts by WHO, foundations such as the Gates Foundation and the Clinton Global Initiative, and many other NGOs have supplemented what national health planning agencies have been able to do to mobilize resources for expanding health staffing. The challenge remains to bridge the boundaries between national child protection initiatives and community-based child protection; creating two parallel, under-resourced systems seems far less likely to succeed than training and deploying workers with multiple competencies and roles.

Health staffing can also reinforce gender equity outcomes. A report on health staffing by community health workers (CHWs) prepared by The Earth Institute at Columbia University noted

> Females, even if less schooled than male counterparts, often are superior CHWs because of the cultural acceptability for them to conduct household visits, their familiarity with child health, their attachment to the community, and their less common use of alcohol in evenings – a common time for care-seeking for child illness.[183]

This report describes how use of mobile-based technology can multiply the effectiveness of CHWs. The effort to scale up use of CHWs in sub-Saharan Africa is linked to the Millennium Villages, which are hosted by ten low-income African countries and sponsored by the Earth Institute and the United Nations Office for Project Services.

The recognition that a professional staffing gap is a major obstacle to child protection and other international development efforts is widespread, but most responses call for more resources for expanded professional training. Utilizing paraprofessionals with relevant life experience is an alternative human resource option that has been explored in a limited fashion, but separately within each area of child protection and not across the whole field. For example, the Open Society Institute has developed a practitioner's guide for paralegals as a means of expanding the rule of law, which George Soros (as well as Gary Haugen and others) has argued could be a global antipoverty strategy.[184] Village-based child protection monitors, as discussed in the section on monitoring efforts, are another example of paraprofessional expansion of staffing capabilities.

The boundaries of child protection: broader, or narrower?

The coordination challenges in sorting out different categories of child protection are evident in UNICEF's different subdivisions, with five thematic areas, four "key result areas," and four categories of "most vulnerable" children.[185] At times this makes it difficult to determine what the real priorities are; UNICEF's budget information on child protection shows allocations across its results areas that range from 8% to 39% of total UNICEF spending. UNICEF's 2011 spending total of $340 million for child protection activities (updated to an annual average of $444 million during 2014-2017) does not include overlapping expenditures by other UN agencies aimed at school attendance, drug trafficking linked with human trafficking, or ILO spending for child labor activities. Spending targeted on vulnerable children spread out across UN agencies, as well as across the agencies of the U.S. and other nations and NGOs, makes the coordination task that much more difficult.[186]

Three broad options may exist for defining the boundaries of coordinated child protection in ways that improve its visibility and expand its resources. The first is essentially re-affirming the status quo: work on each of the sixteen UNICEF-defined categories of child protection separately, intensifying efforts in each area to explain its importance. This approach would involve links to other categories outside child protection with periodic meetings, but without any real merger of categories or attempt to connect projects at the local and national levels. It would also have the advantage of enabling resources in each area to be compared with the others, which is possible within the UNICEF budget but not for other spending.

The second option is to expand the boundaries to include closer connections to a wider set of problems: child survival, child development, and poverty reduction. A stronger connection between projects and policy could result from this approach. This would require both stronger coordination efforts within the UN family of agencies and across the NGOs and national governments involved, tracking indicators of children's well-being even more closely to see what "moves the needle." Within UNICEF, this would require much closer coordination across the entire agenda of the agency, beyond the child protection unit's focus on the sixteen categories of maltreatment. Connecting the separate categories of child protection with the revised SDGs would move substantially in this direction. Beyond the UN, the challenge in pursuing this option is to somehow gain an overview of the hundreds of agencies pursuing child-related agendas and then identify connections among those agencies and agendas that move them out of vertical silos and into closer links at both national and grassroots levels.

A powerful case for this approach was made recently by Santi Kusumaningrum, co-director of PUSKAPA, the Center on Child Protection at the University of Indonesia:

> The priority is situating child protection within broader poverty reduction strategies at the national level, because it gives us a seat at the table with all the important policymakers. A poverty reduction strategy that does not only provide access to school and health services for children but also enables families to care for their children.[187]

Starting with one or two of the single-problem areas that are most closely connected, such as child labor, child marriage, or school attendance, may make the horizontal links clearer, especially if these child protection objectives were linked to measures of child poverty and gender equity.

The third option is to set clear priorities, placing even greater emphasis on those components of the child protection agenda that already appear to have the most visibility and support: gender equity, trafficking, sexual violence, and the effects on children of HIV-AIDS. This might be termed a "momentum option," investing more intensively in those topics with the greatest momentum.

By using "children in adversity" as its rubric, the USAID Center appears to have adopted the second of these, with a portion of the third as well. It has widened its focus beyond the 16 UNICEF issues, but then has proposed selecting only three program goals in its recently announced "3-6-5" approach, as discussed in Chapter 9. Further, implementation may have undercut its impact on child protection by choosing a defined set of "priorities" without resources identified for those priorities, either from new sources or from funding already allocated to those areas.

The second option for broader links to the full range of children's well-being has strong foundations in the Convention on the Rights of the Child. The CRC provides a framework for fitting child protection into a larger perspective on the needs and rights of children. Its seven articles include four core areas:

- Non-discrimination
- The best interests of the child
- The right to life, survival, and development
- The views of the child.

Others have framed the CRC umbrella even more simply, distilling it to the three areas of survival, development, and protection; in some formulations, participation is added as a fourth area. While it is possible to fit components of child protection into each of these, the breadth of the entire CRC places child protection issues in a much larger context that extends well beyond the UNICEF definitions of child protection or those of the major NGOs working in the field. As Woodhouse and Johnson note, Article 6 raises child survival and child development goals that encompass but move well beyond child protection.[188]

In describing the importance of boundaries between child protection systems and other linked systems, the Chapin Hall document on systems-building states

Clarity regarding a shared understanding of the boundary (i.e., the structural relationship or embeddedness) between a child protection system and other formal systems (e.g., education, health, mental health) or informal systems (e.g., family, kin, community) is an important aspect of the child protection system that has implications for how one goes on to define functions, capacities, the process of care, governance, and accountability.[189]

But the document does not specify how the child protection system should be operationally connected to child survival, development, or other key systems that affect child protection.

The revision of the MDGs in 2015 may offer a clear target for those specifics. UNICEF analysis has made clear how much the current MDGs intersect with child protection issues:

Child labour squanders a nation's human capital and conflicts with eradicating extreme poverty (MDG 1) Armed conflict disrupts efforts to achieve universal primary education (MDG 2) Child marriage leads to the removal of girls from school and thus prevents gender equality (MDG 3) Children separated from their mothers, particularly if they remain in institutional settings, are at greater risk of early death, which hinders efforts to reduce child mortality (MDG 4) Female genital mutilation/ cutting undermines efforts to maternal health (MDG 5) Sexual exploitation and abuse hamper efforts to combat HIV infection (MDG 6) Environmental disasters make children vulnerable to exploitation and abuse, hence the need for environmental sustainability (MDG 7) Protecting children requires close cooperation between different partners, which consolidates the need for a global partnership for development (MDG 8).[190]

In some areas, the crosswalk between MDGs and child protection goals is more concrete. The commitment to improving worldwide access to clean water is mentioned throughout recent UN and NGO materials. But in the developing world, the responsibility for bringing water to the household is typically viewed as women's work—or girls' work, more often. This subjects girls and young women to long walks through sometimes unsafe areas, increasing risk in the child protection arena due to shortfalls in the provision of basic necessities of life.

If the revision of the MDGs as SDGs emphasizes these intersections among the new goals and child protection outcomes, monitoring the SDGs as a high-visibility task will necessarily involve monitoring child protection progress, or its lack. The question remains whether NGOs and their allies among other international organizations will be able to make this case, or get sidelined again to a lesser set of priorities

The question of how to get greater *visibility* for child protection issues may differ significantly from the question of how much closer linkage to these broader issues will improve the *effectiveness* of child protection programs.[191] The first is about marketing, in part, whereas the second is about the actual content of the message—what works, rather than what is in the international or national spotlight. It is rare to find a discussion of the tradeoffs between narrow niche marketing of single-issue advocacy and the logic underlying an emphasis on the full CRC framework among most child protection practitioners. We will explore marketing options further in Chapter 8.

Coordination around clear priorities: Girls and Women[192]

Kristoff and WuDunn's *Half the Sky* expresses a clear priority that would guide coordination in saying

> In the 19th century, the central moral challenge was slavery. In the 20th century, it was the battle against totalitarianism. We believe that in this century the paramount moral

challenge will be the struggle for gender equality around the world.[193]

Separating child protection issues from the other humanitarian issues that affect it runs the risk of adopting tactics that result in marginal efforts aimed at both. Yet one critical

> The sex ratio for children born in China is 1.13 male-female (the average is 1.06); in India it is 1.1. These figures have changed in the direction of fewer female births since the use of sonograms began in the 1980s. Twice as many girls as boys do not attend school at all.

connection is the link between gender equality and child protection. The treatment of women mirrors the treatment of girls. If these problems are addressed separately, the separation of under-funded reform efforts can weaken both; if they are linked, they can reinforce each other.

That is why the list of eight policy tools that could affect child protection goals set forth in Chapter 7 must be supplemented with a list of "hooks" that bind the tools to cross-cutting efforts to enforce gender-related policies. If foreign investment, for example, is negotiated among multinationals and host governments without gender-specific child labor issues on the table and without considering the effects of parents' migration on children, then new employment due to foreign investment may risk worsening child protection indicators—instead of improving them. And if school attendance efforts do not include a mechanism for monitoring girls' continuing attendance as they move from elementary to secondary school, then the overall numbers may "get better" while gender disparities remain unchanged.

Secretary Clinton's gender equality policy guidance of 2012 presents a framework for such links between child protection goals and a broader drive toward gender equality. Following an Executive Order signed by President Obama entitled "Instituting a National Action Plan on Women, Peace, and Security," the Secretary issued a 32-page National Action Plan on Women, Peace, and Security, December 2011. It stated

> Gender integration involves identifying and addressing, in all our policies and programs, gender differences and

inequalities, as well as the roles of women and men. The goal of gender integration or "mainstreaming" is to promote gender equality and improve programming and policy outcomes.

> ...foreign assistance indicators tracking the performance of programs implemented by USAID and the Department of State now include specific indicators on gender equality, women's empowerment, sexual and gender-based violence (SGBV) prevention and response, and women's participation in peacebuilding.[194]

Beyond U.S. policy, international agencies and NGOs need a similar framework to ensure that their child protection efforts are not divorced from more serious campaigns for gender progress. Of the sixteen UNICEF conditions of child maltreatment, the following ten have definite gender content:

- birth registration,
- children without parental care,
- child recruitment by armed forces/groups,
- female genital mutilation/cutting,
- child marriage,
- sexual violence against children,
- child trafficking,
- child labor,
- gender-based violence in emergencies, land mines and explosive weapons, and
- psychosocial support and well-being.

But if child protection policies occupy one box on the organization chart and women's issues occupy another, the risks of fragmentation worsen. Secretary Clinton's priority efforts around gender equality offer an organizing principle that could link a majority of the UNICEF child protection conditions to an over-arching concern for gender equality. But that linkage would require closer working relationships across separate units of the U.S. government—and of other governmental and private organizations as well. It is a fair question, on which little data appears to be available at present, to ask whether that kind of coordination is happening across the most important public and private agencies working in this arena today.

Another critical intersection of women's rights and child protection is domestic violence. Women who are abused at home by husbands or partners are often unable to protect their daughters from physical or sexual abuse. If the community enforces sanctions against domestic violence, girls will be safer; if domestic violence is a norm—as it is in many cultures—girls are at greater risk. One of the saddest statistics produced by research into family violence is the finding that

> Data from 68 countries indicate that more than 50% of girls and women 15-49 years old think that a husband is justified in hitting or beating his wife under certain circumstances.[195]

Should child protection be *primarily* devoted to protecting girls? Putting the question that bluntly calls the question on whether human rights should be part of the larger context for child protection. That choice seems on target in part because sooner or later, when human rights as a universal challenge to cultural pluralism is raised, the Taliban is mentioned. And when the Taliban is mentioned, sooner or later their banning girls from attending schools comes into focus.

This is not the only child protection issue, obviously. But it is the one that Laura Bush and countless others brought up when asked about U.S. presence in Afghanistan under the last administration. It is at the core of Nick Kristoff and Sherrie Wu-Dunn's skillful efforts to keep their work on *Half the Sky* visible through book and video sales. And the tragic case of the Taliban attack on Malala Yousafzai in Pakistan reminded the world of the persistent strength in some parts of the world of absolutist interpretations of religion and culture as they affect the lives of hundreds of millions of girls. It should be emphasized that it is not only "outsiders" who understand that damage; that issue was also addressed in the 2002 Arab Development Report (and in subsequent reports in 2005 and 2009)[196] commissioned by the UN and by countless activists in nations and cultures that still subordinate girls and women.

We should not invest more in protecting girls solely because of the Taliban. But if one criterion for deciding what priorities to choose across the entire field of child protection is comprehensibility, we should acknowledge that the human rights implications of forbidding girls to attend school (and the reputations of those who are doing the forbidding) are understood by many more people than most other child protection issues. Keeping little girls out of school and hurting them when they try to go to school is, along with trafficking, the child protection issue that is most visible today. The UN-sponsored Global Thematic Consultation on Education reflects this emphasis in a broad consultation effort to develop higher priorities for education linked with gender equity in the post-2015 Millennium Development Goals.[197]

Human rights, women's rights, and child protection

And yet, as important as gender bias and gender power are as causes of child maltreatment, women's rights should not be automatically equated with the entire array of child protection issues for four reasons:

- Boys are also abused and traumatized as well as girls, and if they grow up to become abusive men, the cycle continues.
- New attention to fatherhood programs in the U.S. and other nations has documented the effectiveness of some of these programs, as well as the continuing cultural importance of fathers in parenting programs and work with formerly incarcerated parents.
- There are some difficult areas in which women's rights and children's rights are perceived by some as being in conflict. One which is visible in the U.S. and also has international implications arises in the area of prenatal substance exposure. Some women's organizations in the U.S. have opposed prenatal screening for drug or alcohol use or toxicological tests at birth as invasions of

privacy. Other groups have demanded universal screening as the only unbiased way of protecting children from the lifelong effects of prenatal exposure. As fetal alcohol research and surveys expand to developing nations, that conflict may deepen.

- Child well-being can at times be pursued in a way that ignores or shifts attention away from parents, just as parenting education and substance abuse treatment for parents can sometimes overlook the effectiveness of family treatment that is designed to adopt two-generation approaches. The tendency in some child welfare agencies to write off "bad parents" and concentrate on rescuing children from such parents is a frequent response of newcomers to these issues—and of some front-line workers as well who have grown tired of parents failing their children.

Viewing child protection through a lens of discrimination against girls and women is justifiable, and deserves even more attention than it has received in the past decade. But care should be taken to acknowledge those areas where child protection issues demand an even larger framework than the rights of girls and women.

Spending estimates: inventories as the core of coordination

Working from the premise, as previously stated, that what can't be counted can't be coordinated, rough estimates of current child protection spending must be made, even in the face of weak data collection capacity. In total, it can be estimated from a review of annual reports and budgets that 10% of the largest NGOs' funds are allocated to child protection activities that fall within the UNICEF definition, which yields (adding in specialized child protection agencies that work on a single issue) an estimated $750 million annual total.

When these estimates of NGO spending are added to the $444 million that UNICEF identifies as separate child protection expenditures, an estimate that 10% of the USAID-compiled total of $2.7 billion is for child protection programs, and estimates of aid from other governments, a very rough approximation can be made that $1.5-2 billion is allocated to global child protection programs annually by governments, the UN, and NGOs.

To this total should be added the significant amounts spent *within* some countries from their own budgets and private sources on child protection activities. Allocating child protection funding by national governments is difficult. For example, in the U.S., nearly $30 billion is spent annually by federal, state, and local governments on the entire child welfare system, for investigative services, prevention efforts, out of home care, and adoption assistance. Out of home care is the largest expense. Apportioning a segment of this spending for child protection activities is somewhat arbitrary, since much of this funding goes for remedial and rehabilitative services after protection efforts have discovered abuse or neglect. If protection is defined as UNICEF does, using the 16 categories of harm to children, then approximately $5 billion would seem an appropriate estimate of the portion of the $30 billion that is spent on *domestic* child protection in the U.S.[198]

That total is still more than twice what international public and private aid programs target on child protection efforts globally. And it suggests that an amount perhaps twice as large (i.e., $10 billion) should be added for the *domestic* expenditures of all other nations on those activities. This results in an estimate of total expenditures of $2 billion for international aid aimed at child protection and $15 billion spent internally in all nations with child protection programs. The derived total of $17 billion for global child protection spending from all sources can be arrayed against the estimated total of 400 million children affected by child maltreatment, which comes to $43 per maltreated child.[199]

Although the estimated U.S. total spending is presumably the largest amount spent on internal child protection in any nation, it does not necessarily reflect results. A recent UNICEF report ranks 29 developed countries according to the overall well-being of their children; the U.S. ranks 26th of 29 nations. The measures include primarily non-child protection issues, but they include exposure to violence. On those measures, the U.S. is in the top half of ranked countries.[200]

This very preliminary estimate of national spending on internal child protection also makes clear that external aid by itself may matter much less than strategic external efforts to partner with and support nations' own efforts to reform their child protection programs—to the extent that national governments will allow other nations and NGOs to help shape those programs. But the fact that this analysis of total spending seems never to have been undertaken by any NGO or international organization suggests either that it is fruitless to attempt to aggregate child protection efforts as a field—or that it is overdue as an indispensable means of understanding how to advance child protection goals. We come down on the side of the second of these, in view of past lessons underscoring again that *you can't coordinate what you can't count.* You probably can't assess its effectiveness very well, either.

The capacity of lower-income countries to expand their spending on child protection programs is greater than sometimes realized. Jody Heymann and her colleagues have reviewed the average spending levels in 191 countries in the work of the World Policy Analysis Centre at McGill University. They point out that "over 80 percent of the countries that do not have enough health professionals to provide basic services spend less than 4 percent of their GDP on health." Similar analyses show the potential to increase countries' spending on education.[201] Some, but not all of these countries could also reap an anti-corruption dividend, if they became serious about enforcement efforts, as discussed in the next chapter.

The further context for this spending is the much larger amount of total foreign assistance from all sources. Spending totals for global child protection are part of much larger foreign assistance funding, which was estimated to be $126 billion in 2012 from 27 OECD (developed) nations. Additional estimates included $12 billion from non-DAC nations and $31 billion from private foundations and NGOs.[202] Within this total of $169 billion in foreign assistance, humanitarian aid can include child protection in some cases, but it is a separate category in other countries' and NGOs' accounting, which adds to the confusion about total child protection spending. Yet working from these (or any other available) estimates of global child protection spending is an essential prerequisite for any serious discussion of improving coordination across programs. In Chapter 7 we will take into consideration the added potential impact of much larger amounts of trade and investment as their secondary effects influence child maltreatment and child protection.

A final difficulty with these totals is that funding for child protection is not entirely spent within the countries to which it is allocated. Staffing costs for UN, NGO, and other extra-national staff, combined with funding for private contractors who provide a significant amount of humanitarian and foreign assistance, can take up a substantial portion of funds "allocated" to projects in specific nations.[203]

An important beginning that may model how to address this problem in at least one segment of foreign assistance came with the recent publication of the Kaiser Family Foundation that aggregates donor spending on HIV/AIDS programs.[204] The Foundation indicated that this was the first in a series of reports on aggregate spending in global health areas.

U.S. officials make an important clarifying point about the inventory function that should be acknowledged. They note that whatever the total in foreign assistance spending related to child protection, it cannot include the efforts made in diplomacy to persuade another government to change its policies and practices. In trafficking, for example, to change another country's laws and enforcement of those laws can accomplish what millions of dollars in grants may not be able to achieve.

This becomes all the more invisible because of the essence of diplomacy: to seek a change in another government's behavior without being seen to pressure that government in any public way. Letting the host government take the credit for making the change—whatever persuasion or more direct quid pro quo pressure is being used—is the nature of diplomacy. Thus any inventory of grant spending may understate the efforts made by the U.S. or any other nation to advance a child protection agenda. It may also overlook the positive effects of human rights monitoring and advocacy efforts aggregated by CRIN and other organizations.

The economics of child protection

If the estimates cited above for global totals spent in preventing and responding to child maltreatment are roughly accurate, the $2 billion is woefully inadequate to make a significant impression on the problem. No one knows what portion of the estimated $32 billion market in human trafficking (not including smuggling drugs with people) consists of profits on child maltreatment, including child labor, sex trafficking, and pornography involving children. But it is highly likely that it dwarfs spending on child protection.

Two perspectives can be used in framing the economic arguments for increased spending to prevent and treat child maltreatment on a global scale. The first relies on estimates of the costs to government and society of child abuse and neglect; the second relies on the positive economic effects of increasing the costs to traffickers and others who benefit from child maltreatment.

Wang and Holton estimated that the direct and indirect costs of child abuse in the U.S. are $104 billion annually in 2007 dollars.[205] Projecting these costs to nations with considerably lower costs of services, as well as those that are closer to the U.S. level of costs, a conservative estimate would be that global child maltreatment has costs in the range of $300-400 billion annually.[206] Thus preventive spending is probably less than 1% of the total costs of maltreatment.

It is far more difficult to estimate the effectiveness of improved enforcement, fines, and other regulatory and legal efforts in increasing the costs of maltreatment to those who commit it. As with the global markets for illegal drugs, the more commercial segments of this economic activity may have great elasticity to adjust prices and operational costs to respond to intensified enforcement. Other methods of increasing financial pressure on commercial forms of maltreatment are discussed in the following chapter.

Fining the poorest parents for allowing their children to work may only make it harder for the whole family to provide children with basic nutrition, health, and education. But creating positive incentives for parents to register their children for birth and to enroll them in school is a well-tested method of reducing some forms of maltreatment. "Conditional cash transfers" is one label for these payments to poor families for meeting conditions such as school attendance and immunizations.[207] Rather than penalizing parents, this rewards them for improving child outcomes under their control. Mexico, Brazil, and other Latin American nations have been leaders in using such transfers to marry incentives for positive treatment of children with social protection spending. Nationwide evaluation of the Progresa program in Mexico begun in the mid-1990s has been used to justify expansion of the program, and its adoption by other countries has been cited as based on the powerful evidence gathered by a rigorous evaluation in Mexico.

India has recently been debating expansion of its use of conditional transfers. The nation is already using monthly stipends based on enrollment in the national biometric database, the unique identity (UID) project, to replace commodity distribution that was estimated to be losing as much as two-fifths of the value of the transfers.[208] This may create new incentives for parents to ensure that their children are attending school and not working. It is also an excellent example of an intersection between economic development/child poverty efforts and child protection.

Soft vs hard power in child protection

Another form of coordination in child protection involves coordination among those using different tactics to achieve change. The distinction first made by Joseph Nye in comparing "soft" with "hard" power in international relations has relevance to child protection as well.[209] The truism that social norms only change through consensus and cannot be imposed from outside a culture or community can at times obscure the possibility of a "harder line"—strengthened enforcement of laws and prosecution of those who abuse children. Persuasion through careful consensus-building needed to change norms can be contrasted with "naming and shaming" tactics used in human rights advocacy, which can in turn be contrasted with aggressive law enforcement—both within and across national borders.

Along this spectrum from soft to hard power, in politics and among interest groups, there is at times a kind of creative duplicity, in which allies agree to take "good cop" and "bad cop" roles, with advocates working outside the system and supporters working within it. In child protection, those within the government may at times take a softer, more consensus-building position on maltreatment. But the value of consensus does not negate the benefits of harder positions being taken by outsiders who are willing to target unfavorable publicity on those tolerating or committing abuse, to take legal action to prosecute them, or, ultimately, to seek financial sanctions or to use police or military power to protect endangered children in natural disasters or war zones. While using different tactics, continuing communication among those working at different points along the consensus-naming-prosecution-sanctions spectrum can ensure that unified pressure is brought for change.

Those adopting consensus-building tactics have the advantage of a less confrontational stance, which can lead to lasting change over time. But the ultimate question child protection advocates might ask is "If genocidal leaders can be prosecuted and brought to trial, why can't traffickers in children?"

A recent review of the track record of non-military sanctions is instructive for policymakers considering sanctions for human rights violations. The track record is mixed, suggested one recent assessment of sanctions including Cuba, South Africa, Iran, North Korea, and others.[210] The growing sophistication of the financial tools to enforce sanctions, arrayed against the multiple ways to bypass or circumvent sanctions, makes clear that this struggle is continuing, with financial weapons and technology used by both sides to the conflict.

It should also be recognized that sanctions are a very double-edged sword, in which many different kinds of human rights violations could come into view in countries that decide to sanction other countries. For example, if sanctions were used against countries with poor child protection records, a sanctioned country would seem likely to suggest sanctions against countries that have not ratified the Convention on the Rights of the Child or the convention on disabilities, including the U.S.

The lessons of Haiti for coordination—real and perceived

With the fourth anniversary of the Haiti earthquake in January 2014, several recent reviews assessed how well international aid has been coordinated with national efforts and how well it has responded to the crisis in Haiti. A recent book by a journalist who was based in Haiti and a lengthy article in the *New York Times* have been fairly critical of the recovery effort, while praising some elements of the initial humanitarian aid.[211]

Haiti is possibly one of the most difficult settings for any form of coordination, with the nation itself ranked high in corruption and low in governmental capacity to deliver services on nearly every index of these factors. At one point in the Senate's consideration of the aid package for Haiti in 2010, Senator Richard Lugar referred to "the self-destructive political behavior that has kept Haiti the poorest country in the Western Hemisphere."[212] While the taunt ignored the history of two invasions of Haiti by the U.S. in the 20th century—one lasting 19 years—it summarized many U.S. lawmakers' perceptions of Haiti.

The reality is that three years after the earthquake there were still 358,000 internal refugees in Haiti who lacked permanent housing and were living in camps. Jonathan Katz and the *New York Times* described the flow of a promised $16.5 billion in aid, which became an actual $7.5 billion allocated (substantial amounts of which are not yet spent) after payments for U.S. military expenses and shortfalls in donor pledges. Half the funding was for immediate relief assistance and not intended for reconstruction. Only a small percentage of the aid actually flowed to the Haitian government; the rest went to NGOs, contractors, and cash payments to Haitians to allow them to rent existing housing rather than wait for construction.

One should not generalize from Haiti's experience with a devastating earthquake in a devastated country. Progress has been made in specific child protection projects that have expanded school attendance efforts, HIV prevention, and services for street children,[213]and a problematic election was held in the middle of the recovery effort. Blaming the Haitian government for the bulk of the problems with foreign assistance overlooks a great deal of evidence that there is blame enough to go around to all participants in the effort, especially since so little of the aid went directly to the national government. But this remains the most visible, recent experience of U.S. and international agencies with a major disaster outside the U.S.—and the lessons are neither comforting for official agencies nor persuasive for taxpayers.

It is easy, writing in a setting removed from the realities of humanitarian crises, to suggest that child protection should be coordinated more effectively with immediate humanitarian aid. But reading Samantha Power's extraordinary biography of Sergio Vieira de Mello--or the latest headlines from Syria—it becomes powerfully clear that humanitarian crises trump long-term strategic planning. Protecting children from indiscriminate shelling or homelessness and starvation must take precedence over the longer-term, and sadly, this happens over and over. The immediate drives out the longer-term, and ad hoc arrangements for getting supplies to those who need them—"delivering the groceries," as Vieira de Mello put it— justifiably dominate the operations of underfunded agencies.[214]

Yet to allow immediate crises to consistently divert the attention given to longer-range protection goals means that funders' claims to be involved in system-building have little substance.

Coordination: Summing up

To summarize the case for coordination: Children are indivisible. The harm done to them and their futures cannot be separated into categories as neatly as those we create in government or philanthropy. Vulnerable children rarely have a single condition caused by a single form of maltreatment. The children at risk of child marriage are those at risk of female mutilation, poor secondary school attendance, and sexual violence, among other conditions. The children living on the street are at risk of violence, recruitment into child trafficking, and many other conditions that will worsen their odds of success. If each of these is treated separately, with separate fund-raising and separate projects—the results will remain fragmented, and the resources will be stuck in silos of funding and staffing, with few opportunities to work across systems.

As noted at the outset of this chapter, coordination is a frequently proposed remedy, often without the substance or resources to ensure its effectiveness. But the case for coordination in child protection is a strong one in view of the widespread evidence of how much its absence weakens overall efforts at protecting children.

The case for improving coordination in child protection rests on three major arguments:

1. In the absence of an overview of total funding for child protection, it is impossible to assess the relationship between resources and results. Each project is justified on its own merits, without reference to its impact on larger needs or funding streams.
2. Without a forum or mechanism by which individual projects can be adjusted to others—such as deciding whether a child labor project will be connected with efforts to increase school attendance—each project may reinforce or undermine other projects, but without useful information about which is happening.
3. Projects can at times serve as a buffer to systems change, by responding to a need but at a scale that is enough for visibility but with no intent or capacity to change the larger system or improve national indicators.[215] A prime example is the data base of projects compiled by USAID, including about 1900 ongoing projects in 109 countries and totaling $2.7 billion. The data base documents activity, but does not reveal results that cut across the field of child protection or the multiple needs of vulnerable children.

This chapter's recommendations may seem modest in the context of 400 million children who are being harmed. Better inventories and wider discussion of the links across the 16 UNICEF categories are not the same thing as in-depth collaboration among dozens of agencies and organizations. But more elaborate coordinative mechanisms would be unrealistic at this point, and these steps toward broader coordination would signal that critical prerequisites for a higher priority for child protection are in place. As such, they would be important steps forward, and those working in this field would recognize them as major steps beyond the status quo.

Coordination is essentially about leadership in building consensus among actors who are not each other's subordinates but equal partners. The paradox—leaders without followers who must follow —is at the heart of the blend of accountability and trust that coordination demands in order to affect resources and results at non-token levels. The need for such leadership in global child protection seems obvious, but its sources seem less certain.

Where could that leadership come from?

It could come from UNICEF, if its strains with the U.S. Congress could be healed in a compromise on adoption and institutional care and its primacy among UN agencies on child protection were made clear. It could come from the U.S. if the President and Congress worked on the common themes of child advocacy that have motivated leaders on both sides. It could come from Europe, whose nations and NGOs often show more willingness and ability to take the lead on child protection issues than the U.S. And it could come from China and India, whose improvements in child well-being indicators remain the largest steps forward in the history of child protection—despite the accompanying negative policies and cultural barriers to their own protection of their own vast numbers of children at risk.

And it could come from a true alliance of NGOs and foundations, if their narrow definitions of child protection were broadened to a point where a new network of shared outcomes became a source of unifying accountability and mutual trust.

CHAPTER SEVEN

Eight Remedies

This chapter reviews eight other strategies beyond coordination that have been emphasized in our interviews and research. The following chapter focuses on a tenth strategy—marketing child protection to external audiences in order to increase overall resources available to the field.

These eight remedies include:

- Grass-roots organizations and civil society: The bottom-up agenda
- Listening to the voices of children and youth
- Corporate aid, operations, and decision-making
- Technology applied to child protection
- Drug and alcohol prevention and treatment
- Achieving balance between institutional care and adoption for children without parents
- Law enforcement and legal action, including anti-corruption efforts
- Evaluating what works

This review of remedies for improving child protection programs and policies begins with bottom-up civil society strategies for two reasons:

- Coordination itself has a top-down connotation in which centralized control is sometimes mistaken for collaboration across a wide network of independent actors. But coordination also demands a bottom-up and a horizontal dimension, because it is about voluntary cooperation with voluntarily given support—not mandated conformity. Civil society organizations are vital players in creating and mobilizing that kind of coordination, and must not be relegated to marginal sideshows.

- Many of the other strategies in this chapter require civil society roles to be both legitimate and effective. For example, to call for use of technology that is restricted to national agencies and not disseminated to grass-roots organizations is to ignore the nature of networked communication and the potential power of new connections among smaller community-based groups throughout a nation or region.

Grass-roots organizations and civil society: The bottom-up agenda

For all the language about both top-down system-building and bottom-up strengthening of civil society, there remains an important tension between working with governments to improve their child protection efforts and working with grass-roots organizations to improve their capacity to hold governments accountable. To their credit, UNICEF, USAID, other national governments, and NGOs have done both. However, in the absence—often cited in this work but often relevant—of inventories that distinguish between the two kinds of grants and support, it is impossible to gauge how much of either type is being supported or how the balance is struck in individual aid programs.

A refinement on the proposed inventory of funding that has been suggested as a coordination tool throughout this work would be to develop distinctions of the kind made by analysts who differentiate between top-down and bottom-up methods. A further refinement would be a recipient-based evaluation tool that would survey local groups receiving aid as to their perceptions of how much involvement they had in choosing the targets and the methods of carrying out a given project.

We have already cited what is arguably the best single example of civil society efforts to change social norms affecting children: UNICEF's efforts to reduce female mutilation through working with CSOs that rely on village elders in East Africa. In Peru, *defensorios* (defense centers) or child protection committees based in schools or communities have been formed with funding from the national government in some cases and as voluntary organizations in others.[216] The Council of Europe has endorsed "child helplines" as a locally based tool to ensure that children and youth can make reports of abuse safely to responsible officials.[217]

Some writers and policy analysts make an important distinction between international NGOs with their inevitable overhead and staff turnover and locally based NGOs and civil society organizations with deeper roots in local cultures and realities. A recent ethnographic study reviewed two NGOs with different approaches to their work in Haiti, finding the one that was more open to community leaders' suggestions to be more effective than the other, which adopted a more top-down style.[218]

Some of our interviewees noted that on occasion civil society organizations have refused to accept UN or US-based assistance, both out of a concern about security and the difficulties of funders' oversight that can, in these organizations' views, constrain local efforts led by local leaders.

Civil society-based programs have other challenges that can give funders pause, as well. In nations where corruption or tribally- or ethnically-based reward systems are widespread, some civil society efforts will not be funded if the conduit is from national decision-makers to local organizations. Others have only rudimentary information systems that can't fully capture the results of what they do. Parents in lower-income communities may be able to free up some of their time for participation in CSOs, but they face difficult choices in deciding whether agricultural productivity, water systems, economic development, or child protection will be where they invest their scarce time. Participation of males who are elders in local settings may exclude women from civil society efforts.

Talk of system-building at the national level is hardly relevant if the system at the level where children are most able to be protected—the community—does not involve a fundamental acceptance of the need to report abuse and the certainty that something positive will happen when reports are made. The compilation of national reports undertaken by Dubovitz and Merrick in 2010 documented that reporting systems are barely in existence in some of the 25 nations reporting.[219] A reality test of system-building, then, is the somewhat counter-intuitive indicator of *increasing* reports of abuse, as evidence that the bottom rung of the system is in place and is being taken seriously. The report from the Philippines in this volume was very candid on this point:

> Reporting is mandatory for attending physicians, nurses or heads of any public or private hospital or medical clinic… in reality, very few report and no one has been penalized for not reporting.[220]

At that point, it is the workings of civil society organizations as much as it is the national system that will determine whether there is any effective follow-up to reports. If children are removed, who will care for them, in what kind of home or institution? If parents whose abuse or neglect is partially poverty-driven need basic economic assistance, who will provide it, through what networks of care and support? If community leaders are to be convened to raise issues of school attendance, female mutilation, or child labor, who will convene them and with what credibility?

This is where civil society organizations can play a critical role. Yet by definition, civil society projects risk being fragmented, disconnected projects with little connection to other, similar projects. That is the challenge of collaboration among CSOs—to transcend project status and to link with other CSOs. In East Africa, the efforts of the African Child Policy Forum based in Ethiopia have strengthened networking among these various civil society organizations, working to improve a situation described as community-based and unrelated to national policy:

> The Child Protection Units in Ethiopia initiated over a
> decade ago are still being supported by NGOs instead of
> being incorporated into the government structure....most
> of these initiatives just continue as projects here and there
> with very limited impact.[221]

Some of the technological innovations mentioned later in this chapter may
be helpful in building such networks among CSOs. Equipping CSOs with
networked communications (and the generators, satellite connections, and
fuel or solar power needed to keep them operational) could increase the
links among these organizations and reduce the sense of isolation among
such groups.

Finally, some CSOs work effectively in areas that address the causes of child
maltreatment, and their efforts could also benefit from better networking
among the full range of CSOs. Sometimes that takes the form of very
direct action. A women's self-help group in India decided they would go
after the problems caused in their village by the liquor *arrack*. A woman
in a World Bank focus group explained: "One year back we initiated a
movement to eradicate the consumption of arrack. We went to the liquor
shops and threw away all the liquor."[222]

Idealized and romanticized "power to the people" may at times ignore all
the other pressures that prevent "the people" from exercising power. Yet
participation has a cumulative effect, at times, in which a greater sense
of solidarity provides a foundation for the next effort—and the next one
after that.

Some of the causes of child maltreatment reviewed in Chapter 5 may yield
more readily than others to civil society efforts and grass-roots activism.
Getting teachers in the classroom and nurses in clinics who are not showing
up may be easier that reversing millennia of gender inequity, Like NGOs,
CSOs and their funders need to pick their targets carefully, calculating
where resistance may be greater or mobilization may be easier.

Listening to the voices of children and youth

In Dr. Yanghee Lee's framing of the three categories of child rights—child welfare, child rights, and child empowerment—the third category is increasingly relevant as child protection agencies experiment with and learn the lessons of how to listen to the voices of children and youth. This form of participation is at times seen by long-time professionals in the international field as politically correct, "patronizing participation," in which children and youth are just one more group that gets a chance to have its say, however token, before decisions are really made.

But for several reasons, the movement toward fuller participation by children and youth is of much more than symbolic importance:

- Listening to the voices of victims adds to knowledge about the specific practices of their abusers and how to stop them, as well as the most effective forms of therapy, including self-help and peer support;
- Encouraging youth to speak out in civic forums builds their self-confidence and their sense that they are part of the process of governance, as an important counter-force to their feelings of isolation and guilt as survivors of abuse; this can be especially powerful when girls as well as boys are part of the dialogue, demonstrating that girls and women have something to add to the process, rather than being passive spectators;
- Encouraging youth to speak out on maltreatment adds to the pressures for changing social norms, making clear that generations to come will not view abuse as tolerable, whatever their parents' generation might believe or tolerate as social norms.

In response, UNICEF and many NGOs have provided forums that allow children and youth to express themselves on child protection issues, both as victims and as citizens active in prevention and treatment efforts. The label "child protection" can itself be seen as paternalistic, implying that children and youth are inert victims, unable to speak or act for themselves. Expanding the opportunities for youth participation demonstrates concretely that it is not token paternalism. The extraordinary participation of Malala Yousafzai in a recent youth session of the General Assembly was powerful evidence of how effective some youth can be in addressing global child protection issues with a global audience.[223]

Two-way learning can happen when genuine listening involves youth who have been abused or neglected. Listening to youth who are part of prevention efforts, or who are simply trying to understand child maltreatment, can also be enlightening. As one international professional powerfully expressed it: "what we think they need isn't the same thing as what they think they want." She went on to point out that a surprising number of lower-income youth are already aware of the standards of the rest of the world, through their ubiquitous internet connections and their growing awareness of youth culture outside their own nations and cultures.

This familiarity with technology, even in lower-income communities, also provides a role for youth as monitors of policy. In their pathbreaking studies of the factors that enabled families in four provinces of India to break out of poverty, a World Bank team mentioned a very specific option for addressing corruption that would be greatly enhanced with technology:

> ...school children can become involved in monitoring whether teachers and health care workers are present at their posts; this will prepare children for citizenship and problem[224] solving and also help address a countrywide problem in which government programs targeted to poor people perform poorly.[225]

Adding a few students with smartphones to this proposal would ensure that daily reports on non-attendance would be immediately available to provincial and national officials. And adding inexpensive video capability for youth to tell their own stories in their own words would provide millions of witnesses to child maltreatment and the possibilities of child protection.

UNICEF's 2014 annual report adds further evidence of this trend:

Innovations in data collection are opening new avenues for children's participation. UNICEF, the Massachusetts Institute of Technology, Public Laboratory for Open Technology and Science, and Innovative Support to Emergencies, Diseases and Disasters are developing a mapping platform that enables real-time data collection using web and mobile applications. Young people in low-income communities of Rio de Janeiro, Brazil, and Port-au-Prince, Haiti, have used mobile phones loaded with a Geographic Information System application to take geotagged photos documenting neighborhood problems.[226]

The Global Partnership for Children and Youth in Peacebuilding is a community of practice uniting international, national and local organizations, scholars and champions to strengthen the role of young people in peacebuilding. In a process termed 3M (multi country, multi-partner, and multi-donor), the Global Partnership is evaluating the impact of youth participation in peacebuilding.

The other side of listening to children is the challenge of hearing those children who lack the right to speak or be heard. In some repressive societies, the idea that children should participate in debate about their futures is threatening to the very basis of order in such nations and cultures. Devising new forms of participation for children has different meaning in nations where there is little participation by anyone outside the ruling elite. In such cases, basic human rights to express opinions can be reinforced by the newer emphasis on listening to children as subjective participants in devising policy that seeks protection and development of children. Many observers have noted the youth of the street participants in the Arab spring movements. The right to speak out and be heard seems unlikely to disappear as a trend, especially with the much greater facility of adolescents and young adults in accessing new methods of grass-roots cybercommunication.

Giving "amplifiers" to grass-roots groups of youth could also strengthen the message of change in ways that Western organizations with credibility problems could never achieve. Some have cited the "Malala effect"—the immense power of one brave, articulate girl on the world's stage speaking truth to power.

A strategy that cuts across several of these other strategies— listening to youth, use of technology, corporate action—is the effort to shift social norms toward child protection and away from acceptance of norms that lead to abuse and neglect.

As much as youth tune into social media, however, larger and more strategic action is needed to address social norms that form barriers to child protection. This is an area where several NGOs, UNICEF, USAID and others have begun making important progress—but more needs to be done at scale.

Finally, it must be realized that addressing social norms is seen by some in non-Western nations as imposing a Western agenda on other cultures. This charge occurs at times in nations whose importation of Western forms of entertainment, weaponry, and other goods and services is enormous. But the charge has power, even when inconsistent or unjustified.

And it is not always unjustified. To preview the corporate-targeted strategies discussed below, it is clear that multinational operations in developing nations often bring unwanted changes in values, lifestyles, and even where children and families can live.

Corporate decision-making

The Gates Foundation, the Open Society Foundations, Google, Facebook, Apple, and ...even the Walt Disney Company have arguably projected more influence in the Middle East and Africa...than the Department of State. These corporate and philanthropic actors have sometimes

bigger budgets but also strategies that are better attuned
to changes in technology, demography, and culture...[227]

In assessing corporate impact on child protection, two broad arenas are relevant: *Corporate assistance programs* and *corporate operations*. Since the latter includes much of the flow of international trade, it is far larger than corporate grant-making and other assistance efforts. Those different magnitudes are important to keep in mind as we review each in turn.

Corporate aid through UNICEF and other international child protection organizations includes several categories, as summarized by UNICEF in early 2012 in announcing its new Corporate Social Responsibility efforts:

- strategic philanthropy through cash & in-kind contributions
- employee-giving programmes
- humanitarian relief & support of emergency appeals
- cause-marketing initiatives
- events & sponsorship
- innovations & program solutions for children
- policy & advocacy for child rights
- promoting corporate responsibility
- training & capacity building[228]

Monitoring these commitments will be challenging, in view of the difficulty of critiquing corporations and corporate foundations that have funded child protection agencies and consortia. The emphasis on corporate giving is typical of corporate responsibility efforts which are typically drawn from a set-aside of corporate resources, rather than changes in the core of corporate operations. The latter emphasis was given more visibility in the release of a new document on "Children's Rights and Business Principles" developed by UNICEF, the United Nations Global Compact, and Save the Children.[229]

Corporate social responsibility is a subject that encompasses a wide range of approaches, from total laissez-faire to social impact investing by corporations and their foundations. When the focus is narrowed to child protection, both corporate/multinational action and inaction can have powerful effects.

Histories and reviews of foreign aid have often segmented out—or largely ignored—the impact of trade and investment on development goals. The financial scale of each, however, is unmistakably relevant, given the much larger amounts involved in trade and investment. The trade vs aid debate has intensified recently, and has been reframed by some as trade *reinforcing* aid, as demonstrated by the fact that in December 2005, the World Trade Organization (WTO) pledged its support for the concept of Aid for Trade (AfT).[230]

As a share of international capital flows to developing countries, foreign assistance has fallen from 70% in the 1960s to 13% as of 2012, "due to the takeoff in trade, remittances, equity, and foreign direct investment."[231] Total world trade in 2011, according to the World Trade Organization, was $22 trillion. This total is composed of $17.8 trillion in merchandise trade and $4.2 trillion in commercial services.[232] This compares with estimates of total international development and humanitarian assistance of $169 billion, as noted above. Most of this flow is among developed nations, but the portion of it that flows to developing and recently developed nations is a critical component of the elimination of poverty for hundreds of millions of children and families, as made clear in the World Bank and UNICEF data on progress toward the Millennium Development Goals. Least-developed countries' exports in 2011 were $202 billion; their imports were $205 billion (this excludes China and India).

Foreign assistance that expands infrastructure and education is a key bridge between trade and aid. It can equip developing nations with missing ingredients such as transportation upgrades that enable trade to provide new fuel for economic growth, rather than becoming merely extractive or a basis for corrupt elites to skim off the benefits of international economic flows. Yet agricultural subsidies within developed nations, along with requirements that food aid be from sources in developed nations rather than from the products of developing nations, have a definite undermining effect in the trade vs aid debate. Debt payments worsen the equation, although both "tied aid" and debt payments have been reduced by policies in some developed nations in recent years, and proposals are pending in the U.S. to further reduce requirements to purchase food commodities domestically.

A recent compilation by the Brookings Institution of essays on scaling-up issues focused primarily upon private sector solutions, though some public–private partnerships were also featured.[233] The prospects were assessed for business development of products benefitting poor families and communities, with foundations providing experimental support and public sector investments and markets then taking innovations to scale.

If the slogan "trade, not aid" is to have meaning, and if we are to take seriously the far more important data on the impact of global trade and investment in moving hundreds of millions of poor families onto a higher economic rung —without denying the negative effects of globalization on many of the world's poorest people—then multinational firms have an important role to play in reducing child maltreatment that results directly or indirectly from their efforts or their inaction.

For example, a rising number of children in the Sudan who have been abandoned or separated from their parents are victims of the war between Sudan and newly independent South Sudan. At the heart of the war is disagreement between the two countries about division of oil profits.[234] Oil purchasers, including China, cut checks to whichever oil source they have contracts with—which gives them at least partial leverage over the dispute. But no known oil buyer has ventured into the conflict, which prolongs it through inaction. The recent collapse of a clothing factory in Bangladesh spotlighted the broad ignorance of developed world retailers concerning the conditions that allow production of their lower-priced goods, along with the lack of enforcement of basic building standards.

The examples serve a second purpose, to make clear how often *inaction* supports or underlies the causes of maltreatment, in addition to the actions of parents, child traffickers, or other malefactors. For corporations—or governments, or advocacy groups—to simply do nothing can have policy content.

Leadership in the past decade has begun to connect children's rights and international business practices. The Organisation for Economic Cooperation and Development (OECD) Guidelines for Multinational Enterprises and the ILO Tripartite Declaration on Multinationals and Social Policy[235] provide important references to children's rights.[236] Other references include the UN Global Compact and the Children's Rights and Business Principles[237] developed by UNICEF, Save the Children and the UN Global Compact. The London-based Business and Human Rights Resource Centre website includes information on the practices of over 4,000 companies in more than 180 countries. One international authority on human rights issues describes the Centre as "the first place to check for those seeking information on a corporation's human rights practices."[238] Jody Heymann has compiled numerous examples of corporations that have improved their bottom line by improving the working conditions of their lowest-level employees.[239]

A new connection between corporate contracting and anti-trafficking measures was announced in November 2012 by the two co-chairs of a new Anti-trafficking Caucus, Senators Richard Blumenthal of Connecticut and Rob Portman of Ohio. The senators introduced an "End Trafficking in Government Contracting Act" (S.2234), which seeks to ensure that overseas contracting dollars are not spent in a way that encourages trafficking. The bill was attached to the Defense Authorization bill in 2013.

Nicholas Kristoff and Sherry WuDunn point to another arena of corporate action that has great potential for public-private impact on child protection and child poverty, in citing tariff reductions as they affect manufacturing incentives for multinational corporations in Africa and other developing regions. They argue that these changes, especially if coordinated with similar changes in European tariffs, would also create expanded employment for women.[240] If such policy shifts were accompanied by better child labor enforcement and efforts to anticipate migration effects that could result in children being separated from their parents, this would represent a significant income stream for some parents from poor families, as expanded trade has already done in China and India.

Again, we are not equating poverty reduction with a consistently direct and positive effect on child maltreatment. But families under reduced economic stress may also be under less pressure to view their children primarily as economic units. And corporate decision-making about foreign trade and investment could definitely pay more attention to who gets hired, where they migrate from, where they live, and what happens to their children. Corporate decisions about the types of energy they use and develop, as noted in the discussion of involuntary resettlement above, also have a significant impact on children and families forcibly relocated from their home communities. Corporate marketing of "green" products from developing countries has been successful; corporate marketing of "family-friendly" products could also enhance their appeal for some consumers.

The Hippocratic principle of do no harm could serve as a useful component of corporate policy as regards children and families affected by corporate operations. The resettlement effects discussed in Chapter 5 are one example where corporations in extractive industries and energy are supposedly bound by recent agreements on minimizing harm to existing communities. But oversight and enforcement of those agreements remains weak, in the view of those NGOs that monitor them closely.

Some progress is reported in a few sites in implementing these principles. UNICEF's 2011 annual report on child protection cited action in Thailand, Iran, Pakistan, and Nepal in working with business groups to reduce the reliance on child labor. CRIN has set up a Business and Human Rights Resource Centre to review progress on The Committee on the Rights of the Child's General Comment on Children and Business principles.[241]

Employment by large corporations has effects on children that go beyond child labor issues. The near-abandonment of many "left-behind" children by parents who have left rural areas to take jobs in urban regions has resulted in millions of children not seeing their parents and being raised by elderly grandparents or other relatives (as discussed below in the Appendix which reviews China's role in child protection). Corporate policy on parental leave and other efforts to facilitate more contact between parents and children does not appear to be a visible issue in any of these statements of business principles. Corporate action on employees' housing and parenting roles is far from a priority in most developing nations. Low-cost manufacturing employment is deliberately stripped to the basics, with some employees living in corporate housing that has few amenities. Those workers who are parents, numbering in the millions, see their children only rarely, at holidays. The problem is most severe in China:

> Researchers estimate that at least 58 million — nearly a quarter of the nation's children and almost a third of its rural children — are growing up without one or both of their parents, who have migrated in search of work. More than half of those were left by both parents.[242]

Global financial institutions also have a critical part to play, as well as multinational manufacturing and service firms. Their processing of the profits of traffickers and pornographers aids child abusers by enabling them to build protected empires of prostitution and crime. These firms' actions can be viewed as enabling terrorism. They profit from systematic, commercial abuses of children, using the Internet and financial hideaways to keep those profits concealed. The arcane techniques of law and finance that are used in asset identification and recovery, including the technological research capacity discussed in the next section, must be aimed at these criminal enterprises just as intensely as they are now aimed at financial flows that benefit organized terrorism and drug cartels. Restitution principles should be used to fund services and support for the abused children—many now young adults—who generated those profits. The total of international criminal profits is estimated at hundreds of billions; the portion of this generated by child-related enterprises that are linked to drugs and human trafficking is unknown, but it is sizable.[243]When global banking and investment firms aid the shielding of these profits, they are an appropriate target for child protection advocates and law enforcement.

A final example of corporate impact on children and families, while indirect, is potentially very large. Corporate success in shielding multinationals' profits from taxation has been pointed out by some as a very large subsidy to these firms from other taxpayers, while others view it as a stimulus to overseas investment. Dedicating some portion of any increases in taxation to foreign assistance (or investments with impact on lowest-income groups) in countries where the profits were earned might soften the opposition to any increases, while enlisting those countries in support for the changes.

Another corporate option: Protection by private security forces?

The logic of child maltreatment in armed conflict and in refugee settings may lead in some situations to prescriptions for private security services as a protective mechanism. It is not difficult, given the widespread use of private security forces in recent conflicts in the Middle East (in a pattern that some have likened to medieval private armies and privateers operating as armed forces under contract to states and military leaders) to envision UN and even humanitarian agencies hiring private contractors to provide strengthened security for at-risk populations, especially in light of recent attacks on refugee camps and traffickers' access to those camps.[244]

Technology

> "We are turning the tables on the traffickers. Just as they are now using technology and the Internet to exploit their victims, we are going to harness technology to stop them."
>
> —*President Barack Obama's Address to the Clinton Global Initiative, September 25, 2012*

The use of technology in child protection is expanding, but a review of available materials suggests that it lags behind the uses of technology in the related fields of policing, surveillance, and international law enforcement. Because it relates to acts within the family and in society that can be illegal in some contexts and culturally acceptable in others, child protection inevitably overlaps with issues of privacy and the rights of the accused vs. victims' rights.

As noted in a recent paper by staff of UNICEF's Executive Office, making the case for locally-driven monitoring of assistance programs,

> It is somewhat difficult to imagine from the vantage point of 2012, but at the time when the MDGs were crafted, Facebook, YouTube and Twitter did not exist; mobile phones did, but they were certainly not that "smart" and their use outside of a handful of developed countries was virtually non-existent; Google was still in its infancy; very few people were 'texting' and no one was 'blogging', 'podcasting' or 'tweeting'... Technology is, potentially and actually, a transformative agent for socio-political change and for ecnomic development [245]

Technology can affect social norms directly. Cable television isn't high technology—unless you live in a village that has never had television. Kristoff and WuDunn describe how watching middle class families in soap operas has had a remarkable effect in some developing nations when women realized that in many parts of the world women go to college and hold professional jobs as well as being parents.[246] Expanding the many forms of televised and recorded performances available to residents of rural villages, including handheld devices, can have a similar impact on social norms.

> A professional with many years of experience working with women in a Middle Eastern nation described the effects of television and the Internet on social norms that restrict women's roles at the village level: "They see that it doesn't have to be this way in other Muslim nations."

Technology is also relevant to the challenges of children, especially girls, who don't or can't attend school. Given the recent developments in distance learning, both in secondary schools and higher education, it is conceivable that the question will shift from whether girls are going to school to whether schools are going to where girls are. Home-based learning may be safer for some children, and may permit access to much higher quality instruction, than attending schools that are not welcoming to girls or whose teachers are not always there. The costs of providing wireless connections, laptops, and learning software could be considerably less than the combination of school staff and security that may be the alternative in some areas.

Three examples of recent use of technology by UNICEF in child protection efforts were reviewed in the 2012 Report of Executive Director Tony Lake:

> ...This is where UNICEF demonstrates a comparative advantage. An example is U-Report, a system developed with the support of UNICEF Uganda in 2011. The initiative uses SMS (text messaging) to inform decision makers of the opinions and feedback of young people in 'real time'. U-Reporters have provided input on issues such as female genital mutilation/cutting (FGM/C), disease outbreaks and other health issues, water availability, early marriage and education. Results are discussed locally and are also presented in newspapers and television shows.... Programme innovations include birth registration and family tracing and reunification through mobile handheld devices.... UNICEF developed a highly successful training programme on "Socio-economic policies for child rights with equity", which attracted approximately 5,000 online participants – 4,000 of whom were external.[247]

The European Council has recommended that an abduction hotline be used in child protection efforts; three European nations have already adopted such a system.[248] Another form of the use of technology that may have important implications for improved reporting of child maltreatment is crowd-sourcing, in which identified or anonymous "reporters" may be able to bring sustained publicity aimed at abuses and what happens to abusers. Cyber-reporting on abuse, with reporters given means of protecting their identities when necessary, could widen the nets of enforcement and community consensus, once reports are aggregated in the ways that a tool like Twitter can do.

In the words of the Google website "Ideas,"

The increasing ubiquity of connection technologies will both empower those driving illicit networks as well as the citizens seeking to curb them. These networks have been around for centuries, but one thing has changed— the vast majority of people now have a mobile device, empowering citizens with the potential to disrupt the secrecy, discretion, and fear that allow illicit networks to persist. As illicit networks grow in scope and complexity, society's strategy to reduce their negative impact must draw on the tremendous power of technology.[249]

Eric Schmidt, Chairman of Google, used the phrase "Basic connectivity is a force for good," at a conference on illicit networks held in Los Angeles in July 2012.[250] The conference was sponsored by Google Ideas, the Council on Foreign Relations, and the Tribeca Film Festival. Schmidt cited an example of use of mobile phones to report on and locate incidents of sexual violence as evidence that technology can reinforce national laws that are often ignored by enlisting citizens in reporting violations. Patrick Meier's recent book *Digital Humanitarians* makes a similar case that better-connected groups can respond more rapidly and accurately to natural and man-made disasters.[251]

For all this progress in the use of technology, in the program area of trafficking it remains to be seen whether the full capacity of financial tracking technology will be used to document and prosecute trafficking. The U.S. Treasury Department's Office of Foreign Assets Control (OFAC) "administers and enforces economic sanctions programs primarily against countries and groups of individuals, such as terrorists and narcotics traffickers. The sanctions can be either comprehensive or selective, using the blocking of assets and trade restrictions to accomplish foreign policy and national security goals."[252] These functions are used against firms and banks that trade with or launder funds to prohibited activities in Iran, Cuba, Sudan, Syria, and other nations. The phrase "terrorists and narcotics traffickers" has been used repeatedly in OFAC materials to indicate the targets of its actions to freeze funds. But these functions have not as yet been widely used against human traffickers.

Comparing the use of technology and invasive cybertechniques in anti-terrorism efforts with the efforts to deal with trafficking becomes even more relevant if one accepts Paul Farmer's framework of structural violence as applying to systemic violence against children. Sexually abused children are subjects of a kind of terror that is far less visible than the attacks on the World Trade Center and other 9/11 targets, but they are no less abhorrent if one considers the lifelong damage done to millions of children. Slavery was a global industry; trafficking children and others is today a global industry, and the full powers available to curtail the harm done by that industry are not presently being brought to bear.

It must also be recognized, however, that technology has a double edge, in the use of technology to exploit children on the Internet and in human trafficking. UNICEF has devoted resources to developing guidelines for safer use of the Internet, as the tension continues between privacy and commercial use of the Internet on one hand and the obvious exploitation of children on the other. What the European Council calls "cybersecurity for children" is a significant focus of efforts in Europe, as well as in the U.S.

A recent publication by the University of Southern California's Center of Communication Leadership and Policy described the continuing contest between traffickers' use of the Internet and efforts by law enforcement to use mobile technology to locate and prosecute traffickers.[253] The report noted that the adoption of mobile phone technology has become the most rapidly developed technology in history, with the World Bank estimating that 75% of the world's population has access to a mobile phone. Sexual trafficking of minors has moved from websites and commercial online firms such as Backpage and Craigslist to mobile technology that is much more diffuse and harder to track. The report mentions "vigilantes" and digital activists and use of crowdsourcing as counter-measures aimed at firms and individuals who are trafficking minors.[254] "Technology forensics" is described as being in its infancy, less advanced than developments in mobile networks and one-time cellphones that make detection very difficult. An overlap is clear between these changes and the role of major cell network carriers whose cooperation with courts and law enforcement is hampered by privacy concerns and impact on profits. The report notes briefly that improvements in tracking traffickers can be used against dissidents as well, raising a further human rights implication of this issue.

While NGOs and government agencies in this field are aware of these changes, the larger field of child protection seems much less engaged in these technology wars as they affect sexual violence and virtual enslavement of minors. These issues seem likely to play out further in the U.S., as the President's 2012 vow to crack down on traffickers moves toward implementation with new levels of public and private resources combined with a brighter spotlight on results. Recent controversy over use of technology to review phone and e-mail accounts obviously raises the visibility and sensitivity of these issues, but aiming these techniques at traffickers seems likely to be much less controversial than using them as widely as has recently been revealed.

Drug and alcohol prevention and treatment

In a thoughtful column in July 2012, Nicholas Kristoff cited a study in Kenya that revealed that "men, on average, spent more of their salaries on alcohol than on food." Kristoff summarized:

> The suffering associated with poverty is sometimes caused not only by low income but also by self-destructive pathologies...It's a vicious circle: despair leads people to self-medicate in ways that compound the despair.[255]

Kristoff went on to describe a CARE program for "village savings and loans" that had been able to reverse some of the negative spending drains in some families.

In Sri Lanka, the Foundation for Innovative Social Development has launched an Alcohol, Drugs, and Development program aimed at

> a reduction in the incidences of health problems and gender based violence associated with these substances as well as an improvement in the status. of economic

planning for youth. The long term strategic goal of the ADD programme is to bring about the improved performance of the state and civil society actors in managing the supply and demand of alcohol, tobacco and other drugs throughout the country.[256]

The recent attention given by WHO to "non-communicable diseases" is a hopeful sign.[257] The WHO initiative, incorporated in a proposed 2013-2020 action plan, is a move toward recognizing how important these factors can be, and how much some of them may worsen as family incomes improve. As globalization and aggressive marketing affect both diet and nutrition in developing nations, the results of increased access to and use of alcohol and tobacco have begun to add to the overall impact of non-communicable diseases in these nations.

A meeting to review the progress of the WHO initiative with respect to alcohol, titled "Global Action in Focus," was held in Washington in October 2012 and involved 45 nations.[258] Its sponsorship by alcohol manufacturers was a cause for concern for some NGOs, given the strong preference of the industry for identifying the problem as binge drinking to be addressed by law enforcement agencies and individual drinkers, rather than a public health issue for which the firms themselves share responsibility based on their marketing campaigns and efforts to expand use in developing nations.[259] A few alcohol firms have gone beyond token warnings about misuse of alcohol in their advertising to support significant prevention efforts. The link between alcohol and child maltreatment is rarely addressed in these meetings, however, despite ample research documenting the connection. Yet the link between childhood trauma and domestic violence remains a critical underlying factor in child maltreatment.

In a wonderful use of vivid acronyms, the NGO coalition calls for WHO to "develop guidelines to distinguish between PINGOs and BINGOs (Public Interest and Business Interest NGOs)." A dispute between these public interest and business organizations appears to be affecting decisions within the WHO bodies responsible for the alcohol policy, as reported by the Global Alcohol Policy Alliance:

> In the monitoring framework for the prevention and control of non-communicable diseases, the World Health Organization has removed the target to reduce per capita alcohol consumption. The first draft of the framework included a target to achieve a 10% relative reduction in per capita consumption of litres of pure alcohol among persons aged 15+ years... The Global Strategy points to effective, evidence-based public health interventions. Including a target on per capita alcohol consumption would be in accordance with the Global Strategy to reduce the harmful use of alcohol. To exclude the target of reducing alcohol consumption from the NCD monitoring framework is ill advised. It is imperative that WHO continues to adopt a public health approach to tackle the growing burden of alcohol harm. Now is the time to move forwards not backwards.[260]

Despite this recommendation, the work program reviewed at the WHO Assembly in May 2013 in Geneva did not include any goal for access to treatment; the 10% reduction by 2025 was kept in the draft. The draft does not refer to any link between alcohol consumption and child abuse.

The International Center for Alcohol Policies (ICAP) is a nonprofit organization created by the multinational alcohol industry. It has advised numerous governments on alcohol policy, emphasizing control of inappropriate use of alcohol by individuals rather than reduction of overall consumption. Its materials include a review of different treatment and prevention methods, including some efforts made in developing nations. A review of the organization's role in four African nations found that its opposition to alcohol tax increases appeared to be a major motivation for participation, with four nearly identical documents produced as "national policies."[261] This would suggest that WHO will face sizable obstacles in setting clear guidelines that address the alcohol issue as a public health problem in developing nations (as well as in the developed world), and suggests that a counter-balancing role by NGOs concerned with child maltreatment would be critical to making the guidelines effective.

WHO reports progress with pilot projects in four countries:

> Innovative portals on alcohol and health with a web-based self-help intervention tool have been developed with the support by WHO in four pilot countries, Belarus, Brazil, India and Mexico. The portal was launched on December 6, 2012, and provides information not only for policymakers and professionals, but also for the public at large. They include a self-screening tool for hazardous and harmful use of alcohol and a fully computerized self-help programme for people who wish to reduce or stop drinking alcohol.[262]

The training of public health professionals and paraprofessionals is an important arena of action in developing nations. Success has been achieved with "recovery coaches" who are themselves in recovery and can engage and retain persons with substance use disorders. This is a lower-cost alternative to fully professional staffing at expensive facilities.

Prevention approaches should not obscure the equal importance of treatment; while treatment in developing nations is unlikely to approach the intensive and expensive forms of treatment in developed nations, it is clear that one of the most effective forms of prevention for children at risk of substance use disorders is effective treatment for their parents. If global health goals omit this critical element in behavioral health progress, children will be among those affected by such an omission. But public health activities and maternal and child health in particular usually do not emphasize substance abuse treatment in their portfolios. As mentioned above, the relationship between HIV/AIDS and alcohol adds further urgency to addressing alcohol issues in greater depth.

Finally, it has proven challenging to weave together an emphasis on child well-being and parents' services in child protection efforts. A recent review of international child protection policies did not mention substance abuse as a policy issue, referring to it only once in passing in chapters assessing ten countries' practices. The systems (all in North American or European nations) were described as moving toward a "child-focused orientation," which was summarized as "defamilialization;" "the child-focused orientation puts children's rights above parents' rights and emphasizes parents' obligations as caregivers." Yet services to parents that improve caregiving were addressed only in terms of evidence-based practices that provide therapy, rather than those that provide treatment for substance abuse.[263] This outlook tends to under-emphasize the potential for a significant portion—but not all—parents to benefit from services that address co-occurring substance use disorders, mental illness, and family violence. The emphasis upon child well-being rather than family well-being further tends to diminish attention given to parents' treatment and recovery as a key factor in child protection for some children.

Closer links among UNICEF, USAID, NGOs in the child protection field, and the expanding efforts of WHO to address substance abuse as a factor in child maltreatment are obvious directions for reform. This is another area where the general prescription about better coordinated efforts could become very concrete, if these links were strengthened.

Achieving balance between institutional care and adoption for children without parents

"Institutional care" has been a target of several recent reports by U.S. and international agencies, based on the view that children are more likely to be mistreated and to miss out on the benefits of living in a family environment when they are in group care in large institutions. But for a large number of "rescued" children, many of whom cannot and should not return to the care of families where the abuse took place or where they were sold into de facto slavery in the first place—institutional care is literally a life-saving option. And for others who are in "orphanages" because their parents cannot care for them for economic or other reasons, international adoption may not be the best way to achieve child well-being.

For the formerly trafficked girls in Somaly Mam's shelters in Cambodia and the former child soldiers in the Democratic Republic of the Congo who cannot be reunified with their families, institutional care is where healing is happening. The stereotypical forms of group care that have been critiqued in some of the recent reviews of alternative care are group homes for AIDS orphans in Africa and horrific orphanages in Eastern Europe where children were severely neglected. But the importance of finding permanent homes for these orphans should not obscure the value of homes that are sheltering groups of children and young people from the violence, trauma, and loss they have endured.

With tribal and family loyalties as deep as they are in some of these cultures, it would be futile and cruel to consign these abused children to "family care" that means living with a close relative of the abuser. And setting as an alternative goal the adoption of children by a distant family, however loving and well-motivated that family may be, could mean breaking the positive ties of a familiar culture that can be part of the healing process. Religious congregations in the country where abuse happened can fill a part of that gap. But we have seen, sadly, across the globe, that religious settings offer no automatic guarantees of safety for children.

The difficult issues of institutional care are too often debated in a polarized, either-or approach that ignores the realities of trauma, broken families, and inter-country adoption. The 2003 UNICEF-sponsored report on institutional care frames the issue more carefully, citing the references to institutional care in the Convention on the Rights of the Child and stating that

> the Convention provides support for a well-prepared and planned process of developing
>
> alternatives to institutionalization for as many children as possible, a process that is itself fully respectful of children's rights and best interests.[264]

The key phrases here are *for as many children as possible* and *best interests* of the child. To prescribe turning away from institutional care without precise definitions of which children are being discussed ignores the critical distinctions between children who can be reunified with family members and those who need safe shelter above all, at least in the initial stages of their treatment and recovery. Lumping all these children in a single, over-simplified category obscures important differences in the categories of children without parents, both permanent and temporary. These include

- Children who need a healing environment based on their trauma
- Children who can live safely with relatives with adequate support to prevent re-institutionalization
- Children who can live safely in a foster or adoptive family
- Children with disabilities or minority status that affects their likely adoption or institutional care

The current scale of international adoptions into the U.S. is relatively small. According to the U.S. Department of State, 8,668 international adoptions were made by U.S. citizens in 2012.[265] This is a significant decrease from the peak in 2004 of 22,991 children. The 2011 U.S. total compares with an estimated 25,000 adoptions to all countries. It is also important to compare these numbers with the total number of 18 million children estimated to have lost both parents from all causes.[266]

The Hague Adoption Convention that went into effect in 2008 is seen by some proponents of adoption as a major barrier, while those who object to hasty and sometimes illegal adoption procedures welcomed this codification of international adoption procedures. One recent review of international adoption statistics attributed the recent decline to crackdowns on illegal baby-selling, worsening conditions in the international economy, and expanded efforts to promote intra-country adoptions of children without families.[267] Guatemala and other countries have struggled with backlogs of adoption cases due to poor record-keeping and accusations of baby-selling, which has stalled thousands of adoptions from these countries and left children in orphanages in some cases for several years, even though they have willing adoptive parents.[268]

The 2003 UNICEF report calls for comprehensive, "upstream" remedies that address the reasons that children are placed in institutional care before placement occurs. This is good child welfare practice, but it is not relevant to millions of the children who have been sold or trafficked, kidnapped and recruited as soldiers or military auxiliaries, or whose parents are dead. All possible efforts should be made to reunify those children whose families are functional and safe places to grow up, but those criteria are impossible to meet for many children in the above categories. An over-polarized approach to the debate that automatically rejects either family care or institutional care ignores the critical impact of *time* in a child's life: a child may need an intermediate period of shelter and group care before she is ready to live in a home that is likely to be a very different place from the one where she was born.

In the U.S., the Congressional Coalition on Adoption and its research and advocacy arm, the Congressional Coalition on Adoption Institute, have kept adoption issues in the spotlight in recent years. CCAI's board and advisory board includes members of Congress from both parties, foundation executives, and corporate executives of major multinational and investment firms.

A recent book on international adoption describes the regulatory oversight of adoption as an "ethical Wild West," citing numerous scandals of children with parents who were virtually sold as "orphans" by unscrupulous adoption agents in several countries.[269] The book describes tensions between U.S. Sen. Mary Landrieu, other U.S. legislators, and UNICEF. UNICEF is accused of blocking legitimate adoptions by U.S.-based advocates. UNICEF responds by pointing out the hazy definitions of who is an orphan, its documentation of unethical practices by some adoption agencies, and the underlying reasons for the agency's preference for in-country adoption. The book also discusses the strong connections between political leaders and faith-based adoption agencies motivated by their interpretations of scripture. The author points out that poverty and development issues form a critical, but often overlooked part of the context for international adoption from poor countries, with agencies and couples seeking children being much more willing to pay sizable fees for adoption than to contribute to stabilizing families in the children's own countries and cultures.

Reformers in the international adoption field have begun a corrective analysis of the adoption movement that in some cases is theologically based. One of these reformers, David Smolin of Cumberland Law School at Samford University, has written about

> ...errors of scriptural and theological analysis [that] have produced, and are producing, practices that in scriptural and Biblical terms would be called "sinful" and in more secular language can be called exploitative... virtually every premise of the modern evangelical adoption and orphan care movement is false... All too frequently, adoption has been practiced in a way that expressed contempt for the original parents and family, due to their religion, culture, poverty, or status as unwed parents... The intercountry adoption system routinely is willing to spend $20,000 to $40,000 on an intercountry adoption, while not being willing to spend even a few hundred dollars on the preservation of the original family... The movement has yet to learn that taking away the children of the poor and vulnerable is neither a Christian nor a humanitarian act... The Christian adoption and orphan care movement has failed to think in a truly scriptural and Christian manner about either orphans or adoption, and ended up distorting both....[270]

Smolin points out that some of the most exploitative adoption practices amount to child trafficking. On the positive side, Kathryn Joyce's book carefully describes other reforms, notably those of Saddleback Church's international efforts, especially in Rwanda, to enhance in-country foster care and adoption involving local churches and national efforts to de-institutionalize children in orphanages, with international adoption as a genuine last resort.[271] A rapprochement between the Saddleback leaders and UNICEF is suggested as a vital new area of middle ground in the adoption/institutions debate.

A final element of this problem is the overlap between institutional care and children with disabilities. In some cultures, disability remains stigmatized, and parents with this attitude may abandon their children to institutions. Adoption that requires specialized care can be quite different than adoption of a generally healthy child.[272] Yet the institutions in developing nations that care for children with disabilities are often staffed by non-professionals who lack training and familiarity with the causes and effects of disability. Easy slogans about adoption are not responsive to this sizable segment of children living in institutional care. A more elevated debate is needed between advocates of adoption and critics of institutional care and those who actually care for those children who cannot go home and should not be dislocated from the positive supports of their culture and communities.

Law enforcement, legal action, and responding to corruption

From village police to international courts, children are harmed or protected based on the capacity and willingness of law enforcement and legal institutions to treat children as having value and rights. Many venues and forums exist in which the rights of children can be addressed, but in many countries, the relative power of these institutions to protect children is not strong. In a recent international conference, a senior representative of a UN agency described the Convention on the Rights of the Child and the role of the Human Rights Council as providing a new "basis for legal action." When questioned about the statement after the session, she explained that she was referring to new legislative action enacting policy about children's rights rather than actual legal action against governments or firms that harm children.

The International Criminal Court (ICC) is an independent, permanent court that tries persons accused of the most serious crimes of international concern, namely genocide, crimes against humanity and war crimes. Only one person, Thomas Lubanga from the Democratic Republic of Congo, has been brought before the Court for a case related to children. In 2006, Lubanga was charged with the war crime of enlisting children under 15 and using them to participate actively in hostilities; the case was closed in 2011. The ICC is also currently investigating situations in Uganda, Darfur, the Central African Republic and is monitoring Cote d'Ivoire. It issued an indictment against five leaders of the Lord's Resistance Army of Uganda including commander Joseph Kony in October 2005 for crimes against humanity which include the abduction and sexual enslavement of children. The first Darfur war crimes suspects were named in February 2007.[273]

President Clinton signed the Rome Statute empowering the ICC, but President George W. Bush nullified the signature in 2002. At present the U.S. functions as an observer in the ICC sessions.

The UN Human Rights Council holds three sessions a year reviewing reports on human rights in a rotating set of nations. The Child Rights International Network monitors these sessions and issues reports on each one, including on its website both UN staff reports and NGO comments as each nation is reviewed in the Universal Periodic Review (UPR) process. In a 2010 report by CRIN on the status of children's rights in the UPR process, the group concluded that although one-fifth of the issues raised touched on children's rights,

> States tend to focus on, and accept, mostly recommendations on 'softer' issues, such as education and health, and neglect, or reject recommendations on more controversial issues, such as corporal punishment or juvenile justice.[274]

CRIN has also compiled a list of rejected recommendations which states have refused to accept from UPR reviews.[275] These include recommendations on birth registration, recruitment of child soldiers, ensuring equality of women and restrictions on child marriage, eliminating discrimination based on gender and disabilities, and providing universal free primary education.

The actual legal standing of the Convention on the Rights of the Child is summarized by CRIN as still emerging. "Although the Convention on the Rights of the Child has been around for more than two decades, it has in many places just begun to make its way into the courtroom."[276] CRIN maintains a case law database that cites use of the CRC in court cases at national and international levls.[277]

The accountability machinery of human rights is slow-moving and ponderous. At times, reading the diplomatically worded disputes in UN sessions among representatives of nations arguing against

> One international leader in child protection who has spent many years in human rights meetings summarized the proceedings, in a moment of great exasperation before an international conference on child abuse, as "sometimes simply stupid."

interpretations of the Convention that seem to infringe on their narrowly defined national sovereignty or cultural traditions, one is reminded of Peter O'Toole in *Lawrence of Arabia*, mocking an Arab sheik with the words "So long as [you] fight tribe against tribe, so long will you be a little people, a silly people—greedy, barbarous, and cruel..."[278]

As a remedy, relying on these arenas of justice is both important and often unreliable. They can spotlight egregious offenses, but it is the strength and persistence of NGOs that most observers feel represent the best defense of child protection in these forums.

At local and national levels, law enforcement practices concerning child protection vary widely, affected by the issues of corruption discussed above, the low pay and status of local police forces in many developing nations, and the cultural norms that assume that children are the property and exclusive concern of their parents. Enforcement of laws concerning sexual violence and trafficking also ranges widely, with some nations using the technological innovations referenced above, along with registries of offenders and residency restrictions.[279] But national mandates enacted into legislation are merely rhetorical when they require reporting child maltreatment, but have neither protocols for local law enforcement officers, nor any nationally or regionally aggregated data on the total number of reports. Such mandates set a standard, but then undermine it by a lack of enforcement of that standard.

Advocates might wish for an aggressive legal attack using the CRC as the basis for activist pursuit of national and multinational corporate policies that harm children directly or indirectly. But the unanimous Supreme Court decision in April 2013 dismissing the *Kiobel* case against Royal Dutch Shell's actions in Nigeria was a major setback for human rights advocates seeking to hold multinational firms accountable in U.S. courts for human rights abuses committed in other countries, using the Alien Tort Statute (ATS) of 1789 as the basis for the claim. However, the door was not completely shut.

> The Supreme Court, considering the broader question of whether the ATS applies to conduct committed outside the United States, held that the ATS only applies to conduct committed within the United States or on the high seas... The Court noted that a claim based upon acts occurring outside the United States may be appropriate under the ATS if the claim touches and concerns the United States with sufficient force to dispute the presumption that U.S. law does not apply internationally. Although the Court did not address the question of corporate liability directly, it did imply that corporations may be subject to claims under the ATS which satisfy the aforementioned requirements.[280]

Thus trafficking and other practices that involve the United States might still apply. Yet for advocates of children's rights, returning to the arenas of CRC interpretations and applications country by country, multinational by multinational, would seem more appropriate than trying to find ways around the *Kiobel* ruling.

Clearly, U.S. policy toward international organizations and issues often has to steer a careful course between expanding multilateral efforts and recognizing the strong views of some U.S. legislators on national sovereignty.

A more reasoned statement of the opposition to some international treaties and conventions was set forth in a recent *Foreign Affairs* article by three conservative spokesmen, who argued specifically against U.S. ratification of the Convention on the Rights of Persons with Disabilities and cited what they referred to as the "transnationalists" who are seeking to subject the U.S. to international law.[281] Their larger point was that

> The transnationalists challenge not merely the technicalities of lawmaking but the very essence of democratic accountability...When it comes to determining what constitutes binding international law, the answer should be officials accountable to the American people.

However much one might disagree with this perspective, it is clear that it is a view widely held among conservatives and others who are reluctant to subject U.S. agencies and firms to international courtrooms. And if the point Senator Kyl and his colleagues made is valid—that we are international leaders on disabilities rights whether or not we sign the Convention—then it could easily be extended to child protection, where we are not yet international leaders, but could be.

However, an opposing view was set forth by David Kaye in a subsequent article in *Foreign Affairs* that followed the Kyl group's statement. In his "Stealth Multilateralism: U.S. Foreign Policy Without Treaties—or the Senate," Kaye argues that the U.S. has lost credibility due to its abdication of treaty-making roles and its absence from the human rights treaty bodies of the U.N.[282] At the same time, he points out that the White House under both Bush and Obama has found ways to participate in institutions created by treaties the Senate would not approve. Ultimately, he concludes, this tactic weakens the U.S. capacity to influence human rights standards on which its foreign assistance programs spend billions of dollars.

The final legal arena that some advocates for child protection have suggested might hold promise is the extension of the responsibility to protect (R2P) doctrine to protection of children. A growing literature on this subject, an international journal, and NGOs dedicated to R2P all suggest the growing power of this idea.[283] Responsibility to protect as a doctrine arose out of a deep concern about genocide—the deliberate attempt to destroy life based on ethnic or racial divisions. Can divisions by age or gender be considered as serious? Pro-life advocates would quickly answer yes, in theory, and would point to abortion based on gender and infanticide as examples of ultimate harm to children. Others would point to a continuum of severity, from trafficking and severe sexual violence on one hand to less harmful forms of gender inequity and child neglect on the other, and might argue for use of the R2P doctrine on the farthest, most severe end of the spectrum. But advocates remain unclear about how to translate the doctrine of responsibility to protect into implementation in a way that would add to child protection mandates and effectiveness.

Secretary Clinton's remarks on International Anticorruption Day in 2011 emphasized the effects of corruption on foreign assistance:

> In September, President Obama and partner nations from around the globe launched the Open Government Partnership (OGP), a program that supports national efforts to promote transparency, fight corruption, and empower citizens. At the State Department and USAID, we launched a new initiative called Domestic Finance for Development that will help developing countries create reforms in tax administration, budgetary transparency and anticorruption to attract private investment, create jobs, and reduce poverty. And in the G20, the U.S. worked tirelessly with the largest emerging economies to create concrete, practical anticorruption commitments.

> International Anticorruption Day commemorates the 2003 opening of the UN Convention against Corruption for signature. Since that time, 158 governments have joined, making commitments to prevent corruption, criminalize corrupt acts, and help recover stolen assets. This year, the United States and other countries completed the first-ever reviews to monitor implementation of the Convention.[284]

The annual Country Reports on Human Rights Practices which are submitted to Congress by the State Department are opportunities for serious spotlighting of corruption that is well beyond the norm. Inevitably, these reports are irritating to the countries that are profiled, but without specifics, the anti-corruption efforts of the U.S. government are simply rhetoric.

In 2012, the annual reports for 2011 provided a good example of such an opportunity. As summarized by Sahara Reporters, an online community of international reporters and social advocates focused on media reports from Nigeria,

> The United States has again dismissed Nigeria's anti-corruption efforts as mere talk, describing the Goodluck Jonathan era as one in which the government is not implementing the law, and officials engage in corrupt practices with impunity.

> "Massive, widespread, and pervasive corruption affected all levels of government and the security forces," it said of Nigeria in its 2011 Country Reports on Human Rights Practices, which was submitted to Congress by Secretary of State Hillary Rodham Clinton. The department submits reports on all countries receiving assistance and all United Nations Member States to the U.S. Congress in accordance with the Foreign Assistance Act of 1961 and the Trade Act of 1974.[285]

Global Integrity Report prepares an annual review (not a ranking) of more than one hundred countries based on detailed scales of more than 300 criteria across 23 domains. As their website indicates, "The index assesses integrity, not corruption — it measures the actions being taken to fight corruption, not the extent of the problem itself."[286] Transparency International publishes a Corruption Perceptions Index (CPI) based on polling data (CPI) and the World Bank issues a Worldwide Governance Indicator. Across these three sets of assessments of anti-corruption efforts, there is an aggregate of useful information that could guide U.S. allocations more than they do at present. The State Department's Country Reports on Human Rights Practices serve this purpose in part, but their focus is human rights, not the full range of corruption as it affects implementation of child protection programs and other humanitarian aid.

The World Bank's summary of anti-corruption efforts is helpful as an overview:

> …[anti-corruption] means investing considerable thought and resources into protecting development projects against corruption. This includes enforcing the use of proper financial and procurement guidelines including financial and technical audits, setting up complaint databases and follow up processes, beneficiary involvement in project design, implementation and monitoring or participation by civil society organizations and the media. Increasing transparency also proves to be an effective deterrent for corrupt behavior.[287]

The reference to civil society and transparency raises some of the same issues touched on in the technology section above, since the spread of cellphones provides a wider potential group of whistle-blowers—if there is a trusted central point to which reports of corruption can be directed.

But a serious discussion of corruption and foreign assistance eventually has to confront the hardest question: will you deny aid to those children and families in the most corrupt nations because of their leaders' greed? And that question has an even more painful consequence when it is harm to children that may be affected rather than building another dam or providing more loans. Bypassing corrupt governments and directing aid to NGOs and civil society organizations has worked in some settings, but this tactic may restrict aid to small projects.

Corruption also has a cultural dimension in which crony capitalism can be masked so well that it appears to be the normal operation of a global economy. Again, Americans should keep in mind that clean hands are in scarce supply. In a recent issue of the *New York Times,* an article referring to corruption of police officers in India who allowed children to be trafficked into child labor and prostitution was printed a few pages away from another article explaining the negative effects of U.S. ethanol subsidies on worldwide hunger.[288] A single corrupt judge or cop may appear to be different from a strategically located industry that is able to bribe elected officials with campaign contributions—but the effects of both kinds of corruption are to increase harm done to children.

The Millennium Challenge Corporation established during the Bush administration has tackled corruption issues somewhat more directly than USAID and other U.S. agencies have done, although the list of MCC recipients includes some perceived kleptocracies. President Obama has requested an 11% increase in the MCC budget to a total of $1 billion in his FY2015 budget proposal, suggesting both the relative popularity of its anti-corruption goals and its relatively small size in the overall foreign assistance budget. The continuing annual reports of U.S. and international bodies, combined with greater use of technological means to detect and intercept illicit financial flows, also offer some apparent hope on this front. Yet until progress is visible, the case for expanding child protection support will be tarred with the same corruption brush as most other international assistance.

But the rule of law in the final analysis has to come down to the streets and villages where children live. Haugen and Boutros' excellent book mentioned above, *The Locust Effect,* sets forth a powerful argument that the reduction of poverty requires the reduction of lawless violence against the poor. Their examples, drawn from the field work of International Justice Mission, make clear that crime without punishment and with consequences only for its victims is a fundamental force that keeps poor families poor and victimized children traumatized. They are also critical of the international public and private aid donors who avoid projects that seek to strengthen local justice systems because they are not seen to be direct aid to the poor.

Although the book does not focus on child protection, its examples and model projects are drawn from the trafficking arena in which IJM focuses its efforts, and which involve millions of children from developing nations. With pointed historical descriptions of 18th and 19th century corruption and incompetence in police forces and courts in the U.S., England, France, and Japan, the authors make their case that local leadership, external aid, and model programs can combine to strengthen a rule of law that is virtually unknown to millions of the poor in developing nations.

Baselines and evaluating what works

Numerous reviews of child protection policies and programs have stressed the need for deeper evaluation efforts to determine which approaches provide the strongest evidence of impact.[289] As previewed in Chapter 1, data collection problems hamper evaluation efforts, including the frequent lack of disaggregated data on lowest-income children, families, regions, ethnic, religious, and caste groups, the difficulty of involving those most affected by child maltreatment, and the cultural barriers mentioned above.

The survey work mentioned previously is providing an important foundation for evaluating from baseline levels of child protection indicators toward national and regional improvement. In addition to national surveys, recent projects have also experimented with use of SMS technology to develop surveillance systems that would allow incident reports to be filed at the local level throughout a district or an entire nation.[290]

Evaluation is also critical in two other tasks in child protection:

- Scaling up the approaches that work best from individual projects to wider impact on child maltreatment
- Moving from quantitative indicators to addressing the need for quality in services and supports: not just attending school, but attending good schools with qualified teachers who show up regularly; not just sending abused children to treatment but ensuring that evidence-based treatment is available.

Debates about evaluation methodologies can be intense, relying on academic specialists whose entire careers have been based on use of these methodologies. With the passage of the Government Performance and Results Act (GPRA) in 1993, U.S. domestic programs have been subject to evaluation and performance assessments in much greater depth than was the case twenty years ago. But foreign aid takes place in widely varying settings, as one former federal official familiar with the GPRA process notes:

> This approach [GPRA]…had several serious limitations when applied to foreign aid. The data used for indicators were sometimes unreliable, and attributing changes in the indicators themselves to aid interventions—especially after a short period of time—was problematical…The most important result—learning how to be effective in a particular kind of aid intervention in a particular time and place—was typically not included as an indicator of results.[291]

Evaluating what works in settings in which the availability of resources can have a great effect on results increases the importance of cost analysis, which is even less frequent in most of these evaluations. Cost analysis is much more prevalent in health innovations, where the costs of immunizations or oral rehydration therapy can be allocated across a specific head count. But effectiveness in many child protection programs must be proven by more than head counts, and this data can be much more difficult to assemble in developing nations.

Evaluation also requires cultural sensitivity and an awareness of behavioral health issues that are too infrequently linked with the growing literature on behavioral economics. In our review of the impact of addictions, we quote sources that note how significantly male use of alcohol affects family income in some cultures and developing nations.[292] Evaluations that overlook gender inequity as underlying forces may fail to consider the full range of factors that really drive outcomes. A recent review of the work of child protection committees at the local level in several countries, undertaken by Save the Children, noted that gender bias issues have generally been neglected by these grass-roots efforts.[293]

Evaluation can also provide powerful evidence for the connections among different child protection programs, as well as how much child protection results may depend on interventions outside the child protection arena. School attendance outcomes have been shown to be linked to specific problems with children's health, as well as the more obvious links to family income. Deworming programs have proven that they can increase school attendance markedly, in an example that bridges a child protection outcome and a child health outcome.[294]

It is also important to mobilize *appropriate* forms of evaluation, rather than relying on a single type that may not be relevant in all settings and for all programs. Lisbeth Schorr and others have written about the over-reliance on "gold-standard" evaluation using randomized control trials, a method adapted from medical science.[295] Schorr has cautioned that multiple methods of evaluation are critical in trying to understand why programs work, in what contexts, and with what prospects for scaling up to greater impact. In settings where context can be critical, to ignore fiscal and cultural realities runs the risk of producing evaluation findings that misallocate resources only to those narrowly designed programs that are disconnected from other causes and effects. And in settings where resources for *any* evaluation are scarce, it is important to recognize that quality evaluation need not be expensive if adequate information systems are part of the original design of the project.

A review of recent reports from UNICEF, USAID, and NGOs suggests that progress in child protection has been greatest in three areas:

- Enrollment in primary and secondary education
- Reduction of poverty and malnutrition that affect child protection outcomes
- Reductions in child marriage

But UNICEF adds that "disparities are narrowing too slowly," pinpointing sub-Saharan Africa, South Asia, and the least developed countries as those that have fallen behind other developing regions on many indicators.[296]

A meta-evaluation of UNICEF programming conducted in 2008 reviewed 59 separate evaluation reports and found that

- UNICEF's best work is at the national level, Strengthening Government Commitments through national plans/policies and building a Legislative Framework…. Technical assistance supports to government and civil society partners are possibly the premier deliverable of UNICEF to CP (child protection) globally. This follows from findings showing that closest to central political power, UNICEF is making regular good use of its status as a convening agency…
- Conversely, Monitoring and Oversight ranks as the most deficient area of the entire PEF. Investments that align to centralized political power –e.g. relating to enforcement of a national plan-- are among the least likely to be monitored for quality assurance
- 27% of the reports say that a lack of basic needs (e.g. water, food) makes families, communities and governments less willing and able to engage in CP issues. Sixteen reports (27%) include reference to child protection needing to be embedded in baseline survival efforts such as water and food.
- Gender should have been a cross-cutting issue…cost-analysis is virtually non-existent but a consistent theme is "do-more-for-less-itus."
- While UNICEF finds and uses its "clout" most effectively with national level government partners, the meta-evaluation finds consistent gaps in enforcement and monitoring…
  It raises the question of whether enforcement weaknesses are basically the price of doing business on CP, or whether UNICEF could better leverage international agreements on aid effectiveness …in forging these agendas with host governments.
- Strategic communications: The absence of investments on this topic could reflect sampling biases, or, alternatively, a weak emphasis on

strategic communications within CP with a corollary need for technical support in design, monitoring, and implementation.[297]

UNICEF deserves credit for commissioning this assessment; few NGOs or national governments have undertaken as hard-hitting and detailed an analysis of their own efforts against the standards used in the 2008 review. Since 2008, it would appear that some of these findings have guided UNICEF efforts to improve their programming, including more emphasis on gender equity, on monitoring progress made, and on balancing bottom-up, community-based with top-down, central government-driven activities.

But governmental responsiveness to the need for child protection enforcement through monitoring mechanisms remains an area where UNICEF and its partners run into major obstacles in many nations. Resources gaps are often cited as barriers, but unwillingness to track progress and the lack of progress are seen as being at least as important as funding shortages in the reports. A recurring theme was voiced by one stakeholder as "an over-reliance on legislation at the expense of how laws get enforced."[298]

A more recent report in 2012 assessed 52 violence prevention programs supported by UNICEF and its partners.[299] Major findings stressed coordination gaps, including

- The child protection sector should better incorporate integrated, multi-disciplinary and intersectoral programming principles; doing so will require forging functional partnerships between different sectors within UNICEF and with other development partners.
- Holistic as opposed to vertical approaches to child protection should be encouraged in order to move beyond the silos of issue-specific programming to more comprehensive and mainstreamed systems approaches.

Again, the message comes through clearly that what is needed is expansion of the capacity to work across child protection boundaries with other UNICEF systems of child survival and development.

Sustaining innovation is a challenge that affects child protection work as well as other social welfare projects. In a 2010 review of more than 19,000 international assistance projects, analysts projected that only one in ten of these projects—half of which occurred during a single year—would be functioning in 2014.[300] This turnover of projects has the effect of wiping out the experience base of some projects, with the result that lessons are not learned from what worked and what didn't. In some assistance projects, an application or proposal for funding needs to include a realistic projection of options for sustaining the project after one-time funding expires, and it may that such requirements should be a larger part of seeking funding and assessing capacity to carry out the project. The lowered expectations and damage credibility that result from seeing a one-time project fall into disuse are a further drawback to weak sustainability efforts.

A paradox of sorts occurred several times in our interviews, in which NGO staff and national officials cited the improved measurement of conditions for children as a major advance in many countries, then explained why it was so difficult to inventory funding for child protection. In essence, this seems to be a contrasting confidence that we are improving our ability to track progress and pessimism about tracking the resources that are making it happen. To be able to upgrade measurements of health, safety, and well-being is unquestionably progress; to be unable as yet to upgrade inventories of the resources devoted to achieving these results remains an important gap in governmental and NGO capacity. Evaluation improvement needs to include improved assessment of the use of resources, as well as the results of programs.

Conclusion

These eight strategies, if pursued separately through siloed, fragmented projects, are unlikely to achieve significant results. On the other extreme, however, to try to carry out all of them at once could dissipate scarce resources and political support.

Each NGO, CSO, and national agency will need to select the mix of these child protection strategies that best responds to the resources available and the results desired. Hopefully this overview will make clear how important the links across these approaches can be. That is the function of a coordinated child protection response: to implement an array of strategies that use all available resources to achieve better results. Those results can serve as the heart of a marketing effort to expand resources—which is the tenth strategy and the focus of the next chapter.

CHAPTER EIGHT

Marketing and Funding Child Protection

Resources: not the only thing, but an impotant thing

Taking child protection problems seriously requires significant resources in both donor and recipient nations. For example, the creation of new governmental units in developing nations can be a step forward, but only if a legal framework, enforcement, and significant resources back up the new unit. Isolated units at the margins of national governance may provide a partial, short-term answer to the question of *what are you doing about this problem?*—but they are not credible in themselves unless they have a genuine impact on the rest of the government and on civil society.

> One federal official described a woman from a developing nation who visited the U.S. and ended up sitting in the official's office weeping because she had been charged with setting up a new child protection office for her nation—and staffing it singlehandedly without any resources.

An initial draft of the USAID Action Plan referred to the U.S. as "a major contributor to child protection efforts," but without any documentation or child protection-specific funding totals to support the claim. The total of USAID-inventoried funding, as mentioned above, includes $2.7 billion for many programs that are not related to child protection as defined by UNICEF and most NGOs.[301] The inventory is developed by a process that involves, as described in the Fifth Annual Report to Congress, an "annual Call for Projects from U.S. Government departments and agencies that fund *interventions to assist highly vulnerable children.*" The language makes clear that this is much more than a child protection agenda, with only 10% of the projects classified as child protection projects. The breadth of that agenda is impressive, despite counting existing aid programs, including food assistance and disaster assistance, as aimed at vulnerable children. But the priority given to child protection is not yet clear.

From the perspective of the UN, resources are stretched as far as possible. Under child protection funding from unrestricted funds, UNICEF reported in its 2011 annual report that

> $5 million was allocated to 33 priority countries to increase birth registration and address violence and harmful practices against children. Funds were focused on the most disadvantaged and marginalized girls and boys, including those without parental care who are placed in large-scale residential institutions, children with disabilities, children exposed to violence in schools, and children at risk of maltreatment in the justice system.[302]

These are appropriate priorities, and important projects. But if $5 million is divided across 33 countries, two major programmatic areas, and four specified target groups—the net impact seems very likely to remain at the project level, rather than rising to the level of systems change and an impact on baseline conditions.

Marketing and messaging for child protection resources

An important distinction should be made between the *marketing* efforts needed to expand child protection resources and the *messages* that would be most effective as the content of that marketing. Marketing involves all the different media and venues in which the message can be transmitted. Both dimensions of making the case for resources are critical, but they are distinct. The messages present perhaps the most challenging parts of the puzzle, since breaking through the ceiling on current child protection resources demands effective counter-arguments to several deeply held attitudes.

Attitudinal barriers to raising the priority for child protection issues: the messages

How could policymakers and the public be convinced that resources for child protection should be expanded? As noted above, the question assumes that some form of baseline inventory has been done to make clearer what resources are currently allocated to child protection activities. But assuming that inventory were to be completed or were under way, it is certain to document that these programs are under-resourced relative to need. And then the question becomes how to get past the marginal status of child protection programs in national and international budgets, as discussed in Chapter Four. This section addresses the U.S. political and media landscape; some, but not all of these arguments would be relevant in other developed nations.

The first task is to deconstruct the "arguments" against a higher priority for child protection, which are often not arguments but mere biases—however powerfully held. These may be classified into at least seven categories:

1. General opposition to foreign aid
    - Inaccurate perceptions that foreign aid is a significant part of the U.S. budget
    - "We need it at home"
    - "They waste it"; "they're corrupt" (a less sophisticated version of the Easterly case discussed in Chapter 5)
    - Anti-multilateral bias: negative views of UN, e.g. refusal to join Human Rights Council (until 2009), candidates' criticisms of UNFPA as population control, recent opposition to ratification of the Convention on Rights of Persons with Disabilities[303]
    - Race and culture bias—"that's just how they are"

2. Fiscal climate change
   - We can't afford it given our deficits

3. The private sector will do it/is doing it
   - Visibility of celebrities' roles in humanitarian programs
   - Visibility of Gates and other large foundations
   - Reliance on religious organizations: "we give to charity through the church/temple/mosque"

4. "Crisis ADD" and compassion fatigue
   - The South Asian tsunami and Haiti: one-time surges of aid and then inadequate follow-up[304]

5. Opposition to the gender equity elements of child protection
   - Religious organizations with supposed theological bases for women's subordinate roles
   - Other forms of misogyny

6. Available resources should be focused on narrower, categorical issues, such as trafficking or child soldiers vs. umbrella efforts aimed at the wider but at times more abstract issues of child protection.

7. Available resources should be focused on child protection projects subordinated to military and foreign aid priorities, which shift as military priorities change, e.g. Afghan schools funded by the military vs. those funded by independent organizations

Responses to the Barriers

Can effective answers be given to these "arguments" against foreign assistance in general and increased funding for child protection in particular? To the extent that they are ill-informed biases, the answer is negative. But to the extent that a serious proposal to expand child protection funding would run head-on into some of the more substantive of these barriers, cogent and persuasive responses are essential. At least four strategies seem worth considering:

1. *Make the case for charitable contributions:*

All U.S.-based denominations and in fact virtually all world religions as well, have a charitable imperative as a major tenet. A focus on children, as mentioned in Chapter 1, is also a central theme in charitable efforts based in religious organizations. The creation of the PL 109-95 legislation and the lobbying for its expansion involved numerous religious organizations, ranging from evangelical, Bible-based denominations and mega-churches to "establishment" denominations, including the Catholic Church. The links between members of Congress with a strong interest in Africa and some of these religious organizations have been strong in recent years, representing a bipartisan alliance which is far from typical in current polarized political environments. These partnerships also ensure that the message is not that government needs to do more by itself, but that government and its partners need to come together more effectively on a broader child protection agenda driven by a goal of reducing specific harm done to millions of children. While a theological, religion-based case will not resonate with all potential contributors, Pope Francis has recently dramatized the role that religious leaders can sometimes play for their own adherents.

2. *Make the economic case*:

UNICEF has begun a body of research on "the costs of doing nothing." A paper published by UNICEF's Innocenti Centre in September 2012, "Social Protection and Equity Stimulate Economic Growth," reviewed

> the available evidence on the impact of social protection and show how equitable distribution of resources can contribute to more prosperous societies. Through the analysis, it argues that additional investments in social protection and income redistribution can be an instrument to enhance economic growth and development.[305]

Although these analyses emphasize social protection defined as income supplements, rather than more narrowly focused child protection, they make clear that cost savings are available from investments in lower-income regions and nations. Analyses have documented the costs of child abuse in the U.S. alone at over $100 billion annually, as discussed above.

The positive side of the argument is also powerful. Recent analysis has shown the long-term payoffs from investments in education for girls and women. That is where the argument from economics and the argument based on policy momentum converge, as noted in the next item. A powerful chart in a recent *Harvard Business Review* article, using research by Booz and Company, ranked more than 100 countries on a matrix of the economic success of women and policies supporting women's access to education, employment, and credit. Their projection was that "if women in the U.S., Japan, and Egypt were employed at the same rates as men, the GDPs of these countries would be higher by 5%, 9%, and 34%, respectively."[306]

Evaluating what works needs to also include evidence of what saves money. In her fine compilation of available data on children's programs, Jody Heymann included a number of citations of studies showing the eventual payoffs from national policies on school attendance, child labor, child marriage, and income support programs.[307] To advocate for eliminating school fees and ignore the initial costs of such a policy in increased education spending for larger enrollments and teacher training is much less persuasive than showing the economic development impact on GDP of such investments, as Heymann points out.

As a partial summary of this argument, Neil Boothby, former head of the USAID CECA staff, recently said at a panel discussion convened by USAID and the CPC Network that "the message of change is how investing in children is building the national economy." He added "It's not going to improve through incremental discussions about child protection or social welfare."[308]

3. *Make the case for linkage—ride other tides*:

As noted throughout this book, several of the items in the child protection agenda overlap powerfully with other efforts aimed at gender equity and trafficking. If child protection is treated as an isolated set of problems, it will not have the same constituency base as these issues that have attracted major support from political and religious leaders and celebrities. There is a risk of submerging issues such as child labor and birth registration in these larger, more media-visible issues, but there is also a benefit that should be weighed that would flow from breaking these issues free of the boundaries around single-focus fundraising. Perhaps it is time for child protection advocates to begin measuring funding for narrow single-issue efforts compared with support for the full range of child maltreatment issues. Again, with better expenditure totals, more would be known about the trend lines in both these larger and smaller slices of the child protection funding pie.

4. *Make the case against corruption*:

The attitude that corruption affects foreign assistance is not only deep-seated among the U.S. public; it has gotten more visibility in the last decade as more books are published that call aid programs into question and make corruption more visible.[309] Afghanistan has been the subject of several exposes spotlighting corruption, and Mexico's struggles with the drug cartels and their infiltration of government have also received a good deal of recent media attention. The World Bank has published a series of reports on their own and others' anti-corruption efforts, as discussed above. Both the realities of corruption and the perception that it is pervasive have to be taken seriously in this climate. To the extent that child protection efforts are more transparent and less influenced by the most visibly corrupt, crony-driven governments, this should be a part of the case for funding those sites.

Marketing child protection

Our expertise is not in marketing social change, but some very thoughtful recent writing has addressed this problem. Experts on social media have turned their attention to many children's programs and efforts to achieve gender equity. Social marketing activities are being refined to undertake the kind of micro-targeting that political campaigns now use to determine which potential donors and volunteers are most likely to respond to specific causes and which kinds of appeals will be most effective. Charitable donations are a highly competitive field in developed nations in the 21ˢᵗ century. Marketing techniques have turned to social media tools such as Twitter and online giving, causing one source to speculate that Twitter could put the UN out of business.[310,311] From initial "child sponsorship" campaigns that sought to identify donations with specific children, more sophisticated efforts have aimed at marketing products linked to humanitarian and development goals through websites such as Hungersite and Kiva.[312]

Academic studies have also looked at marketing and political efforts to generate support for specific ideas in foreign assistance.[313] These reviews emphasize several values that are helpful to increasing support for a given issue:

- The simplicity and concreteness of the message,
- Emotions and stories that help the idea to "stick,"
- Leadership and the presence of "champions" for issues,
- The perceived severity of the issue as assessed by credible measures of the problem,
- The security threats presented by the issue,
- Whether key actors have achieved a consensus on the definition, framing ideas, and effective interventions for the issue, and
- The presence of cross-cutting issue networks that include governments, NGOs, funders, and the UN agencies.

In reviewing the political salience of maternal mortality as a single issue, Shiffman and Smith cite the example of the Task Force for Child Survival and Development, which was formed in 1984 and included the Rockefeller Foundation, WHO, UNICEF, UNDP, and the World Bank. They also cite the opening of "policy windows," which they see as including disasters (such as a tsunami), discoveries (such as vaccines), and international forums (such as global UN conferences).

Marketing expanded resources for child protection to the public is very different from selling it to legislatures, although there is an important overlap in skillful advocacy that builds a wider constituency for a legislative measure. Since both would be needed to make non-trivial increases in child protection program funding, the issue of coordination between outside advocates and "inside" agencies remains critical. Again, advocates tend to work down single-issue tracks in their legislative efforts, and a missing ingredient, at least in the U.S., may be unified issue networks that market their ideas *across* child protection categories.

Religious denominations conduct campaigns specifically oriented to foreign aid and humanitarian assistance. Some denominations that require a set percentage of income for giving, whether tithing or some other form, emphasize the percentage as much as they do the targets of the assistance. Despite declining overall church membership in the U.S. and Europe, some denominations remain active participants in humanitarian funding efforts. The presence of Catholic Relief Services and World Vision in the list of the largest NGOs is further evidence that appeals through religious organizations belong on the list of marketing ideas in child protection.

It is also possible that some NGOs will use a new leverage point aimed at one set of religious organizations, in ways that may affect marketing that seeks to correct public perceptions. The Vatican will be reviewed during the Committee on the Rights of the Child's 65th session beginning in January 2014. A recent CRIN newsletter noted that

> During its pre-session stage…, the Committee asked the State to supply all the information it has on child sexual abuse committed by members of the clergy, monks and nuns that has been brought to the attention of the Vatican. The request for information includes details of any investigations the Vatican authorities carried out, what preventative measures it implemented, and how it assisted and compensated victims.

Some critics of human rights and child rights organizations disapprove of efforts that seek publicity for assistance programs that is framed solely in terms of innocent victims without a concern for those who harm them.

Other have decried the use of celebrities in gaining greater visibility for assistance programs, arguing that these "parachuted-in" visitors to sites where aid programs operate can at times trivialize what is really happening, ignoring how long it takes to achieve lasting change. But media attention in a celebrity-driven era indisputably follows celebrities, and the more important issue seems how those efforts can keep from being merely one more fragmented diversion from unified networks of assistance.

The extraordinary publicity given to the "Kony 2012 video" that focused on child soldiers in northern Uganda, the Democratic Republic of the Congo and South Sudan suggests that marketing through videos can have a powerful, even viral impact. If the entertainment industry were to hold an annual ceremony of awards for videos and films that best dramatize child protection issues, the spotlight on those issues would certainly increase. Social media, again, can surpass print media in total impact in ways that could benefit marketing for child protection issues.[314]

The political dimension of marketing is tempting—and challenging. Conservatives have actively supported anti-trafficking legislation, and some NGOs with religious identities have been active in recruiting these members of Congress in support of these measures, as well as HIV prevention and programs benefitting orphans. Yet foreign aid remains a frequent target for many fiscal conservatives.

Can appeals for new funding succeed when they are restricted to those child protection programs backed by conservatives? The modest level of the recently proposed Child Protection Compact as it passed the House Appropriations sub-committee ($5 million) suggests there is a risk in aiming too low.[315] This legislation was originally proposed in 2009. It can be viewed as an example of advocacy "victories" that are at times much smaller than if an equal level of energy were devoted to advocacy aimed at executive branch action. Getting a very small appropriation can be compared with getting the Justice Department and the Treasury Department to shift its priorities to prosecuting traffickers as a higher priority through identifying the financial transactions that fund traffickers. Sustained congressional oversight that pressed departmental officials to report in depth on the effectiveness of these activities would arguably have a wider impact within the US than near-token levels of funding for foreign governments to stop trafficking at their levels.

One advocacy organization described the impact of the Compact legislation expansively:

> It would eradicate the exploitation of children for slave labor or commercial sex by tackling root causes. Child Protection Compacts will allow the U.S. and its partner countries to make a major (and measurable) impact in child trafficking though strengthening countries' ability to protect children and prosecute traffickers.[316]

If the Compacts were funded at significant levels, these claims might be supportable. At $5 million, it may be a stretch to assert that root causes of trafficking—which include family income, lax law enforcement, gender bias, and corruption—will in fact be affected significantly.

And yet it is a viable political goal to try to build a broader coalition that goes beyond those members of Congress whose support for foreign assistance programs is constant. As noted above, the religious motives for support of child protection are widespread and not confined to progressive denominations. And the argument for trade and corporate investment may appeal to pro-business legislators in ways that proposals for expanded public funding will not. If one believes that capitalism and free markets are good for the world economy, it may be possible to expand the constituency for ensuring that corporate policies do not harm children by creating economic incentives for actions that are harmful.

What are the prospects for increasing child protection resources through a concerted, sustained marketing campaign using all these techniques? The policy and political environment in the US will influence that outcome greatly, and those environments are certain to include debate over foreign aid and discretionary spending as part of the overall effort to reduce US federal deficits. If leadership in such a campaign came primarily from the public sector, it is difficult to predict significant expansion. But the federal government could do two things that would have a great effect: coordinating its own efforts more intensively with more accountability for results (as called for in the new Action Plan) and calling on private firms, foundations, and individuals to both increase and better coordinate their giving to child protection activities.[317]

The rise and multiplicity of NGOs, as Joseph Nye and others have pointed out, is a form of soft power that can compel governments to pay more attention to the issues that NGOs espouse. But the varied agendas of those NGOs may have a negative effect, along with all its potential impact. Fragmented advocacy can cancel itself out, as pressures on governments lead to token or mere rhetorical responses to each cause, rather than real shifts in priorities. In the absence of clear priorities from hundreds of advocacy organizations, governments can more easily resist the need to make significant changes in their budgets and policies.

Again, if NGOs in the child protection field are to have a wider and deeper impact on their field, it will take a more unified effort. Small-scale increases in a few line items in the federal budget may satisfy some advocates, but they are unlikely to make a substantial impact on the lives of children or measures of child well-being around the globe. Alternatively, NGOs working together with foundations, religious organizations, and corporations on a unified child protection agenda could potentially amass more non-governmental resources for expanding child protection programs than they could possibly leverage in federal spending.

Funding options

Calling for an increase in spending, even if the case has been made, without any idea of how to finance it is hollow public policy. What follows is a preliminary set of options that may be fleshed out if a more serious effort were to be made by public or private stakeholders.

The options, each of which could be developed in more detail by the USAID Center, congressional coalitions, or NGO consortia, include

1. A line item increase in the foreign assistance budget specifically allocated for child protection activities, including but going beyond the 3-6-5 approach of USAID to reward nations, NGOs, and CSOs with proven results
2. Social venture funding or social bonding, using the models developed by a number of foundations, in which returns to funders are paid from the longer-run benefits of projects
3. Joint funding with foreign governments or private foundations
4. A combination of lowered tariffs and taxes levied on US firms that benefit from increased imports or distribution of imports from developing nations, or stronger incentives for lowered trade barriers for nations or firms with strong enforcement of child labor provisions
5. A tax checkoff (which could replace the presidential campaign funds which appear to be defunct at present)[318]
6. An option to match funds provided directly by U.S. children for international child-focused projects approved by U.S. charities
7. Alcohol taxation which has been proven to reduce consumption while generating revenues for prevention and treatment programs

Innovative financial models must also be explored in more depth. Restitution funding has been used in the U.S.by state governments to transfer resources from criminals to their victims. Garnishing wages has been used in child support programs, and whistleblowers have been reimbursed with rewards from the Internal Revenue Service and the Securities and Exchange Commission for reporting criminal behavior in their firms and organizations. Negotiations are under way with international banks that have been identified as accepting funds from illegal organizations. Each of these is a model for funding action in support of those harmed by illegal behavior. Rewarding civil society organizations that report child abuse may also be a model that can be adapted from these precedents.

More funding—for an uncoordinated system?

Merely to increase funding from US governmental sources—or from any single source—may not improve coordination or effectiveness across child protection programs. It could even worsen it, if the funding were dropped into existing programs without determining what positive effects it might have in achieving critical mass for some of the most effective efforts.

Funding increases may be easier to justify for priority areas, and at the same time they may have wider effectiveness if they are linked to other investments in those priorities, seeking new leverage on existing funding rather than always trying to launch a new project. Such increases should be multilateral, which will require more consultation than unilateral funding. They should reward either national governments or NGOs that are working on both top-down and bottom-up, social norm-shifting agendas. And they should include serious evaluation efforts to determine both the impact of the programs to be funded and whether overall levels of the problem are reduced.

It may well be that new funding should come in at least two stages: a first stage in which multilateral efforts to compile a genuine global inventory of child protection projects is undertaken, and a follow-up phase in which the inventory is used as the basis for a priority-setting exercise among the UN, national governments, and NGOs active in the child protection field. The annual reports to Congress of the USAID Center now offer an opportunity to summarize the annual reports of major NGOs in a companion volume; the appearance of such joint products for the first time, rather than a completely fragmented series of separate reports issued by each organization, would in itself convey a message of closer coordination. Each organization would continue to issue its own reports, but the USAID effort could assemble (or offer US-based NGOs an opportunity to compile) a more unified product with a broader overview. Expanded cooperation with UNICEF could improve links to an international information base.

CHAPTER NINE

The U.S. Role: A Summary

Four questions emerged from our interviews and literature review in assessing the U.S. role:

1. Is U.S. policy toward child protection coherent?
2. Is U.S. policy proportionate?
3. Is U.S. policy effective?
4. If not—could it be?

Several sources have critiqued U.S. policy in the broader field of foreign assistance that encompasses global child protection. Michael Mandelbaum has scoffed at "foreign policy as social work," David Rieff has dismissed "pervasive Wilsonianism" that seeks to make the world safe for democracy and has pointed to U.S. endorsement of "military-humanitarianism," citing Colin Powell's references in 2001 to NGOs in Afghanistan as a "force multiplier" and "an important part of our combat team."[319] Some NGOs and others find the U.S. wedded to a more unilateral role than other nations' multilateral efforts, expressing concern that the U.S. role in child protection is not as effective as it could be if the U.S. were more engaged in UN-sponsored efforts and had closer ties to NGO projects.

The world's largest economy and the world's largest military power will inevitably attract criticism, some deserved, and some aimed at the biggest target available. But from the vantage point of child protection, a more focused review is essential. These four criteria seem justifiable in undertaking such an assessment, which will address both U.S.-based public and private actors in the child protection field.

First, however, a review of the history of the PL 109-95 functions will be helpful in understanding its current directions.

The origins of PL 109-95 and U.S. progress to date

As noted above, the passage and signing in 2005 of PL 109-95, the Assistance for Orphans and Other Vulnerable Children in Developing Countries Act, was originally supported by 130 co-sponsors in the House. The congressional support emerged in part in response to efforts of a coalition, Global Action for Children, which had emerged in 2003 from 21 organizations that had worked together on AIDS legislation. A grant from the Jolie-Pitt Foundation provided initial funding for GAC, and Angelina Jolie was named its honorary chairman in 2006.

In the U.S., given the importance of gender bias in child protection (as many as ten of the sixteen UNICEF child protection issues relate to gender bias), an overlapping focal point on child protection issues is the focus on gender equality throughout USAID and the State Department, under the leadership of then-Secretary Hillary Clinton. In March 2012 a separate report on gender equality issues was published by USAID.[320] The United Nations has also devoted major efforts to addressing gender bias and violence against girls and women.[321]

The USAID Secretariat for PL 109-95 committed in 2011 to producing by July 2012 a child protection strategy that includes "guiding principles for U.S. Government assistance to affected children." In June 2012 a "framework" in the form of a 22-slide PowerPoint was provided to a coalition of agencies concerned with vulnerable children and posted on the Internet for comment. In December the full U.S. Government Action Plan for Children in Adversity (APCA) was issued, with three major priorities:

- Build Strong Beginnings: Increase percentage of children surviving and reaching full developmental potential.
- Put Family Care First: Reduce percentage of children living outside of family care.
- Protect Children: Reduce percentage of girls and boys exposed to violence and exploitation.

The Plan is reviewed below in more detail.

Now operating as the Center of Excellence on Children in Adversity (CECA), the USAID office currently (late 2013) has a staff of six led from 2012 to 2014 by Dr. Neil Boothby, who was previously at Columbia University's Mailman School of Public Health where he served as Director of the Program on Forced Migration and Health. Boothby's title was U.S. Government Special Advisor and Senior Coordinator on Children in Adversity. The current Director, Rob Horvath, also has responsibility for non-CECA activities.

The origins of the legislation in HIV/AIDS concerns are clear in its background materials, which emphasize the problems of orphans of AIDS. Organizationally, the PL 109-95 office was initially under the Bureau of Global Health in USAID, underscoring its origins in the agency's HIV/AIDS efforts. It has since been moved to the Bureau of Democracy, Conflict, and Humanitarian Affairs.

The office has conducted an initial inventory of U.S. government programs for "highly vulnerable children." This phrase underscores the fact that the USAID office has a much broader definition of child protection issues and "vulnerable children" than UNICEF's categories.[322] Different umbrella terms have been used in the Office's recent history. The PL 109-95 enabling legislation refers to "Orphans and Vulnerable Children," some USAID documents refer to "highly vulnerable children," and the Action Plan draft uses the overall phrase "children in adversity." Included in these categories are child development, child survival, child poverty—and child protection. With that breadth, the USAID unit appears to be more comparable to the whole of UNICEF than its Child Protection section. Of the six goals set forth in the Plan, three mention child protection issues explicitly. But in the listing of 1710 projects in the 2012 Report to Congress, only 171 of them are classified as "protection from abuse, violence, exploitation, or neglect." An additional 100 projects are classified as "capacity building for national child welfare and child protection programs."

In the first annual report on vulnerable children, the USAID office included comments by a coalition of NGOs. One comment addressed the lack of collaborative efforts at the local level.

The NGOs also called for a widening of the focus of the office beyond HIV issues:

> The reference to Highly Vulnerable Children is particularly welcomed, as OVC has become synonymous with AIDS-affected. Vulnerability extends beyond HIV and AIDS, and, as many reports have demonstrated, targeting this specific group is often stigmatizing and counterproductive...Some of the examples of "progress" given (e.g., page 9 of the draft annual report) are results of interventions or programs targeted at adults living with HIV, rather than highly vulnerable children or their caregivers per se.[323]

In December 2011, USAID held a Summit on Evidence-based Programs. The focus was on children living outside of family care, defined as "those living on the streets or in institutions, trafficked, participating in armed groups, or exploited for their labor."[324] An impressive array of experts attended, and several presentations emphasized the effects of no parental care, the importance of gathering better data on these children, and the benefits of a "whole-of-government" approach to improved coordination across U.S. agencies. But there was no overall plan presented with dollar amounts to implement the plan. One presenter stated that "There is currently little sharing of practical experience across agencies or across NGOs."

Two members of Congress have played major leadership roles in the PL 109-95 process, along with several colleagues who also track these issues. Former Senator Mary Landrieu of Louisiana and Rep. Barbara Lee of California are recognized as the most actively engaged congressional sponsors, and their staff play important roles in monitoring the implementation of the legislation. Former Senator John Kerry, Rep. Karen Bass, and former Rep. Michele Bachman have also been active in oversight activities related to PL 109-95. The departure of three of these leading members of Congress raises questions about current leadership which remains unclear.

It should also be noted that congressional oversight and concern about child protection and child survival issues include prohibitions and sensitivity in some areas of funding, such as adoptions, family planning and reproductive health, children's rights vis-a-vis parental responsibilities, and opposition to ratification of the Convention on the Rights of the Child. In November 2011 a conference was held on the Way Forward Project sponsored by the Congressional Coalition on Adoption Institute (CCAI) which brought together African and U.S. officials and experts in this field to make recommendations for strengthening child protection systems in six African countries.

Congressional activity is also affected by the fragmented nature of child protection efforts. One congressional staff member familiar with the advocacy efforts of NGOs and other U.S.-based groups summarized the process by saying "Each group lobbies for its own programs and its own view of the problems. *There is very little lobbying for child protection as such.*" Strong concern for international adoption affects some efforts, trafficking attracts other groups, and so on. Coalitions of advocates exist, but the comments by advocates posted on the website inviting reactions to the first framework versions of the PL 109-95 Action Plan focused primarily on each group's concerns.

One congressional aide noted "When there's an executive order behind it, the agencies pay much more attention to it." The executive order issued at the time of the gender report in 2012 was cited as an example in which Secretary Clinton's clear priority and the White House support reflected in the executive order elevated these issues to higher priority than other foreign assistance-related efforts. Some of the NGOs, in fact, indicated that they have been seeking a broad executive order on child protection issues for that reason. The remarks by President Obama at the September 2012 session of the General Assembly on trafficking were seen by some observers as strengthening the U.S. government's focus on these issues.

A new initiative, the Protecting the Future Alliance, is being developed by the USAID office as part of its rollout of the Action Plan. In July 2012, the USAID office released the following statement on its website:

> Protecting the Future Alliance is envisioned as an innovative alliance model for improving the security and well-being of children growing up in severe deprivation and danger. It seeks to reach critical protection and childhood development goals more quickly, cost-efficiently, sustainably, and at wider scale through innovation and partnership. A set of common objectives is emerging around the U.S. Government's National Action Plan through discussions with public-private and bilateral donors and senior representatives from priority countries in Africa, Asia, the Middle East, and Latin America. A tentative February 2013 prelaunch gathering at the Rockefeller Foundation's Bellagio Center would serve to finalize a set of impact-oriented objectives and indicators.[325]

The Alliance has been relabeled the Global Alliance on Children in Adversity, following the Bellagio conference in February 2013. This session included representatives of fifteen organizations from eleven nations.

To summarize the recent history of the U.S. role in child protection, the U.S. is an important player in some segments of the child protection agenda, but is not at present a leading player in addressing child protection issues proportionate to its resources. Former Secretary Clinton famously said, in 1995 in Beijing that "human rights are women's rights and women's rights are human rights." President Obama directly addressed trafficking issues in his 2012 address to the General Assembly. Yet it must also be noted that there is no serious effort under way within the executive branch or Congress to move toward US ratification of the UN Convention on the Rights of the Child.

Eventually official U.S. leadership may raise the children's agenda to greater visibility, but in the meantime, U.S.-based NGOs, funders, and civil society organizations are attempting in various ways to make the case for global child protection as a problem deserving higher priority within the U.S. government. Reviewing the current role against specific criteria may help understand the prospects for that higher priority.

Coherence

By coherence, I mean at least these ingredients:

- Interagency focus on clear priorities, including an inventory that focuses on child protection spending and goals across all U.S. agencies involved, whether they are separate programs or subsumed under other categories of programs
- A "dashboard" of the most important indicators of progress which U.S. agencies are seeking to improve and monitor over time, assessing progress made against resources and the scale of the total problem
- An ongoing effort to share information with the UN, other governments, and NGOs that includes these first two elements
- An effort to address the issues of resources and the barriers listed above, including a marketing plan.

It is not difficult to conclude that while progress is being made, these ingredients of coherence are not fully present.

Some officials in the U.S. government have thoughtfully made a virtue of necessity, pointing out that having little funding of their own is not a detriment, but actually an asset in working across agency lines. It is true that some coordinating efforts get caught up in "their own" projects, driving away potential partners when the message begins to sound like "let's collaborate with your funding for my projects." One NGO familiar with the Action Plan process described the stance of the new office as being "the resources are already there in the agencies"—a perspective that may not be welcomed by the agencies.

It has been said that nothing coordinates like cash, and it remains to be seen whether the lack of funding for the new USAID Center's agenda is a positive or negative factor. The support given from the White House, the Office of Management and Budget, and the Secretary of State is likely to have much to do with the outcome.

Coherence is also affected by Congress, and Congress has its own narrowing, fragmented approaches to child protection. International adoptions, HIV-AIDS, trafficking, and a few other issues have much brighter congressional spotlights than most of the rest of the agenda. Coherence may be affected as much by cross-cutting congressional action as it is by what happens in the executive branch. Congressional oversight of the new PL 109-95 functions may reinforce the breadth of the proposed Action Plan (reviewed below) or may reveal further fragmentation.

Finally, coherence in policy is affected by the budget process and the priority given to any given policy by White House staff. Dov Zakheim, who was responsible for U.S. reconstruction efforts in Afghanistan while serving as Comptroller of the Department of Defense, describes continuing barriers put up by the Office of Management and Budget in its desire to micro-manage budget allocations even after congressional approvals were secured.[326] On the positive side, Zakheim mentioned the use of financial forensics by the Treasury Department to determine which banks and other institutions were trying to circumvent the U.S. efforts to block embargoed financial transactions in Iraq, noting that these tools provided powerful reinforcements to military action and added to the versatility of U.S. diplomatic efforts. The National Security Council staff can also accelerate or block foreign assistance programs, as shown positively by the efforts to spotlight anti-trafficking efforts in President Obama's 2012 remarks cited above. Whether these agencies will fully support the Action Plan and the Global Alliance with actual resources will certainly affect their coherence in implementing child protection policy.

One set of positive signals began to emerge in early 2014, with action in congressional appropriations committees that included a recommendation for $22 million in new funds

> for the Office of Displaced Children and Orphans Fund to support programs and activities that address the needs of vulnerable children, of which not less than $9,500,000 shall be used to implement the United States Government Action Plan on Children in Adversity in three to five countries which embrace an integrated approach to fully implementing the three objectives of the Plan, and which shall be administered under the direction of the USAID Senior Coordinator for Children in Adversity.

It has also been decided that USAID's Center of Excellence on Children in Adversity (the PL 109-95 team) will merge with USAID's Displaced Children and Orphans Fund, which may achieve further intra-governmental coherence.

Proportionate

By proportionate, I mean to raise the question of whether U.S. assistance is proportionate to what the world's largest economy could achieve in supporting child protection and proportionate to what others are doing in the child protection field. Given the importance of the private and nonprofit sectors, this question needs to extend to those sectors and not just focus on U.S. governmental action.

Yet in the absence of a clear total of what U.S.-based NGOs, foundations, religious organizations, and private donors currently fund in total child protection activities, this question is hard to answer. If the U.S. is compared overall with European nations and private agencies, it would appear that the answer is negative, even allowing for the contributions of the federal government and mega-foundations like Gates. US private donations are often ranked above all but a few nations when aid to international agencies is broken out separately, but these typically include donations to religious organizations; US contributions are in the mid-range at best when national wealth is taken into account. OECD reported that in 2014 aid from countries reporting to the Development Assistance Committee stayed flat at $135.2 billion, averaging .29% of donor countries' gross national income. The US percentage dropped from, 21% to .19% in 2014.[327]

It should also be noted that a recent study found that only one-third of charitable contributions in the U.S. were devoted to efforts targeting the poor, while religious organizations, which receive one-third of all charitable contributions, spend three-fourths of those funds on organizational maintenance rather than aid to the poor.[328]

If child protection were 10% of total governmental U.S. foreign assistance, it would rise from the $270 million we have estimated within the totals compiled by USAID to a level closer to $3 billion. That could double the total of estimated external global financial aid to child protection programs. As noted, these numbers are approximate because the totals have never been compiled; simply undertaking that task with the help of the major private donors would in itself elevate the importance of child protection efforts.

These numbers also need to take into account the much larger economic impact of trade and investment from the private sector, as discussed above. Some proponents of private sector leadership in foreign assistance have noted that it is American consumers, operating through Walmart and other retail firms that stock mostly Asian-manufactured goods, who have created an Asian middle class through their purchasing habits. Buying retail electronic goods for children in the U.S. is hardly a child protection strategy, but its impact on some Asian children who can go to school because their parents have jobs and can afford the fees—while other children may be working to produce the goods themselves or are cut off from their parents in distant villages—all needs to be taken into the equation. The net impact must also take into account the fact that Walmart and other firms have been found to be out of compliance with the existing ethical standards set by business consortia and NGOs that are expert in this field.[329]

There are some important exceptions to this finding of disproportionate funding. In HIV/AIDS funding, the US share is significantly greater than its share of world GDP—the standard usually used to determine proportionate contributions.[330] The US contributes 61% of all donor funding to HIV/AIDS programs, according to the Kaiser Family Foundation compilation referred to above.

It may be off the mark to bring up another critical resource, but as a U.S. veteran, I cannot avoid pointing out that there are girls attending schools in some regions of the world, notably Afghanistan, who did so, at least in part, under a military umbrella funded substantially by the U.S. and involving ultimate sacrifices by some Americans and their families. It does not require validating the original decisions to initiate military action to recognize its powerful side-effects, both negative and positive—and to note that sometimes they are paid for with the resource of American lives and lifelong disability. Whether any of those positive effects on girls' education will be lasting is as yet unknown, but the U.S.-supported NGOs and civil society organizations that will be there long after U.S. military forces have departed will have much to do with that answer, along with the shifting norms of gender equity that those organizations are working to strengthen. The U.S. contribution in some of these concrete efforts to support gender equity—along with other, far more debatable goals—has been at least proportionate.

Effectiveness

Effectiveness must be judged by the impact of U.S. assistance to child protection efforts that "move the needle," even though establishing direct causation runs into the inevitable evaluation conundrums of attribution. We have previously set forth the distinction between evaluating specific programs and assessing the net effect of all child protection programs. Did child marriage decline in a nation where U.S. aid was concentrated because of that assistance, because of national leadership in that country, or for some other reason? Yet what is remarkable is how infrequently any attempt is even made to detect correlation of improved (or worsened) indicators as they relate to U.S. aid. The success of individual projects is assessed, not whether those projects, combined with other nations' and NGOs' efforts when relevant, have made an overall difference in the magnitude of the problem. Project-only evaluations are not assessments of whether the problem is being reduced, whatever the quality of the evaluation.

Effectiveness, of course, depends on both sides of foreign assistance relationships: donors and recipients. The beauty of a limited strategy targeting a small number of countries for more intensive child protection efforts lies in the ability to bypass much of the difficulty of working with a passive or blocking national government by choosing leadership that wants to move forward. The "3-6-5" effort set forth in the USAID proposals discussed below may offer such an opportunity to choose national leadership in six countries that is willing to lead, rather than simply serving as a conduit for aid to NGOs and local government.

As numerous studies of the decision-making in Iraq and Afghanistan have stressed (and as borne out in countless earlier studies of the problems with the U.S. strategy in Vietnam), when there is lack of leadership at the national level, efforts to reform government and enforce the laws at the provincial or local level invariably fall short.[331] This problem is repeatedly cited as a barrier to both military and economic development efforts. Weak, corrupt, or criminally entangled national leaders cannot succeed in child protection efforts (or any others) that demand centralized, coordinated resources at the national level and trusted leaders able to rally support at local levels.

When there are perceived to be unavoidable military or economic reasons for the U.S. to be involved with such national leaders, the original decisions leading to American involvement can be second-guessed. But when there is an opportunity to start with a much cleaner slate, based on criteria chosen to identify the best models of national leadership most likely to succeed with law enforcement and support of strong civil society efforts—there is a much better chance of making progress. The discussion in Chapter 6 of approaches to assessing governmental capacity is relevant here, since the challenge is getting the criteria right. Not only leadership, but also data systems, the legal frameworks, and enforcement machinery on the ground in the designated nations will determine much of the ultimate effectiveness of U.S. assistance for child protection programs.

Effectiveness can also, of course, be assessed in donor nations by reviewing the message of its own record—how much a nation's own child protection efforts move the needle within that nation in setting standards of responsiveness to the needs of maltreated children. As noted, on those measures, the U.S. is in the top half of ranked countries.

Given the importance of U.S.-based NGOs and major wealthy international donors, the effectiveness of the US role can also be assessed based on the government's track record in working with these providers and donors. The Clinton Global Initiative, the Gates, Ford, and other foundations, and dozens of advocacy organizations all pursue child protection agendas along with many other issues in their portfolios. Yet there remains no aggregate assessment of the child protection elements of these donors' funding. As a result, at present each of these is far more driven by its own internal targets than by any efforts to link its priorities with those of USAID or UNICEF. The negotiations now under way to frame the Global Alliance may affect those linkages.

Effectiveness can also include an assessment of the external actors outside government. Greater unity among the U.S.-based NGOs and foundations could be seen as part of the coordination agenda described in Chapter 6, since it is fragmented advocacy and project support that creates the need for coordination in the first place.

It is clear from the efforts of the National Rifle Association, agribusiness, and banking and investment firms that unified, targeted lobbying can have great effect on the current political process. One does not have to endorse the political process as it exists in the second decade of this century to recognize that minorities in numbers can muster majorities in legislatures, especially when fueled by substantial funding.

The current advocacy efforts of child protection organizations are occasionally impressive, but the evidence for their weakness and misguided targets is clear in the agendas of recent conferences. Those conferences often have many more sessions on how to deal with USAID contracts than on political advocacy for a unified child protection agenda. For all the advocacy efforts of these agencies, no proposal for unified lobbying on a broad child protection agenda has ever come from a coalition of child protection agencies. NGOs have banded together on single-issue legislation such as trafficking and HIV prevention, but not on a cross-sector agenda that encompasses the full range of child protection issues.

Our interviews suggest, however, that some NGOs are rethinking this separation—at least in their choices of funding projects jointly, if not their choices for joint advocacy. One major NGO official said "Our basic premise is *don't do it alone.*" While other NGO staff members were less sanguine about either joint funding or joint advocacy, the movement by some of them toward more unified efforts suggests the trend is worth watching carefully.

Perhaps it's naïve to suggest that deeply committed organizations and the individuals staffing them should make common cause in ways that might risk their own funding and visibility. But it makes sense as a strategy that could enhance both these goals. If we are right in our premise that expanding non-token levels of support for child protection is possible, then greater unity of advocacy is a critical ingredient for that expansion. And with that greater unity could come increases in all of the components of child protection, rather than a continuing zero-sum contest in which some are winners and some are not.

Some of our interviewees expressed concern about the extent to which the governmental response lags behind the private and nonprofit sectors. Others pointed out that this is a traditional strength of U.S. roles in international affairs in which religious and other social welfare organizations have provided much broader assistance to international activities than the U.S. government. As noted above in Chapter 7, the volume of private trade and investment also dwarfs US governmental responses in its impact on global family income and working conditions.

U.S.-based charitable organizations have long-standing roles in carrying out programs that benefit children throughout the world, and for the U.S. government to attempt to coordinate these could be seen as inappropriate over-reaching. Yet what *is* appropriate is asking the extent to which governmental leadership provides a credible source of information on the full range of what public and private agencies are doing to improve child protection outcomes. The U.S. government collects a vast amount of information on the economy, most of which comes from its careful monitoring of the private sector. Preliminary efforts now under way within USAID and among some NGOs to monitor private and nonprofit agencies are an important beginning, but have as yet made little impact in assessing how resources affect results in the child protection arena.

Whether efforts to reform child protection policy in the US will be reinforced by proposals for wider reforms of the foreign assistance field also remains to be seen. The advocacy efforts of the policy advocacy group Modernizing Foreign Assistance[332] and the issuance of the Global Development Policy in 2010 by the Obama Administration, along with legislation introduced by Rep Howard Berman, the Global Partnerships Act of 2012, all raise the possibility of a wider overview of U.S. foreign assistance policy, including a broader consideration of trade policy as it affects global poverty. While these efforts do not address child protection in any direct way, greater attention to foreign assistance in general may have the effect of better understanding its components so that the child protection, child survival, and child well-being goals are more visible as a part of overall assistance and more likely to be assessed for their effectiveness.

Potential

If priorities were clearer, it seems likely that proportionate impact and effectiveness would be clearer. The potential remains for the U.S. government to be more coherent, more proportionate with its resources, and more effective in making an impact, and in providing more leadership for private firms and U.S.-based NGOs that work on global child protection.

The gender equity agenda and the trafficking effort are the two clearest candidates for a higher priority that builds on and expands current U.S. efforts. It also seems important not to neglect the strong base of achievement and a clear priority given by former Secretary Clinton to the girls and women agenda. As she transitions to whatever role she will play on these issues in other venues, it would be a major setback if her successor and Secretary Kerry's colleagues were to lose the momentum developed since she first spoke out on these issues as First Lady in Beijing in 1995.

The U.S. governmental role has a positive trend line that is visible in recent events. This includes the creation and expansion of the USAID Center out of the original 109-95 office and its issuance of an Action Plan, remarks by the President at the UN in the fall of 2012 and new legislation aimed at trafficking, the existence of an Office on Women and Girls in the White House, former Secretary Clinton's emphasis on gender equity, and the multiplication of U.S. foundations' and NGOs' efforts to target more resources on some of the child protection problem areas. As noted, Secretary of State Kerry has been a leader in some of these efforts in his prior role as Chairman of the Senate Foreign Relations Committee. The total U.S. contribution to all UNICEF programs in 2011, including both governmental aid and private grants, rose to $432 million, despite congressional reservations about some UN-sponsored programs.[333] Whether these positive trends and events come together into a more coordinated and better-resourced overall effort remains to be seen, but taken together, these steps represent more activity in international child protection than the U.S. has ever seen.

Yet the essential fact remains: nothing we are now doing to protect the world's children from harm is moving in the direction of operating at a scale that responds to our potential or their needs.

An Assessment of the United States Government Action Plan on Children in Adversity

The full Action Plan issued by the PL 109-95 office in December 2012 is the biggest single step ever taken by the U.S. in the field of global child protection and related children's issues. Responding to the congressional mandates of PL 109-95, the Plan is ambitious, comprehensive, and appropriately specific in many respects. It reflects a remarkable compilation and consensus-building process by U.S. government officials working in a widespread interagency effort, advised at many points by their contacts with NGOs, academic centers, policy organizations, and advocates.

The plan sets forth three primary objectives and three supporting objectives.[334] It proposes a set of projects organized on a "3-6-5" basis: three sets of objectives, to be carried out in six countries yet to be chosen, implemented over the next five years. The plan is informed throughout by a deep commitment to evidence-based practice and to the intensified monitoring and survey-based evaluation efforts it will take to develop better evidence to inform practice.

Properly framed, it is not a "child protection plan" as such, since it includes child development, child survival, and family income components as well as some of the accepted elements of global child protection policy. It refers to several other national planning documents as context for the Action Plan.[335] Its breadth creates its own coordination challenges, since the definition of "children in adversity" ranges well beyond child protection to encompass the subject matter of many other U.S. and international agencies. While protection of children is the third goal, with some useful detail behind that objective in eight specific outcomes (Outcomes 3.1-4.4), these outcomes are worded very generally, e.g. "support programs," "support initiatives."

The Plan is, as described, the first whole-of-government effort to work across agencies on a child protection policy agenda that rises above project levels. It includes clear links between family income strategies and child protection strategies—a critical element of overall coordination. It is backed up by a revised website and explanatory materials that are increasingly detailed. It proposes coordination among country and regional teams as well as across thirty separate units of seven federal agencies involved with child protection.

The shortcomings of the Action Plan are far more a product of the political and fiscal environments surrounding child protection issues today than of the proponents and developers of the report. Furthermore, some of the comments that follow are inevitably based on the inherent limitations of an introductory plan which is backed up by much more extensive materials, not all of which are available for review. References to ongoing interagency efforts are made in the Plan, and these are likely to respond to several of these comments on the current Plan.

- The Plan is resource-free. It does not make clear what new and redirected resources would be allocated to carrying out its extensive proposals for change. The proposed allocation of $9.5 million to implement the Action Plan is difficult to assess against the five-year, six-country goals set forth in the Plan. Leveraging other partners' resources is mentioned, without any process by which that leveraging would be implemented or whether that seeks a net increase or simply redirection of existing resources. Resources are essentially taken as given; there is no reference to marketing or messaging that could expand resources for the full array of child protection programs.
- The Plan is what it says it is: a *national* plan. Its references to international donors are few and generally stated. A concurrent effort to work with other leading public and private agencies to develop an *international* plan would add credibility to what the U.S. is doing internally, especially in light of the dominance of private U.S. sources of assistance (and the volume of trade and investment decisions originating in the U.S. that affect children and families)

relative to governmentally coordinated resources. The multilateral dimensions of the Plan are not specified; while multilateral, UN, and NGO model programs are referenced throughout the Plan, the efforts to implement the Plan have a much more unilateral and bilateral tone. This is unavoidably related to the resources issues and the prospects of leveraging other nations' and NGOs' funds. The emerging role of the Global Alliance for Children, as discussed below, may answer some of these concerns.

- The Plan lacks specifics on coordination methods. Awareness of the lengthy history of prior efforts to coordinate among federal (as well as state, local, and private) agencies working toward shared goals would be helpful. Since the early 1960's, under the successive banners of community action, services integration, collaboration, interoperability—and others—a body of experience has grown up that includes many different forms of coordinated efforts. Some worked, some didn't—but all offer lessons that should not have to be repeated anew. It may be useful to extract some of that experience as background materials as federal agencies seek another round of coordinated activities. Eugene Bardach, Lynn Kagan, Dov Zakheim, and others have written excellent reviews of the challenges of agencies working together toward common ends, as noted in Chapter 6. In addition, some federal agencies whose cooperation would seem essential to carrying out the Plan are not mentioned or cited in the matrix of responsibilities at the end of the report.

- The Plan could be strengthened by a more detailed inventory of current U.S. and global funding streams and programs. Not to know how much is spent on children's programs in international forums is a signal of the difficulty of coordinating those streams; again, you can't coordinate what you can't count. The $2.7 billion inventoried by the USAID office (including food assistance) is a beginning, but it will be a challenge to both NGOs and USAID and its federal partners to get a better handle on what is already being spent as it seeks to coordinate those efforts. A revised version of the US inventory, using different criteria, was included in the Seventh Annual Report to Congress presented in 2014.

It listed "contributions addressing APCA objectives" totaling $463.2 million. Under its third goal—protecting children from violence, exploitation, abuse, and neglect—it stated that in FY13 USAID allocated more than $17 million to support "programs aimed at building knowledge, tools, and capacity to address child protection" in 15 conflict and disaster-affected countries.[336]

- The Plan does not address in much depth the barriers created by social norms, cultural practices, and religious interpretations that underlie exclusionary policies at the community and national levels. The reference to gender bias is appropriate, but one child in five is today abused or neglected in ways that risk her future—and those barriers should be as explicit a target as nutritional goals. Existing social norms curricula should also be addressed more fully. To be sure, inciting congressional over-reaction to some of these cultural themes—both for and against—is a risk that is avoided when these issues are ignored. But the issues remain major barriers to child protection.

- The objectives and indicators of the Plan are yet to be specified in many cases, and some are stated in very general terms, as noted above. The implementation plans refer to recurring tasks described as seeking to "support programs," without the resources or extent of those programs being clarified.

- NGO roles in implementation are mentioned but not emphasized, despite the large volume of US foreign assistance now delivered by and through NGOs. Nor is there any reference to the need for NGOs themselves to work in a more collaborative manner.

- The Plan does not refer in any depth to technological means of advancing child protection, at a time when other U.S. agencies and private organizations have emphasized these advances. One of the action steps refers to technology, but without any detail.

- Specific tools and approaches already in use by federal agencies that may lend themselves to international adaptability could be described more than the Plan now does. These include, for example, adapted versions of tools for assessment of the quality of child care, the tools developed for screening and assessment for substance abuse under the SAMHSA Screening, Brief

Intervention, and Referral to Treatment (SBIRT) effort, and protocols for reviewing child fatalities. Referring specifically to these and other tools already in use would place a greater burden on an "adaptability assessment" of these methods that may have international relevance.

- The process by which the 3-6-5 projects are to be implemented and the criteria to be used in selecting them are not specified. The focus on six nations is not clarified in terms of how much concentration of resources will be attempted and whether those resources will be supplemented from non-USAID or non-U.S. government partners. The three primary objectives—early childhood programs, family care, and child protection—are an amalgam of other Administration priorities and congressional priorities which omit major areas of child protection.

- If these six countries are able to focus on capacity-building efforts, including measures of each country's improved capacity for child protection, the 3-6-5 approach could potentially escape the trap of funding isolated projects and instead funding (together with each countries' own resources) genuine capacity improvements.

- The operations of the USAID Center itself are not assessed as part of the Plan, and the staffing and other resources required to implement the Plan are not described. A senior policy group and a technical group are described without indicating who serves on these groups and how they are staffed in ways that will ensure interagency accountability. The coordinating unit is described on the website as having six staff members; the additional staffing from the 30 agency units mentioned is not listed.[337]

- The transparency of the planning process thus far is impressive, but reports on the responsiveness of the 30 governmental agencies mentioned as partners will be a deeper test of transparency. That reporting could include exemplary, standard, and perhaps even sub-standard performances—as is done in other federal agency ratings done by self-assessment and by external evaluators.

The Global Alliance for Children, as it supports USAID's 3-6-5 strategy, may be able to respond to some of these concerns about resources, but the initial signs of its scale are not clear. Its website states

> Foundation and government donors have pre-existing priorities, strategic frameworks and calendars that commit substantial portions of existing funds for the next several years. The Alliance has therefore adapted a flexible approach to resource mobilization that includes reprogramming existing funding, coordinating funding, co-funding, and pooling funding. Securing private sector contributions to fill gaps is also a priority.[338]

What this "flexible approach" consists of is still emerging. As stated throughout this assessment, a critical prerequisite to increased commitment from the US public and private sectors includes an answer to the unavoidable question—"compared to what?" That is, without an inventory of all public and private funding from US sources, the scale of the GAC's efforts will inevitably become yet another list of projects, essentially separate from earlier activities and funding streams. The USAID compilation of federal agency support is a beginning, but does not encompass NGO efforts or other donors. Whether the GAC focuses solely on its own fund-raising or frames its efforts as part of a larger context of documented funding will be an important signal of its scale and scope. If the GAC rejects the view that token projects are good enough, its efforts may move beyond projects to at least identifying the resources needed to move policy.

The CECA office, like any new governmental agency, is a work in progress. Making a judgment about its likely success at a moment in time is hazardous, but can be informed by what its own staff and others familiar with its work have said about the agency. Assessing its prospects is also aided by a comparison of the resources available to achieve the goals it has set. As admirable as those goals may be, they will depend on both the financial and coordinative resources brought to bear on the tasks CECA has set for itself. And both factors lead to concern about its future.

The number that jumps out of a cursory review of the 2014 report to Congress from USAID is the 60.6% of all the funding assigned to the National Plan goals is for PEPFAR—the HIV/AIDS initiatives. The U.S., led by the Bush and Obama administrations, deserve a great deal of credit for initiating and sustaining these funds directed at HIV/AIDS, which have unquestionably saved millions of lives. But if "the budget is the plan," as the adage puts it, then this is the most important target for protecting children. Yet the numbers of children affected by the other forms of child maltreatment make clear that what is missing is a proportionate commitment to the other forms of abuse and neglect experienced by children around the world.

This same inventory indicated that only $13 million was allocated to the USAID office coordinating the Action Plan. The Global Alliance for Children is described as a coalition of the principal funding partners for USAID in the 3-6-5 program, but the total funding to be made available from these sources is not specified in assessing the overall US response,

It should not be overlooked that there will be an election in 2016 that may affect these issues in at least marginal ways that cannot be anticipated as of mid-2105. Front runners at a very early stage include an articulate spokesperson for gender equity, an internationally-minded ex-governor familiar with Latin America, as well as nativist, isolationist, misogynists who would probably reject many of the premises of global child protection.

But the most likely outcome of the election in the context of child protection seems likely to be to confirm its marginality. Trafficking may get a mention or two, the foreign policy credentials of the candidates may be reviewed by the media and the public—but the arena of global child protection is likely to be essentially invisible.

Finally, it should again be noted that the reference in the framework to ratification of international agreements raises the continuing "clean hands problem" of the U.S. not having ratified the Convention on the Rights of the Child. While many of the nations that have done so have a long way to go to enforce their adoption of the Convention, the U.S. is at a singular disadvantage, for all its sizable contributions to global child well-being, as the sole non-ratifying developed nation. The gap between preaching and practicing remains important.

The clean hands problem goes beyond what the U.S. has and hasn't ratified. Part of working effectively in another culture is knowing enough about your own to be able to explain its failures as well as its successes. Child protection history in the US is not always the moral high ground. It includes a form of ethnic cleansing in Executive Order 9066—the internment of 110,000 Japanese children and families in 1942, the "orphan trains" that removed children from urban areas and sent them to farms where many worked long hours for no pay, the dislocation of thousands of native American children to boarding schools that sought to strip them of their culture, and, of course, selling children and parents away from their families during more than two centuries of slavery. More recently, a nation with a rising rate of child poverty over the past decade should take care in preaching about family income strategies in lower-income nations. More than nine million children live in families with one or more parents with substance use disorders fueled by international commerce and U.S.-based demand. And our widespread problems with technology-aided sex trafficking, often involving older youth aging out of the foster care system, also suggest caution in labeling this an international problem without examining both the supply and the U.S.-based demand for illegal substances and trafficking in persons, including children.

None of these issues reduces the importance of the Action Plan. Prior to its issuance, there was no attempt to achieve what the Plan seeks in integrating a broad array of U.S. child-focused international activities. The Plan creates a benchmark of institutional progress against which further monitoring efforts can be measured during the five-year period encompassed by the Plan. With adequate staffing and financial resources, stronger accountability for interagency performance, and sustained support from the White House and Congress, the Plan has the potential to mark a sea change in U.S. efforts to take child protection and other child-related issues seriously.

CHAPTER TEN

Conclusion

A Campaign for Child Protection

The word "campaign" can be used in two very different contexts: *military conflict* and *politics*. In the context of global child protection activities, both are relevant. A campaign can be

- a series of military operations taking place in one area over a period of time, intended to achieve a specific objective, or
- a planned and organized series of actions intended to achieve a specific goal, especially advocating or opposing an issue or raising people's awareness of an issue or a candidate.

It will take a campaign, rather than a set of projects, to achieve child protection goals. *Organizing on multiple fronts*, paying close attention to planning for the logistics and human resources needed to support programs at scale, carefully studying and anticipating the moves of the opposing forces—all these are relevant to the fate of the fifth child.

Earlier this review of child protection issues referred to the critical importance of *priorities* in efforts to coordinate, citing the adage that you can't coordinate what you can't count. Here it is the phrase *organizing on multiple fronts* that is critical: in the listing of multiple strategies for advancing the child protection agenda in the prior chapters, some are more important than others. And across the range of UNICEF's separate child protection issues, some of these strategies now receive much more funding and attention than others, in some cases without regard to the much larger numbers of children affected.

So the question of what a campaign would aim at is fundamentally about choosing priorities among the different problems and the different remedies that have been suggested. The answer to the question of priorities cannot be supplied by science, by the indicators themselves, or by the best possible evaluations of what works. Deciding among investments in

- Improved coordination
- Listening to the voices of children
- Civil society-based community programs
- An emphasis on girls and women and gender equity
- Corporate decision-making
- Technology
- Institutional care, reunification, and adoption
- Law enforcement, legal action, and anti-corruption measures and enforcement
- Evaluating what works
- Expanded resources through better marketing

demands a thoughtful review of what is in place now and what has proven effective. That varies in each of the numerous problem areas and in each of the strategies. Corporate action may be far more important in addressing trafficking, while technology may help most in reporting progress and problems in school attendance and birth registration.

A recent review of the progress made in several (but not all) child protection problem areas emphasized improvements in school attendance, birth registration, child labor, and child marriage.[339]

- Failure to record birth registration was reduced from 40% of all births to 36% from 2002 to 2008. The efforts of Plan International in 32 countries were cited as a major factor in this improvement.

- Data from 47 countries shows an increase in the median age for first marriage.
- More than 100,000 child soldiers and conscripts have been released from military roles and re-integrated into their communities, with UNICEF's "Girls Left Behind" project and efforts by Caritas and the International Rescue Committee cited as models of effective programs.
- An overall decrease of 3% in worldwide estimates of child workers occurred between 2004 and 2008, with reduction of 15% and 10% respectively in girls and boys between 5 and 14 in hazardous occupations. The Minimum Age Convention of the International Labor Organization was described as an important development underlying this progress, and efforts in India supported by the ILO and the U.S. Department of Labor, including the National Child Labour Project, were noted as model programs.

Yet this assessment also noted that

> Among many donors, child protection tends to be relegated to a lower priority than other immediate concerns such as food and health care. For example, a recent UNICEF report found that child protection continues to be significantly underfunded in emergencies, In 2009, $129 million was required to respond to child protection in emergencies by the UN Central Emergency Fund; however less than one third of this was received.[340]

Efforts to increase support for and coordination of child protection activities must be based on strong evidence of which approaches are most effective, as well as judgments as to which funders and project sponsors are most effective. As noted, some funders, including the U.S. have a "clean hands" problem, created by their own roles in ratification[341] and enforcement of child protection agreements. These effects can be worsened by the direct and indirect effects of other national policies on child poverty and maltreatment, such as agricultural subsidies and trade barriers. Qualified endorsements of some provisions of the Convention by some nations, stating that religious law and the primacy of the family supersede the Convention, further undermine national efforts to achieve child protection goals.

Yet the progress that has been made in the past decade has undeniably improved some important indicators of child maltreatment. A wider array of national, international, and local groups is working on child protection issues than ever before. The tasks that remain are taking the resources to scale, connecting fragmented efforts, and assessing in greater depth which approaches are effective and which stakeholders are aiding and which are blocking progress for children and families. Making the case for the first of these—increased resources—will depend on the other tasks: better bridges connecting separate efforts and deeper assessment of what works, who can help, and who stands in the way of expanded, effective programs and policies.

As difficult as it is to summarize the broad scope of humanitarian aid, development, and child-specific programs, some keen observers are not afraid to do so. A painfully pointed assessment has been made by Mary Robinson, who served as High Commissioner of Human Rights for the UN. Speaking of overall impact of Western aid programs (not of child protection specifically), she summed up:

> Count up the results of fifty years of human rights mechanisms, thirty years of multi-billion dollar development programs and endless high-level rhetoric, and the global impact is quite underwhelming. This is a failure of implementation on a scale which shames us all.[342]

The needed blend of top-down and bottom-up efforts

What emerges from an assessment of current efforts, though based on very partial evaluation results, is a conclusion that child protection can best be achieved through combined top-down and bottom-up efforts. UNICEF officials have framed this as a "two-pillar" strategy, involving strengthened child protection systems and efforts to shift social norms.[343] In a similar formulation, Save the Children framed two main components to achieving children's rights:

1) ensuring responsive governmental performance, transparency of decision-making and robust accountability mechanisms…

2) supporting an active and well-organized civil society in support of children's rights as an important counterpart and counterbalance to governmental action.[344]

The tension is obvious between bottom-up, grass-roots projects demanding flexibility and adaptability to local conditions and top-down coordination demanding accountability driven by data on results. Well-integrated top-down governmental and NGO/CSO efforts are needed to allocate resources at scale to effective programs and policies that achieve measurable improvements in global, national, and local child protection outcomes. As noted throughout this assessment, strong tendencies toward fragmentation and project thinking must be overcome in implementing these policies and programs. As painful as it seems to critique well-intentioned efforts, stakeholders' narrow approaches are at times part of the problem.

At the same time, bottom-up efforts are needed to provide specific child protection programs in local communities, to build the social capital needed to protect children, and to change cultural norms that allow child maltreatment and constrain child protection efforts. Although most agencies concentrate their efforts on one or the other of these, some have been able to participate in global consortia while operating direct services projects at the same time. Few agencies, however, are able to catalogue and coordinate their current efforts so that top-down vs bottom-up strategies are totaled separately and can be compared and linked together. And it must also be understood that officials and organizations that are skilled at developing lasting partnerships among collaborative agencies at national and international levels are not always those who have the very different skill set it requires to work credibly and with cultural sensitivity at the community level in changing norms.

Taking barriers seriously

In a campaign, assuming that initiatives will succeed with adequate resources and good leadership can overlook the power of barriers to those initiatives. In military campaigns, it is said that no battle plan survives the first contact with the enemy. Without characterizing blockers as enemies, it would be unrealistic to assume those blockers will be inert when initiatives are launched. We have reviewed the power of many of those adversaries and barriers in this assessment:

- Social norms that accept child maltreatment
- Vested interests in lax law enforcement
- The profitability and economic gains possible from some forms of child maltreatment
- Governments' inertia and organizational fragmentation
- Well-intentioned assistance efforts that are confined to siloes restricted by narrow definitions of the problem and success defined as token allocations to pilot projects

Allocating some of the resources now devoted to new projects to analysis of these barriers and direct responses to them might help ensure that efforts are more effective than if these barriers are accepted as norms that cannot be changed. Reports on progress achieved by public and private funders could usefully devote more space to the impact of these barriers, rather than leaving such comments to advocacy organizations alone. "Barrier-busting," as it is sometimes referred to, is controversial, compared with announcing new projects and new partnerships. But at the risk of overdoing the military analogies, ignoring adversaries is as dangerous as assuming that they will do what you want them to do.

The Future of Child Protection

Rather than summarize with predictions, it seems more useful to ask questions about the future.

- Will technology become the tool its advocates claim it to be in strengthening monitoring efforts targeted on child protection, detecting violations, identifying exploiters, and advocating change?
- Will legal action against the worst offenders become a more effective tool in prosecuting child maltreatment?
- Will child protection as a professional field become more appealing to significant numbers of young graduates of higher education institutions around the world?
- Will social norms and cultural practices evolve further toward greater equity for girls and women in the most repressive parts of the world?
- Will the aging of the population in many nations eclipse the issues affecting children as a growing preoccupation of governments and civil society?
- Will the "responsibility to protect" doctrine—to the extent that it is a doctrine rather than a slogan—be understood to extend to a responsibility to protect children when they are known to be harmed on a scale that cannot be ignored or addressed with mere pilot projects? Will it be defined as including non-military means of protecting children?
- Will resources for child protection programs expand, or will additional resources be restricted to single-program areas of emphasis?
- Will the revised SDGs in 2015 include child protection conditions as explicit priorities?

Action-forcing events

In 2015 and beyond several events will allow advocates for expanded child protection efforts to give renewed voice to their agenda. These include

- Continuing efforts to develop revised Sustainable Development Goals for the period beginning in 2015
- The agenda-setting by Secretary of State Kerry and the White House among foreign assistance priorities in the concluding months of this Administration
- Reactions to the Action Plan issued by the USAID Center and the launch of the Global Alliance for Children from U.S. and international foundations
- Continuing efforts to secure passage of an international version of the Violence Against Women Act (VAWA)
- The prospects of congressional leadership that replaces those who have left Congress

As with the entire child protection agenda, a fragmented response from proponents for each element of the agenda will be less effective than a more unified response with more supporters behind it. It remains to be seen if this is possible.

But: imagine for a moment—perhaps only as an intellectual exercise— what could be possible if a convocation of U.S. based and European NGOs in the child protection field agreed to work together to launch a multi-year campaign on behalf of children who have been or may be harmed. If they devoted only 10-20% of their efforts which are usually focused on a single facet of child protection to a broader campaign that worked across the entire field, it could generate a much wider joint effort than any of the ongoing multilateral activities. And it would enable them to see the field as a whole, rather than solely from the vantage point of "their" issues.

Or imagine what a genuine coalition of the leaders of the world's religions could do to spotlight the need to act to reduce violence and harm to children. Convened in Rome, Istanbul, or some other symbolically powerful location, involving Pope Francis and other world religious leaders, addressing the harm done to children by many institutions including their own—that would be a remarkable convocation. And the campaign that followed it could mobilize more "soft power" that has ever been assembled in a single international cause.

Fanciful? Perhaps. But without imagining actions like this that step out of our daily plodding toward marginal improvements with few new resources, the status quo will prevail. International progress at times demands both risk-taking and resources. If funders and policymakers confine themselves to working at the margins, the margins will remain barriers to what is possible.

The evolution of NGOs

Nongovernmental organizations are themselves undergoing significant transitions. Michael Hammer, executive director of Intrac (International NGO Training and Research Centre), is quoted in a 2014 *Guardian* article pointing out that "virtually every large NGO is significantly dependent on governmental or intergovernmental funding."[345] Recent reductions in several nations' funding for foreign assistance, according to the same article, have affected many NGOs. Some of these have relocated their offices, reduced funding to some countries (notably India), and shifted their emphasis from large central offices to country-based teams.

The *Guardian* article further states

> Increasingly these [changes] cluster around the concept of the 'networked NGO' – a network of multi-party stakeholders or partners from civil society, government departments, indigenous communities, even the media, mostly located within the country where the development work is taking place. The NGO's role becomes one of supporting capacity building and knowledge sharing among these stakeholders, rather than designing and implementing projects and programmes... In a networked international NGO model, co-ordination becomes more important than ever.[346]

One could speculate, perhaps optimistically, about whether the shift to country-based strategies and teams, as in the US APCA 3-6-5 plan, means that closer integration of child protection and other child-targeted giving would be easier to negotiate at the country level than across separate NGO headquarters staffs.

The William and Flora Hewlett Foundation in 2013 sponsored a paper by the firm FSG titled "Ahead of the Curve: Insights for the International NGO of the Future." Based on interviews with 50 of the largest US-based NGOs, one of the authors pointed out that the report recommended "conducting systems mapping, gap analysis, and bringing in other players – companies, local NGOs, other INGOs, government agencies – as needed to fill those gaps."[347]

A subsequent roundtable discussion in 2014 among twelve NGOs, organized as a follow-up to the 2013 report, distinguished among *joint projects and programs* on end of a continuum and *strategic alliances and collective impact* on the other end. [348] Yet there was no specific call for an inventory of current investments or programs as baselines for measuring the scale or effectiveness of new partnerships.

While it is difficult to predict future patterns for organizations that range from billion-dollar agencies to much smaller ones, the pressures for greater effectiveness across the field of foreign assistance seem likely to affect those in the much smaller arena of child protection. As noted throughout this book, however, the capacity of these agencies to work together against baselines and total spending may do much to determine the capacity they can build at national and local levels in the future.

Beyond the conventional wisdom

In much of the above, repeated reliance on what has been gathered from the literature and our interviews repeats prior prescriptions and may break little new ground. To be sure, talking with and reading those who have worked in this field for decades is humbling, and one cannot help but agree with many of their ideas on how to improve outcomes.

But sometimes these sources disagree, and sometimes they miss things. The lack of an emphasis on addiction, for example, needs attention. Weighing neurodevelopmental damage against cultural defenses of maltreatment needs more attention. The failure at developing or even calling for an inventory of child protection spending, despite all the fragmentation—indeed, because of it—needs attention. And so this section will briefly review those areas in which our exploration of child protection has seemed to us to raise points that go beyond the conventional wisdom in child protection circles, if only to call for a second look at some of these issues.

1. Without an ongoing inventory of spending for child protection, "priorities" will be merely the aggregate of allocations made without any overview of the system as a whole, and coordination across agencies and NGOs will be more difficult.

2. Without greater emphasis on addiction as a contributing factor in parents' and caretakers' maltreatment of children, this cause of maltreatment will receive disproportionately less attention than it needs in light of its association with maltreatment, neglect, and violence. Its relationship to increases in family income also needs more attention.

3. The boundaries of child protection as set by UNICEF are helpful in specifying the specific conditions that prevention and remediation should be targeting. But beyond those categories, any consideration of the causes of child maltreatment and neglect demands a wider lens and much closer ties between child survival, child development, and child poverty than attempted by most child protection efforts at present. Achieving those closer ties will be difficult, but a greater effort is needed to ensure that narrow, siloed efforts not constrain the impact of child protection policy. Our conclusion is that those boundaries are more often a part of the problem than the solution. The rhetoric is clear, and UNICEF deserves credit for its framing of the broader agenda: *poverty plus, survive and thrive*. But the external resources have not followed the rhetoric. Advocacy is still driven mostly by single-problem, siloed perceptions of segmented child protection, rather than seeing it whole.

4. The decision about priorities must confront the greater visibility of some forms of child maltreatment as well as the greater numbers

affected by others. Maltreatment of girls leads to violence against women, and the positive counter-forces against that dynamic have begun to strengthen in impressive ways. But reversing these outcomes will take continued leadership at the highest levels of governments, as well as in the villages where girls and women are denied their basic rights and subject to life-long abuse and neglect. Weighing the gains of much greater concentration of resources on those issues against emphasis of other targets may be the most important decisions to be made about child protection in the first decades of the 21st century. Pretending to be able to do it all with the thin layer of resources available today is just that—a pretense that ignores the reality of continuing harm to children. The priorities debate is rare—and needs more emphasis.

5. Cultural bases of maltreatment must be carefully weighed against the growing body of evidence that neurodevelopmental damage affects all children when they are abused. The lack of conclusive proof that culture mediates trauma is neither a defense of cultural norms that permit maltreatment nor a final proof of universal values. But in years to come, we are more likely to learn more about the universality of neurodevelopmental harm than we are to find that culturally grounded and religiously sanctioned abuse is not really harmful to the brains of millions of children. This body of evidence will strengthen the policy argument for enforcing the CRC as universal standards that protect all children from neurodevelopmental damage. It will also reduce the logic, if not the power of a culturally grounded defense of maltreatment as a tolerable social norm. And it may require more boldness in confronting abuse that is justified by cultural and religious tradition—regardless of which nations are the sites of the abuse.

6. Above all, as a summary of these points, the field needs a greater emphasis on the *causes* of child maltreatment. As noted above, the lists of causes in this report are not the only way to explain maltreatment, but expanding and better targeting of scarce resources demands greater clarity about causative factors affecting maltreatment.

Markers of progress

It is possible to set forth a set of markers of progress in child protection in years ahead:

- SDG references to child protection
- Girls remaining in schools in Afghanistan after U.S. and other nations' troops withdraw—will social norms have changed permanently?
- Further measurable progress in reducing female mutilation in Africa and other regions
- Net increases in total funding by governments and private donors to child protection efforts
- A broader inventory of spending on child protection efforts
- Congressional attention to child protection efforts that cuts across subcommittee jurisdictions and members' single-issue focus
- Additional commentary by leaders from Islam, Christianity, Judaism, and other religions who cite the harm done by gender inequity in both economic and social terms
- Closer links with WHO's activities on non-communicable diseases including alcohol and drug addiction
- Expanded use of cybertechnology against those who use it to harm children on both commercial and charitable fronts
- Greater protection from reprisals for whistle-blowing aimed at child maltreatment, using the same technological tools that criminals use in child maltreatment
- Expanded funding for networking among civil society organizations using grass-roots forms of technology
- More joint NGO-foundation efforts to work across the entire field of child protection and to do so at scale
- Global Alliance for Children capacity to assemble resources at scale

Child protection and the new SDGs

The fate of child protection goals in the revision of the Millennium Development Goals is one of the most important factors in determining whether child protection will remain a marginal adjunct to development and survival campaigns. A summary of the ongoing consultations on the SDGs, "The Global Conversation Begins," was issued by the UN Development Group in 2012.[349] As cited above, US and other nations' officials and some NGOs feel that these efforts have not been adequate.

For child protection, the unfortunate aspect of this report is the lack of any specific mention of child protection goals anywhere in the report, with the important exception of frequent, but general references to gender equality and gender-related violence. Yet the calls throughout the document for a more human rights-oriented, holistic development framework offer hope that such broadening of the SDG agenda would enhance recognition that the education and health priorities that emerged from the consultation are inseparable from the impact of educational and health choices on children. Gender violence is described explicitly as a public health issue and non-communicable diseases are emphasized, including increasing use of alcohol and tobacco. But the report views children primarily as objects of discrimination or potential beneficiaries of health programs, social protection, and economic development.

Whether child protection advocates, NGOs, and governmental agencies are able to join their voices with the thousands of participants in these consultations remains to be seen. There are several references to active youth participation in the consultations, without any recognition that youth participation is hampered throughout the world by the prevailing levels of abuse of children and youth, by repressive governments, and by a lack of recognition of youth as valid, non-token participants in many nations' consideration of public policy affecting youth.

The *sine qua non* of the SDG negotiations for child protection advocates would seem to be explicit mention of child protection as a field and as a part of the overall goals. For the report not to mention child protection as a major priority would represent a significant setback in the effort to raise the visibility of those issues. The report reviews several advances since the development of the original MDGs in the capacity of information systems and surveys to provide richer qualitative and quantitative data on issues of governance and equity. The relevance of these advances to the task of including child protection as an SDG goal is not discussed, however. For child protection advocates to overcome this subordination of its concerns to other priorities will require unified efforts rather than separate single-issue lobbying.

Our interviews suggest that there is more consensus among the child protection provider agencies on including child protection issues in the SDGs than how or where to do that. One NGO official with a key advocacy role stressed that a single child protection goal added to the SDGs was not what NGOs should be seeking, but rather infusing the child protection goals throughout the other SDGs. Yet it may be difficult to get proponents of each SDG goal to modify those goals with new references to child protection that may be seen as extraneous. This issue will clearly be addressed by child protection advocates as the 2015 MDG revisions come closer to finalization.

UNICEF Executive Director Anthony Lake has called the lack of child protection goals in the original Millennium Development Goals "a serious omission." He added, in a statement to his Executive Board in February 2014,

> child protection must be a part of all of our programme areas — from child health and education, to nutrition and sanitation... protection must be woven into our programming for children's health, education, nutrition and sanitation."[350]

Serious discussions are under way about how much further the reduction of poverty can be taken by the end of the SDG period in 2030. Jeffrey Sachs and others have held out the prospect of eliminating extreme poverty in total.[351] Progress in Africa and other regions that have emerged more rapidly from the worldwide economic downturns has given further impetus to these hopes.

Such progress would be good for children, unquestionably. Yet advancing child protection goals will not automatically follow, and, as noted throughout this review, there are downsides to family income improvements when migration, increases in substance use, and child labor effects are not taken into account. This is a further argument for linking child protection to the revised SDGs in ways that keep both poverty and maltreatment in view.

Whose neglect?

Throughout this document, we have raised the question of whether parents' poverty contributes to a form of neglect that is classified as maltreatment. But there is another kind of neglect that is unmistakable—although it requires a broader view of the rest of the world than most of us are capable of taking.

When you have the essential knowledge about maltreatment in front of you—that one in five children is at risk of losing any chance of achieving their full potential because of trauma, abuse, disease, or some other risk factor—that knowledge creates its own ethical force. To ignore that knowledge is itself a kind of neglect, unless you can develop an ethics in which it is acceptable to completely ignore the harm done to millions of children. Ignoring that reality is not parental neglect; it is human neglect. And then the real question becomes what binds us to other humans—especially the youngest ones.

"Things are getting better" is statistically true in some parts of the world, but it is almost totally irrelevant to the 400 million children who still seem to be near the bottom of our list of concerns. In the final analysis, it is our ethics—personal, social, and cultural—that will determine whether *getting better* is good enough.

The West cannot preach to the rest of the world about its ethics with unclean hands, and only a very few nations have really clean hands. Ours is not one of them, despite all our efforts and recent progress. The resources and sustained commitment required to make a difference are far greater than what our nation has devoted to global child protection thus far. Whatever one thinks about American "exceptionalism," this commitment is one where we are not yet exceptional, except in the gap between our total resources and those devoted to protecting children from harm.

The reality is that there are at least 400 million children who have been abused and treated like property instead of people. They are at risk of being very angry at everyone else and being unable to contribute to a better world economy and to their own future families. We know a great deal about what it would take to prevent this from happening, but we are not doing enough to prevent it.

The essential, moral core of the case

There are powerful economic reasons to expand the resources targeted on child protection, and there are political and even national security reasons. But the core of the argument remains moral and ethical: harm must not come to innocent children. The human potential of those children is precious and should not be compromised for any reason. To reach for an economic rationale is important for many audiences—but it is a reach, whereas the moral basis of the case for resources is indisputable, as has been powerfully captured in scriptures from virtually all world religions as well as in the best humanist traditions.

We can help these children because some of them may become dangerous. We can help them because it would improve worldwide economic conditions. And we can help them because it is right.

APPENDIX

Child Protection in China and India

China and India could each be the subject of entire books on child protection in each nation. These brief summaries, along with the overview of U.S. policy and programs, are included because these three nations have both the largest populations and the largest child populations (although Indonesia's child population will soon exceed that of the United States). More than one-third of the world population of children lives in these three countries.

Child Protection in China[352]

Introduction

It is both critical and somewhat unfair to compare child protection efforts in China with those of any other nation. It is critical because China's population of children is exceeded only by India's (as a partial result of the one-child policy) and because China, as noted throughout this book, has arguably done more to improve the economic position of its children than any other nation, and thus deserves credit for that reduction in child poverty, which is clearly related to child protection. China's progress in increasing school attendance is also noteworthy, and leads the world in totals achieved.

On the other hand, China's per capita income is 95th in world ranking, despite its second-place ranking in GDP. This is interpreted by some international observers as a great constraint on what China can do in its domestic policy, with further economic equity as the unavoidable priority goal of China's government. It should also be noted that China has become a major contributor to official development assistance (not child protection per se) in many nations. This aid is primarily for infrastructure projects.

With the indispensable help of a student from SIAS University in China, we have compiled the following information on China's child protection policies.

Legal environment

The primary law that provides children's rights protection in China is the People's Republic of China (PRC) Law on the Protection of Minors (first passed in 1991 and revised in 2006).[353]The newly revised Minors Protection Law came into force on June 1, 2007, and sets up responsibilities of families, schools, and the government regarding the protection of children and judicial roles in enforcing the law. China has ratified the Convention on the Rights of the Child; China's role in implementing the CRC was reviewed by the Universal Periodic Review process in the Human Rights Council's 17th session beginning in October 2013.

Who works on child protection in China?

Central government

In late October, 2010, the central government announced that 2.5 billion yuan (US$373.1 million) would be spent on infant and child protection in the coming year.[354] The major organizations working on child protection include the China's Women's Federation, the Youth League, State Council, the Judicial Department, the Department of Civil Affairs, all sponsored by the central PRC government. Their work emphasizes homeless and "floating" children as well as trafficking of children. As described in a press release,

Homeless and floating children are those under the age of 18 who left their family and have been living on the streets for more than 24 hours without any supervision of caretakers. They make a living by begging, recycling trash, selling flowers or stealing. Those children are mostly from rural villages in some least developing provinces. Some children are left-behind children, some are from the single families and some children left their family as a result of the extreme poverty. There are about 1-1.5 million homeless and floating children in China every year. Among which 10% are under the age of 7, 23% are at the age of 8-12, 65% are at the age of 13-15 and 4% of which are at the age of 16-18.[355]

Despite these several units, as is true in many other countries, there is no central function that cuts across all the categories of child maltreatment as defined by UNICEF.

In 2011, in order to meet the needs of child development and break intergenerational poverty transmission, the Government of China issued a National Programme of Action for Children (NPA) (2011-2020), proposing major targets and policies on child development from five aspects: health, education, welfare, social environment and legal protection. Meanwhile, the China Rural Poverty Alleviation and Development Program (2011-2020) describes the objectives of rural child development and requires government at all levels to regard women and children as a special target group, to include child poverty reduction in the general poverty alleviation and development planning for unified organization and implementation, and to prioritize child poverty alleviation with more support.

Local Government and Social Service Agencies

At provincial levels, local governments work on specific child protection issues depending on their own priorities. Social agencies work on different areas of child protection according to their own mission or the decisions of the central government, raising funding by themselves. Generally, they work on trafficking and floating/homeless/left-behind children. There are agencies that focus on both the rural and urban areas.

NGOs and other non-profit organizations

Several major NGOs and non-profit organizations work on child protection in China.

- Asian Legal Resource Center
- Children's Council Working Committee
- China Society for Prevention of Child Abuse and Neglect, Child Abuse and Treatment Center
- Compassion for migrant children
- Juvenile Legal Aid and Resource Center
- Plan International- China
- Qingdao Children's TV Development Council
- Save the Children UK-China office
- Society for Community Organization and Hang Kong Human Rights Commission
- UNICEF China[356]

UNICEF's China programs emphasize four areas of child protection:

- pilot programs to help reintegrate street children into society,
- contributing to the development of day care centres that provide services to disabled children,
- facilitating the provision of education and healthcare to migrant children, and
- collaborating with authorities on procedures for responding to child trafficking.[357]

Overview of child maltreatment and enforcement issues

Children in China are exposed to unsafe migration, lack of parental care, HIV/AIDS, human trafficking and other forms of exploitation, violence and abuse.[358]

Present Chinese laws on child protection cover all minors, i.e. all those under 18. But they mainly relate to physical protection, rather than children's rights, especially of those under ten years old. Wang Zhengyao, dean of the One Foundation Philanthropy Research Institute at Beijing Normal University, has summed up current enforcement by noting that many children are still not covered by specific laws. The current PRC Law on the Protection of Minors has established an overall network of child protection, but there is no specific child protection legislation and detailed rules and policies to implement the laws. Nor do the laws that refer to child protection identify the specific responsibilities of the agencies assigned roles in child protection.[359]

Staffing child protection work

In a 2011 survey by Dr. Chen Zhonglin, a professor in Nankai University in China, the government departments and organizations involved with child protection issues indicated a need for professional social workers and psychology counselors based on the fact that the current staff have received no specific training on child protection.

This survey further documented that

- When children are abused or neglected, there is no formal agency that they can report to.
- When children go back home after they sought help from the social agency, there is no follow up work to make sure that they are not going to be abused again.[360]

What are public attitudes and social norms regarding child protection?

Recent surveys have documented the fact that families, schools and communities rarely educate children about sexual abuse, which contributes to the result that when children are abused, they don't understand what happened and how to deal with it. The All-China Women's Federation and the People's Procuratorate in South China's Guangdong Province conducted joint research on children living in parentless homes and found that 2,506 children under 18 had been sexually abused over the last three years, with more than half of the victims under 14, as reported in Guangzhou Daily.

> Research conducted by child advocacy (website chinachild. org) found over 80 percent of child molesters are known by their victims and their families, with most aged between 50 and 82. One factor that contributes to sexual abuse of children and cases being unreported is that children are often unaware about being cautious around strangers.[361]

Another survey reported in "The Evolving Evidence Base for Child Protection in Chinese Societies" published in *Asia Pacific Journal of Public Health* found that there is a large gap between public perception and lived reality in Chinese societies. One example is that violent parenting and severe discipline in school are illegal in China, but there is still a high level of tolerance of these acts by numerous parents and other adults. Also, in China, strong traditional beliefs accept the use of discipline and force to control or punish children.[362]

Overview of Effectiveness

In sum, China faces major challenges in protecting its children and in living up to its ratification of the CRC—as do many other nations. China has clearly accomplished extraordinary results in ensuring that its children attend school, with figures for elementary attendance well above the percentages in other nations in Asia. In addition, the sex ratio in schools, in contrast to the sex ratio of births, is generally in balance.

But in following through on the far-reaching laws that have been passed, and in particular the task of protecting and improving the lives of the millions of children left behind by the vast migration of working parents to urban areas, China has far to go. The gap between its laws and the attitudes of many of its parents and government officials about what is permissible in disciplining children suggests the need for continuing surveys and better record-keeping for child maltreatment in order to determine whether progress is being made in the critical area of social norms. The policy space given to civil society organizations to carry out their work may be a critical factor in making that progress.

As noted in a recent issue of the CRIN newsletter,

> Nine States are under review during September's session which runs from 16 September to 4 October. Eleven NGOs have submitted alternative reports on China, raising issues such as corporal punishment, human rights defenders, HIV and AIDS, and children with disabilities.

Child Protection in India

Introduction

India is home to the largest number of children of any country: an estimated 444 million children. A 2011 report published by the Indian government found that around 40 percent of them were vulnerable to threats such as sexual abuse, trafficking, homelessness, forced labor, drug abuse, and crime.[363] The government has also declared that every second child in India is malnourished, less than one fourth of the rural population has access to toilets, and only four out of ten girls who enroll into school complete eight years of schooling.[364]

India has extensive legislation in force that addresses child protection issues, but its enforcement and monitoring mechanisms are often inadequate to the immense task of implementing those laws nationwide. The Indian Constitution states that all children between the ages of six to fourteen should be provided with free and compulsory education. The Child Labor (Prohibition and Regulation) Act of 1986 defines a child as a person who has not completed fourteen years of age. The Prohibition of Child Marriage Act of 2006 states that a male has not reaches majority until he is twenty-one years of age and a female has not reached majority until she is eighteen years of age.[365] But national statistics on each of these problems underscore how far India has to go to reach the goals of this legislation.

Like China (and not unlike some regions of the US), data on urban areas and data on rural areas diverges widely. For example, the 2012 report of a consultation on child marriage held by the Ministry of Women and Child Development reported 52% incidence of child marriage in rural areas, and 28% in urban areas.[366] In this meeting the Secretary of the Ministry declared that "there is a need for the change in the mindset of society which largely perceives the girl child to be a burden on the families." She went on to describe several efforts under way to "empower the girl child," including guidelines for recording of evidence of vulnerable witnesses in criminal matters, The Protection of Children from Sexual Offences Act 2012, The Child Labor (Prohibition and Regulation) Act, 1986 and amendments in 2006, and The Prohibition of Child Marriage Act, 2006.

To its credit, the report of the Working Group on Child Rights on the 2012-2017 Plan issued by the Ministry for Women and Child Development is candid and includes the results of numerous surveys covering not only child protection issues, but a much broader range of child well-being indicators as well. The report states bluntly that

> sexual offences against children are inadequately addressed by extant legislation." ...Child Welfare Committees and Juvenile Justice Boards, mandated for every district... were not set up;... low allocation of funds by the States/ UTs and availability of services for children in difficult circumstances was negligible in comparison to their needs.[367]

Who works on child protection in India?

Central Government

In the national government, agencies that are related to child protection work include the

National Human Rights Commission, National Commission for the Protection of Child Rights, Ministry of Women and Child Development, Ministry of Labor and Employment and Related Bodies, Ministry of Social Justice and Empowerment, Ministry of Human Resource and Development, and the Ministry of Health and Family Welfare.[368]

A "Children's Policy" document was issued in 2013 by the Ministry of Women and Child Development, which was described as a "National Policy for Children, to reiterate the commitment of the rights-based approach to children."[369] The National Policy was first issued in 1974. The 2013 document states that "survival, health, nutrition, development, education, protection and participation are the undeniable rights of every child and are the key priorities of this Policy." The protection section of the Policy describes both child protection measures and specific groups of children who need special protection.

The Policy also calls for coordination across sectors and indicators to measure progress. It charges the Ministry for Women and Child Development as the central coordinating body and sets up an interagency group, the National Coordination and Action Group, to achieve this coordination. The Ministry is to develop a National Plan of Action for Children, and the separate National Commission for Protection of Child Rights and its state counterparts are to perform monitoring roles as well.

> A continuous process of indicator-based child impact assessment and evaluation will be developed, and assessment and evaluation will be carried out on the situation of children in the country, which will inform policies and programmes for children.

Progress on the Plan is to be reviewed in five years. Budget allocations are to be made to achieve the purposes of the Plan, and expenditures on the Plan are to be monitored. In a separate process within the Ministry, "Gender Budgeting" involves a review of the national budget from the perspective of gender equity.[370]

It is difficult to assess the impact of this Policy without a broader assessment of trend lines in child protection indicators. The role of the National Commission for Protection of Child Rights in monitoring progress will be critical.

Local Government and Social Service Agencies

The 28 states and 7 union territories in India all have specific departments and offices that focus on different child welfare, health care, education and other areas related to child protection. Childline is a 24-hour helpline for children, especially street children, to report abuse and request assistance. The helpline handles more than a million calls a year, working with 415 partner organizations throughout the nation.

Regional and International Mechanisms

India also participates in a number of regional and international organizations and consortia that address child protection issues. These include the South Asian Association for Regional Cooperation (SASRC), the Asian Human Rights Commission (AHRC), the Association of Southeast Asian Nations (ASEAN), UNICEF and other UN agencies, including the International Labor Organization, Child Rights International Network, and Child Helpline International.

What do agencies do in responding to child abuse and neglect in India?

The Government and NGOs operate numerous child protection programs; there are thousands of civil society organizations in India that address some facet of child and family issues. Some of the most visible programs include a Scheme for Working Children in need of care and protection, an Integrated Program for Street Children, CHILDLINE-the 24 hour help line for children in distress; the Rajiv Gandhi national crèche scheme for the children of working mothers, a Pilot Project to Combat the Trafficking of

Women and Children for Commercial Sexual Exploitation in Destination Areas, and many others.

UNICEF/India and the Government of India in January 2012 signed an agreement to implement a Country Programme Action Plan covering the years 2013-2017. UNICEF's efforts focus on three priorities: child labour, child trafficking, and children in difficult circumstances.[371]

Pending issues

Recent cases of severe child abuse and rape have spotlighted the enforcement of child protection and rape laws in India. In a recent report, Human Rights Watch reported child sexual abuse to be "disturbingly common" in India, due to "poor awareness, social stigma, and negligence."[372] The report stated that many of the recommendations contained in the "Integrated Child Protection Scheme" issued in 2006 have not been followed. In response to recent incidents, new legislation was swiftly passed in March 2013 that included penalties for police not responding adequately to rape and reports of sexual assaults.

The Protection of Children from Sexual Offences Act of 2012 came into force in November, 2012, and its implementation is in an early stage. "However, the government should ensure that the provisions of the Act are implemented in letter and spirit," according to Chandan Barman, a child protection consultant to UNICEF/India. The establishment of special courts under the Act is critical for speedy disposal of cases so that the victims get justice and the perpetrators are punished, he added.

In India and several other nations, dowries can be a sizable economic burden for low-income families, with the effect of increasing discrimination against girls as economic drains on family income. A number of advocacy and civil society organizations in India have campaigned against dowries and have developed specific programmatic responses to the problem. A spokesman for one of these groups summed up the problem: Ranjan Karmaker, Executive Director of Steps toward Development, said, "Our society measures women as commodities while men are considered as assets."[373]

Despite legislation that prohibits dowries, Human Rights Watch, UNICEF, and other organizations have pointed out that the legislation is not well enforced. When the Convention on the Elimination of all Forms of Discrimination Against Women was being considered by the UN in 2012, India entered a reservation that indicated it did not intend to be bound by the provisions of the Convention requiring adjudication of violations of the Convention by international courts, in much the same way that the U.S. has entered similar reservations to international jurisdiction. India also issued explanatory statements that referred to its policy of "non-interference in the personal affairs of any community without its initiative and consent."[374]

Public attitudes and social norms regarding child protection

Amartya Sen, who had done some of the original work in the 1990's estimating the "missing women" caused by discrimination against girls' births, has recently updated these estimates, noting significant disparities among Indian states. He points out the apparent effect of sonograms for determining sex, calling it "natality discrimination," and finds that the proportion of missing women due in part to abortion of female fetuses and in part to differential health care has not declined in the total population, despite improvements in women's education.[375]

In summarizing the causes of child maltreatment, the 2012 report of the Working Group on Child Rights stated

> Harmful Traditional Mindsets: Long standing/ entrenched value systems combined with the low socio-economic status of women and children are a source of much social malpractice and gender violence and these manifest in female foeticide, domestic violence, child marriage, dowry, etc. Furthermore, as the child is viewed as a mere extension of the family and not a separate entity

with rights and entitlements, it creates an environment where the voice of the child is not heard, which in turn results in vulnerability to abuse of multiple sort, ranging from incest to children in forced labour.[376]

In a recent chapter in an international compilation of child protection materials, Sibnath Deb of Calcutta University cited the diversity of India as it affects attitudes and social norms concerning children:

> Geographically, India is an amalgam of 28 States and 7 Union territories, each with its own set of cultural beliefs and practices with regard to child rearing social and linguistic identity...In general, Indians do not consider children as an individual who should have freedom of expression of views and opinions. Therefore, changing the mindset of the Indian population towards children is essential for creating child-friendly environments across the society...The efforts which have been made for prevention of child abuse and neglect by different agencies are not adequate as compared to the need.[377]

ACKNOWLEDGEMENTS

I begin my thanks by crediting two classmates from Occidental, Scott Robinson and Carolyn (Toc) Dunlap, for early interviews, inspiration, and invaluable guidance. They have both spent their lives much closer to the realities I was attempting to capture in this book, and I returned to their wise observations many times. Toc's work with Creating Hope International and the Afghan Institute of Learning and Scott's many anthropological, academic, and political interests from his bases in Mexico City and Tlyacapan, Morelos, were tremendously helpful. That we were all part of an era and an institution that valued international perspectives was one of those lasting gifts of a first-rate higher education experience; may it affect more recent Oxy students as well, including the most internationally-minded President in a long time.

We had great support from our Washington-based partners at ChildFocus: Mary Bissell and Rebecca Robuck, in arranging meetings, networking among their rich sets of contacts, careful readings of drafts, and helping us "Washingtonize" our findings where necessary.

As noted in the preface, those we interviewed were candid and perceptive in their comments.

I do not mention them by name, except where citing their actual words, not because of a lack of gratitude but because I do not want to risk omitting any of them. Again, none of them is responsible for our interpretations of their comments or their work.

Huge thanks to Nancy Young and Larisa Owen, my wife and daughter, whose gifts of time are truly priceless, whose support was unending, and whose tolerance for my fascination with this topic was a great resource. Special thanks go to Tarah Garcia and Tricia Gomez in arranging complicated flights and travel (and then re-arranging them at least once and dealing with forgetful, older travelers who occasionally may have mislaid one or two things along the way). Annette Garcia played a critical role in the final stages of production and editing, and Jessica Warbrick added some timely updates. Special thanks also to Russ Bermejo of CFF whose personal commitment to this work has been a true inspiration. Thanks to CFF the institution, which supported some of the time and travel required for this book to take final form.

Selia Wang, who is Wang Min when she is at home in China, worked with us at CFF for three months and shared with us her deep understanding of village life and realities half a world away. Her hard work, keen intelligence, research persistence, and sense of humor when confronted with American oddities were great assets to this project. Now a graduate of SIAS University in China, studying in graduate school in Florida, she has a great future in whatever she chooses to do.

Our extraordinary cover is the work of Shelley Furgason, a talented graphic designer at http://www.behance.net/bluseashell.

BIOGRAPHICAL NOTE

Sidney L. Gardner, M.P.A., M.A.
Email: sgardner@cffutures.org

Mr. Gardner serves as President of Children and Family Futures, Inc. He is the author of *Beyond Collaboration to Results*, and *Cities, Counties, Kids, and Families: the Essential Role of Local Government* (2005), which describes a model for developing strategic policy for children and family policy in local governments.

Mr. Gardner has served as Deputy Assistant Secretary of the U.S. Department of Health, Education, and Welfare, a staff member of the White House Domestic Council, Director of State and Local Affairs at the Children's Defense Fund, Director of the California Tomorrow Youth at Risk Project, Director of the Hartford Private Industry Council, as an Assistant to the Mayor of New York City, and as an elected member of the

City Council in Hartford, Connecticut from 1977 to 1981. He served as Director of the Center for Collaboration for Children at California State University, Fullerton from 1991-2001. He has taught courses at seven universities.

He graduated from Occidental College in 1963 and was awarded a Master's degree in Public Affairs from Princeton University's Woodrow Wilson School in 1965 and a Master's degree in Religious Studies from Hartford Seminary in 1986. Mr. Gardner is a Vietnam veteran, and lives in Mission Viejo, California with his wife, Nancy Young, and two of their four children.

NOTES

I have used international spelling variations (such as "programme" and "labour") where those were used in the original source.

INTRODUCTION

[1] This book is based on a year-long literature review, interviews with key child protection officials and academics in this field, and travel to China, Mexico, and Turkey begun in May 2012. The project has been supported by Children and Family Futures, a nonprofit agency based in Lake Forest, California.

[2] We are using the UNICEF definitions of child protection issues, including birth registration, children without parental care, child recruitment by armed forces/groups, armed violence reduction, female genital mutilation/cutting, child marriage, sexual violence against children, child trafficking, child labor, justice for children, children with disabilities, family separation, gender-based violence in emergencies, land mines and explosive weapons, and psychosocial support and well-being. I have added school attendance as sixteenth issue which is not in the formal UNICEF list but which UN agencies, including UNESCO, include in their agenda.

[3] The estimate that one in five children in the world is mistreated or at serious. risk of maltreatment is based on the following:

- A total of 2.2 billion children under the age of 18 are alive today
- The annual reports from UNICEF on children's indicators, based on surveys and national administrative data, describe prevalence of maltreatment that ranges from a few hundred thousand children for some conditions to hundreds of millions for others, e.g. 215 million children 5-17 years old engaged in child labor, 223 million experienced sexual assault.
- The prevalence of children living in lowest-income families, below the extreme poverty line of $1.25 a day, is estimated most recently at over

400 million children. The overlap between poverty and maltreatment or neglect—while not explaining the full range of causes of maltreatment, as discussed throughout this book, is wide enough to justify assuming that some of these children are at high risk for neglect at levels that constitute maltreatment.

- The estimate that one of five children alive today has been subjected to physical or sexual violence that could impair their full development may seem excessive, especially in the absence of effective data collection in many nations. Yet further context for this estimate is provided by recent surveys of the U.S. Department of Justice and the Centers for Disease Control and Prevention that one in four women in the U.S. has been sexually abused and one in five has experienced physical violence and abuse. (November 2011 Department of Justice/Centers for Disease Control report *National Intimate Partner and Sexual Violence Survey*, was begun in 2010 with the support of the National Institute of Justice and the Department of Defense.)

The Council on Europe has used available data to estimate that one in five children in Europe is a victim of some form of sexual violence (The title of this book was chosen before learning of the Council's aptly named "One in Five" campaign; Save the Children also refers to the "final fifth" of children who have not yet been immunized). Coe.int, (2014). *Council of Europe proposes four-year plan for children's rights.* [online] Available at: http://www.coe.int/t/congress/newssearch/Default_en.asp?p=nwz&id=6926&lmLangue=1 [Accessed 25 Jun. 2014].

[4] We use *child maltreatment* to refer to the forms of abuse and neglect that are categorized by national and international governments and agencies as maltreatment; we use *child protection* to refer to prevention and intervention efforts to reduce and respond to this maltreatment. As noted by one reviewer, the term maltreatment may not fully recognize the illegality, violence, and criminal nature of child abuse and neglect, but it is an encompassing term that is used widely in the field.

CHAPTER ONE

[5] UNICEF (2004). Child Protection: A handbook for parliamentarians available at: http://www.ipu.org/pdf/publications/childprotection_en.pdf

[6] J. Carroll, (2011) *Jerusalem, Jerusalem.*

[7] A Kahn, 'From Child Saving to Child Development' in S. Kamerman, S. Phipps, and A. Ben-Arieh, editors, (2010) *From Child Welfare to Child Well-being: An International Perspective on Knowledge in the Service of Policy Making.* New York: Springer.

[8] S. Pinker, (2011) *The Better Angels of Our Nature: Why Violence Has Declined.* Viking: New York. p.415-447.

[9] This document was based largely on the Declaration of Child Rights, developed by the predecessor organization to Save the Children under the leadership of an extraordinary British woman, Eglantyne Jebb.

[10] His Holiness The Dalai Lama, (1999) *Ethics for the New Millennium*, Riverhead Books, New York. p.123

[11] J. Berryman, (2010) *Children and the Theologians: Clearing the Way for Grace* Morehouse Publishing. http://www.childtheology.org/blog/children-and-the-theologians-clearing-the-way-for-grace/

[12] Violating Children's Rights: Harmful practices based on tradition, culture, religion, or superstition. (2012) The International NGO Council on Violence against Children. The quotation is from Paulo Sergio Pinheiro, who led the Secretary-General's Study on Violence against Children in 2006.

[13] This is not one of the sixteen problem areas in UNICEF's framework; it is monitored by UNESCO and UNICEF, as described below. For purposes of this book, and because of the close links between school attendance, child labor, and gender equity issues, we include this issue under the heading of child protection. UNICEF, in fact, indexes education issues in its evaluation database at http://www.unicef.org/evaldatabase/index_13711.html UNICEF, (2014). *Reports by theme | Evaluation database | UNICEF.* [online] Available at: http://www.unicef.org/evaldatabase/index_13711.html [Accessed 25 Jun. 2014].

[14] UNICEF (2013). Annual Report. Available at: http://www.unicef.org/publications/index_73682.html [Accessed 25 Jun. 2014].

[15] Wulczyn F, Daro D, Fluke J, Feldman S, Glodek C, Lifanda K, (2010) Adapting a systems approach to child protection: key concepts and considerations, UNICEF, UNHCR, Save the Children. John D. Fluke and Fred Wulczyn, (2010) A concept note on child protection systems monitoring and evaluation, UNICEF.

[16] Dr. Yanghee Lee, remarks at the plenary session of the International Society for the Prevention of Child Abuse and Neglect, Istanbul, Turkey, September 10, 2012.

[17] Lansdown G (2005) Can you hear me? The right of young children to participate in decisions affecting them.
Working Paper 36. Bernard van Leer Foundation, The Hague, The Netherlands

[18] Asher Ben-Arieh, "The Child Indicators Movement: Past, Present, and Future," Child Indicators Research, Volume 1, Number 1 (2008), p.3-16.

[19] P. Britto and N. Ulkuer, "Child Development in Developing Countries: Child Rights and Policy Implications," *Child Development*, January/February 21012, Vol. 83. No. 1 p.92.

[20] J. Heymann, (2013) *Children's Chances*, Harvard University Press. 9.

[21] The MCIS data is available at the MICS pages on childinfo.org. Childinfo.org, (2014). *Childinfo.org:*. [online] Available at: http://childinfo.org [Accessed 25 Jun. 2014].

[22] Ipscan.org, (2014). *Nmap - Free Security Scanner For Network Exploration & Security Audits.*. [online] Available at: http://www.ipscan.org [Accessed 25 Jun. 2014].

[23] UNICEF, (2014). *Data and evaluations.* [online] Available at: http://www.unicef.org/protection/57929_57979.html [Accessed 25 Jun. 2014].

[24] Isci.chapinhall.org,. (2014). International Society for Child Indicators. Retrieved 7 July 2014, from http://isci.chapinhall.org/

[25] Ben-Arieh, op. cit.

[26] Besley, T., & Ghatak, M. (1999). Public-private partnership for the provision of public goods: Theory and an application to NGOs. Available at

[27] This study distinguished between humanitarian aid, which was its focus, and "development aid," which was outside the purview of the study. Available at http://www.globalhumanitarianassistance.org/wp-content/uploads/2010/07/2009-Focus.-report-Public-support-for-humanitarian-crises-through-NGOs.pdf
"Public Support for Humanitarian Crises through NGOs," Development Initiatives, November 2008

[28] G. Allard, (2011) "Are NGOs promoting development objectives? In pursuit of empirical data." IE Business School. Available at http://latienda.ie.edu/working_papers_economia/EC8-123-I.pdf

[29] Too Little, Too Late (n.d). Child Protection Working Group of the Child Protection Cluster. Available at: http://resourcecentre.savethechildren.se/sites/default/files/documents/4382.pdf

[30] Rittel, Horst, and Melvin Webber; "Dilemmas in a General Theory of Planning," pp. 155–169, *Policy Sciences*, Vol. 4, Elsevier Scientific Publishing Company, Inc., Amsterdam, 1973. [Reprinted in N. Cross (ed.), *Developments in Design Methodology*, J. Wiley & Sons, Chichester, 1984, pp. 135–144.] Roberts, N.C. "Wicked Problems and Network Approaches to Resolution." *The International Public Management Review.*, Vol. 1, 1 (2000). Weber, E. P. and Khademian, A. M. (2008), Wicked Problems, Knowledge Challenges, and Collaborative Capacity Builders in Network Settings. *Public Administration Review*, 68: 334–349. J. Nickerson and R. Sanders, (2013) *Tackling Wicked Government Problems*, Brookings Institution Press, Washington, D.C.

[31] Weber and Khademian, op.cit.

CHAPTER TWO

[32] UNICEF (2013). Convention on the Rights of a Child. Available at http://www. unicef.org/rightsite/237.htm

[33] R. Jolly, "UNICEF, Economists and Economic Policy: Bringing Children into Development Strategies" in I. Ortiz, L. Moreira Daniels, S. Engilbertsdóttir (Eds) (2012) *Child Poverty and Inequality: New Perspectives*, United Nations Children's Fund (UNICEF), Division of Policy and Practice, New York. p.79-84

[34] United Nations (2008). Economic and Social Council. Available at http://www. unicef.org/tdad/unicefcpstrategyjune08(2).pdf

[35] *Global Monitoring Report 2010: The MDGs After the Crisis*, (2010) The World Bank. p. 131

[36] W. Fengler and H. Kharas, editors, (2013) *Delivering Aid Differently: Lessons from the Field*, The Brookings Institution, Washington, D.C.

[37] Ibid. p. 13.

[38] The most recent data available on the organizations' annual expenses (either 2010 or 2011 fiscal years) was World Vision ($1.1 billion), Oxfam ($1.12 billion), Catholic Relief Services ($820 million), CARE ($805 million), Plan International ($687 million), Save the Children ($619 million), International Rescue Commission ($384 million), Mercy Corps ($334 million), and Doctors without Borders ($178 million). As noted below, these are all-funds budgets, with child protection expenditures not broken out separately.

[39] D. Ignatius, "Drawing down, but still projecting power" *Washington Post* March 30, 2013.

[40] Fifth Annual Report to Congress on Public Law 109-95, USAID, 2012.

[41] Second Annual Report to Congress: Supporting highly vulnerable children: progress, promise and partnership. USAID, December 2008. 19.

[42] H. Dubovitz and J. Merrick, eds., (2010) *International Aspects of Child Abuse and Neglect*. Nova Science Publishers: New York.

[43] OECD (2014). Statistics on resource flows to developing countries. Available at http://www.oecd.org/dac/aidstatistics/statisticsonresourceflow stodevelopingcountries.htm

[44] UNICEF (2014). Partners for change and development: the growing partnership between the European Union and UNICEF. Available at http://www.unicef.org/ about/execboard/files/2014 FRS-Special Focus Session-Concept Note-EU-UNICEF partnership.pdf

[45] The Congress of Local and Regional Authorities (2012). Available at http://www. coe.int/t/congress/newssearch/Default en.asp?p=nwz&id=6926&lmLangue=1

[46] *Championing Children's Rights*, (2012) UNICEF Office of Research. Florence. p.4

47 Ibid. 5

48 Ibid. 10

49 Ibid. 16

50 Ibid. 17

51 Ibid. 19

52 A. Neier, (2012) *The International Human Rights Movement.* Princeton University Press, Princeton, N.J

53 There are some important exceptions to the general dismissal of rights for children in the human rights community, especially within the UN. The UN General Assembly in its fall 2012 session passed an landmark resolution condemning female mutilation that emerged from the Assembly's human rights committee, not the Human Rights Council.

54 M. Ignatieff, (2001) *Human Rights as Politics and Idolatry,* Princeton University Press, Princeton, N.J. p.68

55 C. Martin,"However Long the Night: A Q&A With Molly Melching," SSIR Review blog, June 27, 2013. Available at

   http://www.ssireview.org/blog/entry/however_long_the_night_a_qa_with_molly_melching?utm_source=Enews&utm_medium=email&utm_content=3&utm_campaign=From_Blog

CHAPTER THREE

56 UNICEF, (2014). *Armed violence reduction.* [online] Available at: http://www.unicef.org/protection/57929_58011.html [Accessed 25 Jun. 2014].

57 OECD (2011), *Linking Security System Reform and Armed Violence Reduction: Programming Note, Conflict and Fragility,* OECD Publishing. http://dx.doi.org/10.1787/9789264107212-en; OECD DAC policy paper (2009) *Armed Violence Reduction: Enabling Development.*

58 Geneva Declaration (2014). Best Practice Seminars. Available at http://www.genevadeclaration.org/programming/best-practice-seminars.html

59 *Every Child Counts,* UNICEF January 2014 www.unicef,org/sowc2014/numbers p 83.

60 *Child Protection from Violence, Exploitation, and Abuse, Thematic Report 2011,* UNICEF. Available at http://www.unicef.org/protection/57929_58010.html

61 ILO (2010). *Facts on Child Labour.* Available at http://www.unicef.org/protection/Birth_Registration_Working_Paper(2).pdf

62 *Every Child Counts,* UNICEF January 2014 p. 3 www.unicef,org/sowc2014/numbers

[63] Roadmap for Achieving the Elimination of the Worst Forms of Child Labour by 2016 (2010). Available at http://www.ilo.org/ipecinfo/product/viewProduct.do?productId=13453

[64] ILO (2010). *Facts on Child Labour.* Available at http://www.unicef.org/protection/Birth_Registration_Working_Paper(2).pdf

[65] http://childrenofsyria.info/wp-content/uploads/2015/07/CHILD-LABOUR.pdf

[66] Ibid. p. 4

[67] *Child Protection from Violence, Exploitation, and Abuse, Thematic Report 2011,* UNICEF. Available at http://www.unicef.org/protection/57929_58010.html

[68] *Progress for Children: A Report Card on Child Protection,* No. 8, September 2009 UNICEF. p.26

[69] R. Vogelstein, (2013) Ending Child Marriage: How Elevating the Status of Girls Advances U.S. Foreign Policy Objectives. Council on Foreign Relations Press.

[70] Otunnu. Olara A. "Era of Application: Instituting a compliance and enforcement regime for CAAC," Statement before the Security Council, New York, 2/23/2005. p.3

[71] UNODC.org, (2014). United Nations Convention against Transnational Organized Crime and the Protocols Thereto
[online] Available at: http://www.unodc.org/justice-child-victims/ [Accessed 25 Jun. 2014].

[72] http://www.state.gov/documents/organization/164452.pdf

[73] UNODC.org, (2014). United Nations Convention against Transnational Organized Crime and the Protocols Thereto
[online] Available at: http://www.unodc.org/justice-child-victims/ [Accessed 25 Jun. 2014].

[74] *Progress for Children: A Report Card on Child Protection,* No. 8, September 2009 UNICEF. p.19.

[75] Ibid. 18.

[76] *Child Protection from Violence, Exploitation, and Abuse, Thematic Report 2011,* UNICEF p.31

[77] United Nations Children's Fund, *The State of the World's Children 2013: Children with Disabilities,* UNICEF, New York, 2013, http://www .unicef.org/sowc2013

[78] *Child Protection from Violence, Exploitation, and Abuse, Thematic Report 2011,* UNICEF. Available at http://www.unicef.org/protection/57929_58010.html

[79] *Child Protection from Violence, Exploitation, and Abuse, Thematic Report 2011,* UNICEF. Available at http://www.unicef.org/protection/57929_58010.html p.24.

[80] *Progress for Children: A Report Card on Child Protection,* No. 8, September 2009 UNICEF. 12.

81 *Progress for Children: A Report Card on Child Protection*, No. 8, September 2009 UNICEF 21

82 Ibid. 20.

83 UNODC.org, (2014). United Nations Convention against Transnational Organized Crime and the Protocols Thereto
[online] Available at: http://www.unodc.org/justice-child-victims/ [Accessed 25 Jun. 2014].

84 G. Haugen and V. Boutros, (2014) *The Locust Effect: Why the End of Poverty Requires the End of Violence*, Oxford University Press.

85 *Progress for Children: A Report Card on Child Protection*, No. 8, September 2009 UNICEF 21

86 State.gov, (2014). *To Walk the Earth in Safety (2013)*. [online] Available at: http://www.state.gov/t/pm/rls/rpt/walkearth/2013/index.htm [Accessed 25 Jun. 2014].

87 UN.org, (2014). [online] Available at: http://www.un.org/children/conflict/english/index.html [Accessed 25 Jun. 2014].

88 Violating Children's Rights: Harmful practices based on tradition, culture, religion, or superstition. (2012) The International NGO Council on Violence against Children. The quotation is from Paulo Sergio Pinheiro, who led the Secretary-General's Study on Violence against Children in 2006.

89 UNICEF, (2014). *Sexual violence against children*. [online] Available at: http://www.unicef.org/protection/57929_58006.html [Accessed 25 Jun. 2014].

90 UNICEF, (2014). *Sexual violence against children*. [online] Available at: http://www.unicef.org/protection/57929_58006.html [Accessed 25 Jun. 2014].

91 Cdc.gov, (2014). *Together for Girls|Sexual Violence|Violence Prevention|Injury Center|CDC*. [online] Available at: http://www.cdc.gov/violenceprevention/sexualviolence/together/ [Accessed 25 Jun. 2014].

92 http:www.unicef.org/protection/57929_58006.htm

93 "Abby", "China, Pollution, and Cancer Villages," Available at http://globalvoicesonline.org/2013/02/25/chinese-billionaire-pollution-steering-china-toward-cancer-crisis/ On Sina Weibo, China's internet, a map of the cancer villages was published.

94 Cleanhouston.org, (2014). *CLEAN Archives- Environmental Child Abuse*. [online] Available at: http://www.cleanhouston.org/comments/archives/child_abuse.htm [Accessed 25 Jun. 2014].

95 P. Britto and N. Ulkuer, "Child Development in Developing Countries: Child Rights and Policy Implications," *Child Development*, January/February 2012, Vol. 83, No 1. 101

96 Ibid. 95-6.

[97] *Progress for Children: Achieving the MDGs with Equity*, No. 9, September 2010. UNICEF

[98] Unicef.org, (2014). | *UNICEF.* [online] Available at: http://www.unicef.org/post2015/files/Post_2015_Key_Messages_V07.pdf

CHAPTER FOUR

[99] American Academy of Pediatrics: Technical Report: The Lifelong Effects of Early Childhood Adversity and Toxic Stress; J. Shonkoff, et al. *Pediatrics 2012; 129:1 e232-e246*

[100] *Child Protection from Violence, Exploitation, and Abuse, Thematic Report 2011*, UNICEF 31. As stated in the UNICEF Strategy document, "Preventing and responding to violence, exploitation and abuse is essential to ensuring children's rights to survival, development and well-being."

[101] P. Engle, *National plans of action for orphans and vulnerable children in sub-Saharan Africa: Where are the youngest children*. Bernard van Leer Foundation, 2008.

[102] M. Indyk, K. Lieberthal, M. O'Hanlon, (2012) *Bending History: Barack Obama's Foreign Policy*, Brookings Institution Press, Washington, D.C.; J. Bader, (2012) *Obama and China's Rise*, Brookings Institution Press. Washington, D.C.; J. Nye, (2011) *The Future of Power;* James Mann, (2012) *The Obamians*, New York. Nye has a brief discussion of general foreign aid as an example of economic power in Chapter 3. Mann does not discuss children's issues as such but mentions the Taliban preventing girls from attending school in Afghanistan in the book's final chapter.

[103] C. Lancaster, (2007) *Foreign Aid: Diplomacy, Development, Domestic Politics*. University of Chicago Press, Chicago. 109

[104] N. Boothby, "A Conspiracy of Goodness," proceedings of the 2011 Evidence Summit. Available at http://www.hvcassistance.org/blogs.cfm#boothby

[105] Fifth Annual Report to Congress on Public Law 109-95, USAID, 2012. For example, the USAID office refers to $2.8 billion allocated in the FY10 budget for "assistance to highly vulnerable children" (rather than child protection) in a foreign aid budget that totals $30.4 billion. The CP total includes $858 million of food aid, which makes clear that the funds devoted to strictly CP purposes are relatively small. The PL 109-95 office in USAID refers to this legislation as an unfunded mandate, which explains in part its re-designation of previously appropriated funds as designated for vulnerable children. The definitions of "vulnerable children" do not include all of the UNICEF categories under child protection, and do include some issues of child survival as well as child protection.

CHAPTER FIVE

[106] Fifth Annual Report to Congress on Public Law 109-95, USAID, 2012. The Office of the U.S. Government Special Advisor and Senior Coordinator on Children in Adversity in USAID. At present, this officey, implements Public Law 109-95: the Assistance for Orphans and Other Vulnerable Children in Developing Countries Act of 2005. The legislation calls for an annual report to Congress (the fifth was issued in March 2012) and includes a secretariat which coordinates the efforts of the Interagency PL 109-95 Working Group, consisting of 40 persons from five federal agencies: State, Labor, Agriculture, Defense and Health and Human Services, two governmental agencies (USAID and Peace Corps), the U.S. NGO community, and the UN (represented by UNICEF).

[107] *Progress for Children: Achieving the MDGs with Equity*, No. 9. UNICEF September 2010. p. 8.

[108] An Baijie and Xiang Mingchao, "Youngsters may be left behind, but not forgotten," *China Daily*, May 31, 2012

[109] UNICEF, Thematic Report: Child Protection from Violence, Exploitation and Abuse, 2010. "Measuring and monitoring the well-being of young children around the world," a paper prepared by Asher Ben-Arieh for the *Education for All Global Monitoring Report 2007*.p 4.

[110] UNICEF, Thematic Report: Child Protection from Violence, Exploitation and Abuse, 2010. "Measuring and monitoring the well-being of young children around the world," a paper prepared by Asher Ben-Arieh for the *Education for All Global Monitoring Report 2007*.

[111] UNICEF, (2014). (2014). *UNICEF IRC major publications 2010*. [online] Unicef-irc.org. Available at: http://www.unicef-irc.org/publications/forthcoming/ [Accessed 25 Jun. 2014].

[112] *Progress for Children: A Report Card on Child Protection*, No. 8, September 2009. UNICEF, New York. p.3

[113] For example, talking with older persons about corporal discipline in schools is a very different experience than talking with a child in school today. "If we got out of line—of course they paddled us. And none of us are the worse for it…"

> The Dickens quote on p. 8 was cited by Adam Gopnick in "The Caging of America," *New Yorker*, January 30, 2012.

[114] "Philippines Alternative NGO Report 2011: Optional Protocol on the Sale of Children, Child Prostitution and Child Pornography," ECPAT Philippines. October 2011 p. 10

[115] D. Nepra,ed. Op.cit. p.31.

[116] M. Lewis and C.G. Ippen, (2004) "Culture, Trauma, and Young Children" in J. Osofsky, ed. *Young Children and Trauma*, The Guilford Press, New York. p.19.

[117] M. Schuder and K. Lyons-Ruth, "'Hidden Trauma' in Infancy: Attachment, Fearful Arousal, and Early Dysfunction of the Stress Response System," in Osofsky, op.cit p.69-106.

[118] P. Alston and B. Gilmour-Walsh, (1996) *In the Best Interests of the Child*, UNICEF, Florence, Italy. p.1.

[119] Ibid. p.18.

[120] Ibid. p.31.

[121] J. Lansford at al. "Physical Discipline and Children's Adjustment: Cultural Normativeness as a Moderator" *Child Development* Volume 76, Issue 6, pages 1234–1246, November 2005. As noted, this was one of the few studies that could be accessed that explicitly linked cultural practices and behavioral outcomes. In requesting information from several academic centers of research on child trauma, the question of how culture and trauma were related was met with responses that essentially stated that it was "a good question." This would appear to be an important area where more research is critical.

[122] K. Appiah, (2006) *Cosmopolitanism: Ethics in A World of Strangers*, W.W. Norton, New York. p.85

[123] Ignatieff, op.cit. p.170

[124] For example, guidelines developed by experts at the Chadwick Center for Children and Families on cultural values set forth thoughtful suggestions on how to deal with cultural issues among families in the U.S.. http://www.chadwickcenter.org/ Documents/WALS/Adaptation%20Guidelines%20-%20Cultural%20Values%20 Priority%20Area.pdf

[125] None of what follows in this section is intended to minimize the great and positive work done by religious. organizations and individuals in religious communities in responding to child maltreatment, nor to the spiritual dimension of some forms of therapy for childhood trauma. But to refer to culture without mentioning the explicit overlap of religion and culture in child-rearing—and in some forms of child maltreatment—would be to ignore reality. Nor should it be overlooked that many non-Islamic religious institutions have difficulties providing women with full rights as leaders in the church; within recent months the Church of England and the Roman Catholic Church have had serious controversies over prohibitions on women priests and women bishops, and control of women's religious orders.

[126] L. McClain, (2010) "Child, Family, State, and Gender Equality in Religious Stances and Human Rights Instruments: A Preliminary Comparison." Boston University School of Law Working Paper No. 10-31.

[127] Crin.org, (2013). *UN: Historic Declaration adopted to combat violence against women | CRIN*. [online] Available at: http://www.crin.org/resources/infodetail. asp?id=30542 [Accessed 25 Jun. 2014].

[128] Badawi, J. (1995). *Gender equity in Islam.* World Assembly of Muslim Youth.

[129] The harm done by culturally based gender bias is not a subjective judgment I am making; it relies in part on the extraordinary assessment by the Arab Human Development Study of the UN Development Program issued in 2002 that concluded "...three critical deficits face all Arab countries: freedom; women's empowerment; human capabilities and knowledge relative to income...Utilization of Arab women's capabilities through political and economic participation remains the lowest in the world in quantitative terms...Society as a whole suffers when half of its productive potential is stifled." *Challenges to Human Security in the Arab Countries,* UN Development Programme, (2009) p. 79. Available at http://www.arab-hdr.org/publications/contents/2009/ch4-e.pdf

> In addition, it is not just a lack of participation and a denial of opportunity that affects child protection; it is also the sanctioned violence against women and girls that causes recurrent harm and trauma, often with state approval or a refusal of the state to intervene. A relevant question then becomes whether exercise and defense of male power is a form of addiction as well. "Power is sweet; it is a drug, the desire for which increases with habit." Bertrand Russell, *Saturday Review,* 1951

[130] WHO Facts: *Child maltreatment and alcohol.* World Health Organization (2006)

[131] G. Gonzalez-Alcaide et al. (2012) "Scientific Publications and Research Groups on Alcohol Consumption and Related Problems Worldwide: Authorship Analysis of Papers Indexed in PubMed and Scopus Databases (2005 to 2009)" *Alcoholism: clinical and experimental research* [pre-publication] [italics added]

> http://onlinelibrary.wiley.com/doi/10.1111/j.1530-0277.2012.01934.x/abstract

[132] Preventing Child Maltreatment (2006) World Health Organization and International Society for Prevention of Child Abuse and Neglect. Geneva, Switzerland. p.37

[133] *2012 World Drug Report,* United Nations Office on Drugs and Crime. Available at http://www.unodc.org/unodc/en/data-and-analysis/WDR-2012.html

[134] K. Fritz, "Namibian Community Unites to Curb Alcohol Use and HIV Risk in HIV and AIDS" May 2012. The International Center for Research on Women.

[135] U. Grittner, et al. "Alcohol and Alcoholism" alcalc.oxfordjournals.org *Alcohol and Alcoholism* (2012) doi: 10.1093/alcalc/ags040 First published online: April 27, 2012

[136] L. Gowing, R. Ali, S. Allsop, J. Marsden, E. Turf, R. West, and J. Witton, "Global statistics on addictive behaviours: 2014 status report" *Addiction,* Volume 110, Issue 6, pages 904–919, June 2015

[137] N. Freymond and G. Cameron, eds. (2006) Towards *Positive Systems of Child and Family Welfare: International Comparisons of Child Protection, Family Service, and Community Caring Systems.* University of Toronto Press, Toronto Canada. N. Gilbert,

N. Parton, and M. Skivenes, eds. (2011) *Child Protection Systems: International Trends and Orientations*. Oxford University Press, New York.

[138] Both quotes are from O. Bakke, D. Jernigan, C.Parry, (2011) Alcohol: a key determinant for ill health and an obstacle to development, a paper from the Global Alcohol Policy Alliance in response to the WHO call for papers: Health in the post-2015 development agenda. Citations for these sources include R.. Room, D. Jernigan, C.B. Carlini, O. Gureje, K. Mäkelä, M. Marshall, et al. (2002) *Alcohol in developing societies: a public health approach*. Helsinki and Geneva: Finnish Foundation for Alcohol Studies and World Health Organization; S.C. Kalichman, L.C. Simbayi, M. Kaufman, D. Cain, S. Jooste, (2007). Alcohol use and sexual risks for HIV/AIDS in sub-Saharan Africa: systematic review of empirical findings. *Prevention Science*, 8(2): 141-151; J.C. Fisher, (2007). The Association Between HIV Infection and Alcohol Use: A Systematic Review and Meta-Analysis of African Studies. *Sexually Transmitted Diseases*, 34 (11): 856-863.

[139] K. Shieldl, P. Shuper, G. Gmel, and J. Rehm, Global burden of HIV/AIDS in 2004 resulting from non-adherence to medication regimes and alcohol-attributable non-adherence to medication regimes. *International Journal of Drug and Alcohol Research* 2(1), 19–44.

[140] The Global Alcohol Policy Alliance (GAPA) is a developing network of non-government organizations and people working in public health agencies who share information on alcohol issues and advocate evidence-based alcohol policies. Resource centers affiliated to GAPA are already operating in the EU, U.S.A, South America, India, South East Asia and Western Pacific regions, and will soon be operational in Africa as well. Alliance, G. A. P. (2002). Declaration of the technical consultation to the WHO on the marketing and promotion of alcohol to young people. *The Globe: Drinking it in. WHO targets alcohol marketing*. Available at http://www.globalgapa.org/pdfs/Joint_NGO_Position_WHO_NCDs_Partnerships_Proposal_Final_June2012.pdf

[141] J. Sachs, (2005) *The End of Poverty*. Penguin Books, New York. 312

[142] W. Easterly, (2006) *The White Man's Burden: Why the West's Efforts to Aid the Rest Have Done So Much Ill and So Little Good*, Penguin Press, New York. Critiques of Easterly by Amartya Sen and Nicholas Kristoff can be found at http://swasthyamundial.com/2012/02/william-easterly-and-the-western-student-burden/.

[143] Lest a reader think this is Western hubris at work, it should be acknowledged that many recent critics of U.S. politics, including candidates in Republican primaries in 2012, have used the phrase "crony capitalism" to describe the very close relationships between legislators seeking finance and financial interests seeking legislators.

[144] K. Annan, "Stop the Plunder of Africa," *The New York Times*, May 9, 2013

[145] World Bank. 2000. *Helping countries combat corruption : progress at the World Bank since 1997*. Washington, D.C. : The World Bank.

http://documents.worldbank.org/curated/en/2000/06/828311/
helping-countries-combat-corruption-progress-world-bank-1997

[146] S. Rice, C. Graff, and C. Pascual, editors, (2010) *Confronting Poverty: Weak States and U.S. National Security.* The Brookings Institution. Washington, D.C. p 5-6

[147] R. Norton, "Feral Cities," *Naval War College Review* 66, no. 4 (Autumn 2003): p.98

[148] UNICEF (2011) *The State of the World's Children 2012: Children in an Urban World*, UNICEF, New York.

[149] D. Kilcullen,(2013) *Out of the Mountains*, Oxford University Press, Oxford, U.K.

[150] Accountabilityproject.org, (2014). *International Accountability Project.* [online] Available at: http://www.accountabilityproject.org [Accessed 25 Jun. 2014].

[151] P. Nampungu and D. Kasabiiti, (2012) The Impact of Involuntary Resettlement on children: A Case Study of the International Development Association Funded Bujagali Hydro-Power Dam, Naminya Resettlement Area. Bank Information Center. Udall, L. (1997). *The World Bank inspection panel: A three year review.* Bank Information Center. Available at http://www.bicusa.org/issues/resettlement/; http//www.bicusa.org/wp-content/uploads/ 2012/11/Naminya-Final-Report.pdf.

[152] P. Farmer, (2005) *Pathologies of Power: Health, Human Rights, and the New War on the Poor.* University of California Press, Berkeley, CA.

[153] Ibid 19-20.

[154] *Child Protection from Violence, Exploitation, and Abuse, Thematic Report 2011*, UNICEF. Available at http://www.unicef.org/protection/57929_58010.html p.35.

[155] P. Farmer, (2001) *Infections and Inequalities.* University of California Press, Berkeley, CA.

[156] An Baijie and Xiang Mingchao, "Youngsters may be left behind, but not forgotten," *China Daily*, May 31, 2012

[157] T. Piccone, (2012) *Catalysts for Change: How the UN's Independent Experts Promote Human Rights.* Brookings Institution, Washington, D.C.

CHAPTER SIX

[158] UNICEF uses a similar framework in describing child protection systems with some additional and some consolidated topics: 1) Laws, Policies, Standards and Regulations; 2). Cooperation, Coordination and Collaboration; 3). Capacity Building; 4). Service and Service Delivery Mechanisms; 5). Communication, Education and Mobilization for Change; 6). Financial Resources; and 7). Accountability Mechanisms [from "A Concept Note", op.cit.] The current paper emphasizes advocacy more directly, and also acknowledges the impact of trade, investment, and child survival and development programs on child protection issues.

[159] These are added because of the overwhelming evidence that hundreds of millions of children in China and India—and other nations as well—have been lifted above extreme poverty levels in the past decade due to the increase in higher-paying manufacturing and services employment as a result of expanded trade and foreign investment. The extent to which child labor and other child protection issues are affected negatively by these changes should not be overlooked, but the consensus is strong that trade and investment—at amounts much greater than current levels of foreign assistance (one source estimates total foreign assistance at only 13% of total world trade with developing nations)—have reduced child and family poverty among some of the poorest of the world's population. To the extent that these reductions have positive effects on child maltreatment, these approaches belong on a list of strategies to improve child protection outcomes.

[160] First Annual Report to Congress: USAID, December 2007, p.36.

[161] Interview, June 15, 2012.

[162] Piccone, op.cit.

[163] J. Heymann, with C. McNeill (2013) *Children's Chances, How Countries Can Move from Surviving to Thriving*, Harvard University Press, Cambridge, Massachusetts. p.88

[164] The UN agencies include UNICEF, UNESCO, the International Labor Organization, the World Health Organization, the Secretary-General's Representative for Violence Against Women, the UN Commissioner on Human Rights, the Human Rights Council, the UN Office on Drugs and Crime, and the UN Population Fund.

[165] Interaction.org, (2014). *InterAction Working Groups | InterAction*. [online] Available at: http://www.interaction.org/members/working-groups [Accessed 25 Jun. 2014].

[166] Cpclearningnetwork.org, (2014). *CPC Learning Network*. [online] Available at: http://www.cpclearningnetwork.org/ [Accessed 25 Jun. 2014].
   Crin.org, (2005). *Asian Legal Resource Centre | CRIN*. [online] Available at: http://www.crin.org/organisations/vieworg.asp?id=2336 [Accessed 25 Jun. 2014].

[167] www.cpcnetwork.org.

[168] Child Protection Working Group, (2014). *Child Protection Working Group - Global*. [online] Available at: http://cpwg.net/ [Accessed 25 Jun. 2014].

[169] "Collaboration within the United Nations system on child protection, Report of the Secretary-General"
   Available at http://daccess-dds-ny.un.org/doc/UNDOC/GEN/N13/415/29/ PDF/N1341529.pdf?OpenElement

[170] S. Gardner, (2005), "Time After Time" Available at www.cffutures.org

[171] E. Bardach, (1998) *Getting Agencies to Work Together*, The Brookings Institution, Washington, D.C.

[172] The trust side of the equation is more of a "soft power" ingredient, while the data accountability dimension is harder-edged. Some, including my wife, Dr. Nancy Young, have pointed out that there is a definite gender orientation to the skill sets required for each of these, and thus another form of collaboration is sometimes needed to bring both into play.

[173] L. Chandy, A. Hosono, H. Kharas, and J. Linn, (2012) *Getting to Scale*, The Brookings Institution, Washington D.C. p.30.

[174] Cdc.gov, (2014). *CDC - Implementation Science - What CDC is Doing - Global HIV/AIDS*. [online] Available at: http://www.cdc.gov/globalaids/What-CDC-is-Doing/implementation-science.html [Accessed 25 Jun. 2014].

[175] "Getting to Great for Children 2008-2012; Strategic Directions 2010 Refresh," (2010) Save the Children federation, Westport CT.

[176] Save the Children (2014). Available at http://www.savethechildren.org.uk/

[177] See for example Cffutures.org, (2014). *Collaborative Practice Tools | Children and Family Futures*. [online] Available at: http://www.cffutures.org/resources/collaborative-practice-tools [Accessed 25 Jun. 2014].

[178] Slow Progress in Closing Global Economic Gender Gap, New Major Study Finds | World Economic Forum, (2014). *Slow Progress in Closing Global Economic Gender Gap, New Major Study Finds*. [online] Available at: http://www.weforum.org/news/slow-progress-closing-global-economic-gender-gap-new-major-study-finds [Accessed 25 Jun. 2014].

[179] www.cpcnetwork.org

[180] UNICEF,(2013 Case studies on UNICEF programming in child protection. Available at http://www.unicef.org/protection/files/CP Case Studies Final.pdf

[181] N. Freymond and G. Cameron, eds. (2006) *Towards Positive Systems of Child and Family Welfare*, University of Toronto Press, Toronto, Canada.

[182] Oak Foundation, Plan, REPSSI, RIATT, Save the Children, Terres des Hommes, The African Child Policy Forum, UNICEF, World Vision, (2012). Available at http://www.unicef.org/wcaro/english/strengthening child protection systems in sub-Saharan Africa - August 2012 .pdf

[183] *One Million Community Health Workers* (2012) The Earth Institute, Columbia University, New York.

[184] S. Gardner and D. Nava, *Reforming the Human Services Workforce: The Role of Life-Experienced Workers,* (2006) The Annie E. Casey Foundation. Available at http://www.opensocietyfoundations.org/topics/rule-law

185 The thematic areas are young child survival and development, basic education and gender equality, HIV/AIDS and children, child protection from violence, exploitation, and abuse, and policy advocacy for children's rights. The Key Result Areas include better child protection systems, networks and dialogue on norms, protection of children from impacts of armed conflict and humanitarian crises, and improved country level monitoring and use of data on child protection. The vulnerable groups viewed as priorities are children affected by conflict, child labor, child sexual exploitation, and child trafficking. Child Protection from Violence, Exploitation, and Abuse, Thematic Report 2011, UNICEF.

186 UNICEF uses a rolling four-year budget, in which $1.776.5 billion is dedicated to child protection activities during the 2014-2017 period; if this were equally allocated to all four years (the budget indicates amounts are planned to rise during the four-year period), annual child protection expenditures during the four-year period would be $444 million. Annual expenditures in 2013 were $3.9 billion for all programs and administrative expenses. Available at http://www.unicef.org/about/execboard/files/2013-ABL4-Integrated_budget-ODS-English.pdf

187 http://www.cpcnetwork.org/apr-newsletter/

188 B. Woodhouse and K. Johnson, (2009) "The United Nations Convention on the Rights of the Child: Empowering Parents to Protect Their Children's Rights," in M. Fineman and K. Worthington, eds. (2009) *What is Right for Children? The Competing Paradigms of Religion and Human Rights.* Ashgate, Surrey, U.K. p.7

189 Wulczyn F, Daro D, Fluke J, Feldman S, Glodek C, Lifanda K, (2010) Adapting a systems approach to child protection: key concepts and considerations, UNICEF, UNHCR, Save the Children p.26

190 UNICEF, (2014). *Tools.* [online] Available at: http://www.unicef.org/protection/files/What_is_Child_Protection.pdf [Accessed 25 Jun. 2014].

191 R. Marcus. et al., (2011) *Progress in Child Well-being: Building on What Works.* Overseas Development Institute, London, U.K. p. 109.

192 A personal note: when you watch the extraordinary new film, *Girl Rising*, it is very difficult not to conclude that this arena is the most important child protection issue, with all its emotional power and its impact on many of the 16 UNICEF issues. I have two daughters, and I had the privilege of working with a young woman from China in the preparation of this book. Those experiences deepened my understanding of the importance of girls to the entire world. If it were not possible to work across the entire set of child protection issues, coordination of this critical segment of the agenda would still be a major step toward claiming more resources and using existing resources more effectively. But the child protection field still has a long way to go before reaching that level of coordination.

193 N. Kristoff and S. WuDunn, (2009) *Half the Sky.* Knopf, New York

[194] "Secretary's Policy Guidance on Promoting Gender Equality to Achieve our National Security and Foreign Policy Objectives," March 2012 U.S. Department of State. 1, p.4.

[195] *Progress for Children, A Report Card on Child Protection.* No. 8, September 2009 UNICEF, New York. p.7

[196] The 2009 Arab Human Development report on Human Security says "in societies where women are still bound by patriarchal patterns of kinship, legalized discrimination, social subordination and ingrained male dominance, women are continuously exposed to forms of family and institutionalized violence." *Challenges to Human Security in the Arab Countries*, UN Development Programme, (2009) p.79. http://www.arab-hdr.org/publications/contents/2009/ch4-e.pdf

[197] Unicef.org, (2014). *Basic education and gender equality | UNICEF.* [online] Available at: http://www.unicef.org/education/index.php [Accessed 25 Jun. 2014].

[198] These estimates have been questioned as too low by one reviewer of an early draft, who suggests that if the 16 UNICEF categories are used for comparisons, these totals should include U.S. expenditures for alternative care, kinship care, mental health services, gender-based educational outreach, and a portion of interagency efforts to deal with trafficking. If the point is conceded, and if it is relevant to other developed nations, it makes the larger point even more significant: international aid to child protection programs is dwarfed by internal spending at the national level, at least in the developed nations. Much less is known about spending by less developed nations in these categories, however.

[199] These estimates are obviously gross approximations at best. But no other similar estimates have been found in our literature review or interviews.

[200] *Child well-being in rich countries: a comparative overview.* UNICEF Innocenti Research Centre, Florence, Italy. 2013 Available at http://www.unicef-irc.org/publications/pdf/rc11_eng.pdf

[201] Heymann, op.cit. p.258.

[202] "Aid Statistics," One World. http://uk.oneworld.net/guides/aid Foundation and NGO estimate is for 2010. 28% of this aid is multilateral, consisting of contributions to UN agencies, the World Bank and other regional development banks. See also DAC data at http://www.oecd.org/dac/aidstatistics/50060310.pdf

[203] It is interesting to note that this point is made by UN Ambassador-designate Samantha Power in her 2008 biography of Sergio Vieira de Mello, *Chasing the Flame: One Man's Fight to Save the World.* (Penguin, New York).

[204] J. Kates et al. (2013) *Mapping the Donor Landscape in Global Health: HIV/AIDS,* Kaiser Family Foundation.

[205] C. Wang and J.Holton, (2007) "Total Estimated Cost of Child Abuse and Neglect in the United States," Prevent Child Abuse America, Chicago, Illinois. 2 UNICEF is currently supporting efforts to extend this analysis to global scale.

[206] This is roughly proportionate to the U.S. share of total global economic activity; it is much less than the rest-of-world proportionate share of the total maltreatment that is measurable by global indicators, i.e. 5 million children reported (not substantiated) for abuse and neglect annually in the U.S. vs. much larger numbers globally.

[207] "Latin America: Gini back in the bottle," The Economist, October 13, 2012. p.18.

[208] "Money is where your mouth is," *The Economist*, November 10, 2012. p.41-42.

[209] J Nye, (2005) *Soft Power*, Public Affairs: New York; J. Nye, (2011) *The Future of Power*, Public Affairs, New York.

[210] David Cortright and George A. Lopez, eds..(2002) *Smart Sanctions: Targeting Economic Statecraft*.
New York: Rowman & Littlefield.

[211] J. Katz, (2013) *The Big Truck That Went By: How the World Came to Save Haiti and Left Behind a Disaster*, Palgrave MacMillans University Press, New Brunswick, N.J., New York. D. Sontag, "In Reviving Haiti, Lofty Hopes and Hard Truths," *New York Times*, December 24, 2012.

[212] Quoted in Katz, op.cit. p.200.

[213] UNICEF, (2014). *In Haiti, improving care for children on the streets and in residential care.* [online] Available at: http://www.unicef.org/protection/haiti_61249.html [Accessed 25 Jun. 2014].

[214] S, Power, op.cit.

[215] G.G. Smale, (1996) *Mapping change and innovation*, National Institute for Social Work, London.

CHAPTER SEVEN

[216] C. Molina, (2011) "Defence centres for children and adolescents in Peru," in "Hidden violence: protecting young children at home," *Early Childhood Matters*, Bernard van Leer Foundation, The Hague, and The Netherlands. p.52-55.

[217] Violence Report, Bernhard van Leer Foundation, p.38, 59.

[218] M. Schuller, (2012) *Killing with Kindness: Haiti, International Aid, and NGOs.* Rutgers University Press, New Brunswick, N.J.

[219] H. Dubovitz and J. Merrick, eds., (2010) *International Aspects of Child Abuse and Neglect.* Nova Science Publishers: New York.

[220] B. Madrid, "Child Protection in the Phillipines," in Dubovitz and Merrick, op.cit. p.32

[221] A. Adefrsew and D. Mugawe, "Safeguarding Children: Child Protection Systems in Ethiopia, Kenya, Tanzania, and Uganda" in Dubobvitz and Merrick, op.cit. p.237

[222] Narayan, op.cit. p.251

[223] YouTube, (2014). *Girl Shot in Head by Taliban, Speaks at UN: Malala Yousafzai United Nations Speech 2013.* [online] Available at: http://www.youtube.com/watch?v=QRh_30C8l6Y [Accessed 25 Jun. 2014].

[224] www.GPCYP.com.

[225] D. Narayan, ed. (2009) *Moving Out of Poverty, Vol. 3: The Promise of Empowerment and Democracy in India.* Palgrave MacMillan and the World Bank. New York. p.53

[226] UNICEF 2014 "Every Child Counts"

[227] S.Coll, "Hard on Obama," *The New York Review of Books*, July 11, 2013. p.10

[228] UNICEF, (2014). *UNICEF's Corporate Partnerships | UNICEF's corporate partnerships | UNICEF.* [online] Available at: http://www.unicef.org/corporate_partners/index.html [Accessed 25 Jun. 2014].

[229] Unicef.org, (2014). *UNICEF - Corporate Social Responsibility -Home.* [online] Available at: http://www.unicef.org/csr/ [Accessed 25 Jun. 2014].

[230] Recent assessments of the impact of this policy have been undertaken by ODI, a UK-based policy research institute."The findings are being published, in part, in *World Development*, the top academic journal on international development, in the Commonwealth Economic Paper Series, a technical publication series, as well as in the *Trade Hot Topic*, a periodic publication by the Commonwealth Secretariat with a wide distribution among policy-makers and development practitioners...This research has become an important reference in the AfT debate, widely quoted by the World Bank, the International Monetary Fund, OECD, WTO and other bodies interested in the operationalisation of the AfT initiative." http://www.odi.org.uk/news/382-aid-trade

[231] Chandy et al, op.cit p.17.

[232] *International Trade Statistics, 2012*, WTO (2012) Geneva, Switzerland. Available at http://www.wto.org/english/res_e/statis_e/its2012_e/its2012_e.pdf

[233] Chandy et al., op.cit.

[234] J. Gettleman, "A New Wave of 'Lost Boys' in Sudan War, *New York Times*, July 1, 2012.

[235] Tripartite declaration of principles concerning multinational enterprises and social policy (MNE Declaration) - 4th Edition. Available at http://www.ilo.org/empent/Publications/WCMS_094386/lang--en/index.htm

[236] OECD Guidelines for Multinational Enterprises, (2011) OECD Publishing. Available at http://dx.doi.org/10.1787/9789264115415-en

[237] Children's Rights and Business Principles (2011), UNICEF, Save the Children and UN Global Compact. Available at http://www.unicef.org/csr/12.htm

[238] A. Neier, (2012) *The International Human Rights Movement.* Princeton University Press, Princeton, N.J. p.244

[239] J. Heymann, (2010) *Profit at the Bottom of the Ladder: Creating Value by Investing in Your Workforce* Harvard Business Review Press.

[240] Kristoff and WuDunn, op.cit. p.261.

[241] The principles can be found at http://business-humanrights.org/media/documents/quarterly-bulletin-business-and-children-jun-2013.pdf.

[242] M. Stack, "China raising a generation of left-behind children," September 29, 2010 *Los Angeles Times.*

[243] "Making a Hash of Finding the Cash," *The Economist,* May 11, 2013.

[244] Allison Stanger, "Hired Guns: How Private Military Contractors Undermine World Order," *Foreign Affairs* July/August 2015 163-169. A forthcoming, fictional companion volume to this book, titled *Five Paths*, envisions just such a security force—staffed entirely by women with military experience—charged with protecting women and children from trafficking in refugee camps.

[245] R. Morgan and S. O'Shea, (2012) "Locally-led monitoring as an engine for a more dynamic and accountable post 2015 development agenda," UNICEF. Available at http://www.unicef-irc.org/research-watch/Post-2015--What-Next-/903/

[246] Kristoff and WuDunn, op.cit. p.245

[247] "Annual report of the Executive Director of UNICEF: progress and achievements against the medium-term strategic plan," United Nations Children's Fund Executive Board Annual session 2012, 5-8 June 2012. p.10-11. Available at http://www.unicef.org/about/execboard/files/2012-10_Annual_Report_of_Executive_Director-ODS-English.pdf

[248] ENOC (2009). *The Best Interest of the Child.* Available at http://www.crin.org/docs/FileManager/enoc/enocreportconferenceagparis.pdf

[249] US Department of the Treasury (2014). *Resource Center.* Available at http://www.treasury.gov/resource-center/faqs/Sanctions/Pages/answer.aspx

[250] Official Google Blog, (2014). *Google Ideas: joining the fight against drug cartels and other illicit networks.* [online] Available at: http://googleblog.blogspot.com/2012/07/google-ideas-joining-fight-against-drug.html#!/2012/07/google-ideas-joining-fight-against-drug.html [Accessed 25 Jun. 2014].

[251] P. Meier, (2015) *Digital Humanitarians: How "Big Data" Is Changing the Face of Humanitarian Response,* Taylor and Francis Press.

252 Treasury.gov, (2014). *Frequently Asked Questions and Answers.* [online] Available at: http://www.treasury.gov/resource-center/faqs/Sanctions/Pages/answer.aspx#1 [Accessed 25 Jun. 2014].

253 M. Latonero, (2012). *The Rise of Mobile and the Diffusion of Technology-Facilitated Trafficking.*
Annenberg Center on Communication Leadership & Policy, University of Southern California, Los Angeles.

254 Ibid. p.21.

255 N. Kristoff, "Doughnuts Defeating Poverty," *New York Times,* July 4, 2012.

256 Foundation on Innovative Social Development (2012). Available at http://www.fisd.lk/our-programmes/alcohol-drugs-a-development.html

257 Classifying substance use disorders and co-occurring mental illness as "non-communicable," however, overlooks the extent to which these disorders can be contracted within families through prenatal exposure, genetic predisposition, and family instability. Substance abuse is a family disease, and family-oriented treatment has produced some of the best results in reducing its effects. It should also be noted that the Adverse Childhood Experiences research by Anda, Feletti and associates found substance abuse in the family to be the second most frequent adverse experience of ten that were surveyed. International data on increasing alcohol use as families raise incomes is a further basis for more attention to these NCDs, which are not emphasized in the WHO action plan.

258 ICAP (2012). *Media Advisory.* Available at http://icap.org/LinkClick.aspx?fileticket=s9C4wdxxVYk%3d&tabid=36

259 J. McCambridge, "Dealing Responsibly with the Alcohol Industry in London," *Alcohol and Alcoholism*, Advance Access, published October 2, 2012. "Paying the Piper: The Effect of Industry Funding on Alcohol Prevention Priorities" (1996) Alcohol Policies Project, Center for Science in the Public Interest. Available at http://www.cspinet.org/booze/ppstudy.html

260 Ias.org.uk, (2014). *IAS.* [online] Available at:
http://www.ias.org.uk/resources/publications/theglobe/globe201202/gl201202_p3.html [Accessed 25 Jun. 2014].
Implementationscience.com, (2014). *Implementation Science.* [online] Available at: http://www.implementationscience.com/ [Accessed 25 Jun. 2014].

261 O. Bakke and D. EndaL "Vested Interests in Addiction Research and Policy Alcohol policies out of context: drinks industry supplanting government role in alcohol policies in sub-Saharan Africa." *Addiction.* 2010 January; 105(1): 22–28.

262 Who.int, (2014). *WHO | Management of substance abuse.* [online] Available at: http://www.who.int/substance_abuse/en/index.html [Accessed 25 Jun. 2014].

263 N. Gilbert, N. Parton, and M Skivenes, (2011) *Child Protection Systems: International Trends and Orientations.* Oxford University Press, New York. p.252-255.

264 *Children in institutions: The beginning of the end?* (2003) UNICEF, The Innocenti Research Centre. Florence, Italy. 6

265 Adoption.state.gov, (2011). *Intercountry Adoption.* [online] Available at: http://adoption.state.gov/about_U.S./statistics.php [Accessed 25 Jun. 2014].

266 Childinfo.org, (2014). *Childinfo.org: Statistics by Area - HIV/AIDS - Orphan Estimates.* [online] Available at: http://www.childinfo.org/hiv_aids_orphanestimates.php [Accessed 25 Jun. 2014].

267 M. Mason, "International Adoptions: Number is at Lowest in 15 Years." Associated Press, May 10, 2012.

268 R. Swarns, "A Family, for a Few Days a Year" New *York Times*, December 9, 2012.

269 K. Joyce, (2013) *The Child Catchers: Rescue, Trafficking, and the New Gospel of Adoption.* Public Affairs, New York.

270 D. Smolin.(2012) "Of Orphans and Adoption Parents and the Poor, Exploitation and Rescue: A Scriptural and Theological Critique of the Evangelical Christian Adoption and Orphan Care Movement." *Regent Journal of International Law* 8.2.

271 Joyce, op. cit, p.25-257.

272 Perhaps full disclosure requires indicating that the author and his wife are adoptive parents of two special needs children through the public child welfare system in California.

273 Crin.org, (2013). *UN: Historic Declaration adopted to combat violence against women | CRIN.* [online] Available at: http://www.crin.org/resources/infodetail.asp?id=30542 [Accessed 25 Jun. 2014].

274 Crin.org, (2013). *UN: Historic Declaration adopted to combat violence against women | CRIN.* [online] Available at: http://www.crin.org/resources/infodetail.asp?id=30542 [Accessed 25 Jun. 2014].

275 Crin.org, (2013). *UN: Historic Declaration adopted to combat violence against women | CRIN.* [online] Available at: http://www.crin.org/docs/List_rejected_recommendations_UPR.pdf [Accessed 25 Jun. 2014].

276 Crin.org, (2014). *CRC in Court: Case Law Database | CRIN.* [online] Available at: http://www.crin.org/law/crc_in_court/ [Accessed 25 Jun. 2014].

277 P. Geary, (2012). CRC *in Court: The Case Law of the Convention on the Rights of the Child. The Child Rights International Network*, London, U.K. Crin.org, (2013). *UNIVERSAL PERIODIC REVIEW: Information and Advocacy Opportunities | CRIN.* [online] Available at: http://www.crin.org/resources/infoDetail.asp?ID=22015&flag=report#qn [Accessed 25 Jun. 2014].

[278] This is, of course, a remarkable comment from the product of a continent whose own tribes, sects, nations, and religions spent much of the past two thousand years trying to kill each other.

[279] S. Wurtele and C. Miller-Perrin, "Global efforts to prevent sexual exploitation of minors," in *World Perspectives on Child Abuse*, Tenth edition, International Society for the Prevention of Child Abuse and Neglect, 2012, Aurora, CO. p.86.

[280] Martindale.com, (2014). *United States Supreme Court Decides Question of Corporate Liability Under Alien Tort Statute On Broader Grounds ? Martindale.com.* [online] Available at: http://www.martindale.com/corporate-law/article_Sheppard-Mullin-Richter-Hampton-LLP_1776208.htm [Accessed 25 Jun. 2014].

[281] J. Kyl, D. Feith, and J. Fonte, "The War of Law," *Foreign Affairs*. July-August 2013. p.115-125.

[282] D. Kaye, "Stealth Multilateralism: U.S. Foreign Policy Without Treaties—or the Senate," *Foreign Affairs* September/October 2013, p.116-124.

[283] Responsibilitytoprotect.org, (2014). *Core Documents.* [online] Available at: http://www.responsibilitytoprotect.org/index.php/publications [Accessed 25 Jun. 2014]. ; Globalr2p.org, (2014). *Global Centre for the Responsibility to Protect.* [online] Available at: http://www.globalr2p.org/ [Accessed 25 Jun. 2014].

[284] US Department of State (2014). *Secretary Clinton on International Anticorruption Day.* Available at http://www.state.gov/secretary/rm/2011/12/178568.htm

[285] Sahara Reporters (2014). *News.* Available at http://saharareporters.com/news-page/U.S.-government-dismisses-nigeria%E2%80%99s-war-against-corruption-hot-air

[286] Global Integrity (2014) *The Global Integrity Report 2011.* Available at http://report.globalintegrity.org/globalIndex.cfm

[287] The World Bank (2000). *Helping Countries Combat Corruption.* Available at http://web.worldbank.org/WBSITE/EXTERNAL/TOPICS/EXTPUBLICSECTORANDGOVERNANCE/EXTANTICORRUPTION/0,,contentMDK:20222111~menuPK:384473~pagePK:148956~piPK:216618~theSitePK:384455,00.html "The World Bank has increasingly made this a priority in its work through a four-pronged approach, namely by assisting countries in fighting corruption, mainstreaming corruption concerns in their operations, preventing corruption in World Bank projects and by supporting international efforts to combat corruption."

[288] Sonia Faleiro, "For India's Children, Philanthropy Isn't Enough," *New York Times*, September 16, 2012, SR4; Tyler Cowen, "World Hunger: The Problem Left Behind," *New York Times*, September 16, 2012, SR6.

[289] M. Wessels, (2010), What are we learning about protecting children in the community? An interagency review of the evidence on community based child

protection mechanisms in humanitarian and development settings, Save the Children. (Summary); United Nations Committee on the Rights of the Child, "General measures of implementation of the Convention on the Rights of the Child," 2003. N. Jones and A. Sumner, (2011) *Child Poverty, Evidence, and Policy*, The Policy Press, Bristol, U.K.

[290] Boothby, Stark, Simmons, and Chu, (2009) Child *Protection Information Management Mapping: Towards a Data Surveillance System in Indonesia.* UNICEF

[291] Lancaster, op.cit. p.52.

[292] A fascinating book on evaluation of microcredit as a strategy for reducing poverty repeatedly referred to the findings that men tend to do better in microcredit schemes than women—without ever linking this to references throughout the book to husbands drinking up the profits of microloans! (It should be noted, obviously, that these dynamics operate in developed nations as well.) The power relationships in families and the addictions and habits of men who confiscate their wives' earnings has a powerful echo at the intersection between antipoverty strategies and gender equity. But it would appear that the boundaries between behavioral economics and behavioral health are patrolled as actively as those between other disciplines. (It should be noted, in fairness, that an experiment with smoking cessation was discussed in the book.) D. Karlan and J Appel, (2012) *More Than Good Intentions*, Plume, New York.

[293] Wessels, op. cit.

[294] Ibid. 209.

[295] L. Schorr, Broader Evidence for Bigger Impact," Stanford *Social Innovation Review*, Fall 2012 p.50-55.

[296] *Progress for Children: Achieving the MDGs with Equity*, No. 9. UNICEF September 2010. p. 7.

[297] A. Sheeran, (2008) "UNICEF Child Protection Meta-Evaluation," UNICEF, New York.

[298] Ibid. p.34.

[299] Z. De Sa Kropiwincki, (2012) 2012 Global: Protecting Children from Violence: A Synthesis of Evaluation Findings, UNICEF New York.

[300] Chandy et al. op.cit. p.13.

CHAPTER EIGHT

[301] A more recent compilation, using different methods, was included in the 7th Annual Report to Congress by the USAID office. This total was $463 million, described as aimed at Action Plan for Children in Adversity (APCA)-related work. The submission also stated that a US contribution of $17 million in FY 2013 was

allocated to support child protection efforts in 15 conflict- and disaster-affected countries.

[302] UNICEF (2013). Annual Report. p, 15. Additional funds were allocated from unrestricted sources for improved monitoring of child protection problems, including children affected by armed conflict.

[303] The opposition of a vocal minority in the U.S. to UN enactments was demonstrated in early December 2012 by the defeat in the Senate of the ratification of the UN Convention on the Rights of Persons with Disabilities. The Convention, which is based on the Americans with Disabilities Act, was opposed in part due to language about the best interests of the child. That language was seen by opponents of ratification as supporting possible legal action against parents who choose to home-school children with disabilities—despite language in the ratification legislation that would have forbidden using the treaty as precedent in court cases. J. Steinhauer, "Dole Appears, But G.O.P Rejects a Disabilities Treaty, *New York Times*, December 5, 2012, A19.

[304] In Haiti, 2 1/2 years after the 2010 earthquake, nearly 400,000 persons are still homeless.

[305] UNICEF, (2014). *UNICEF IRC major publications 2010*. [online] Unicef-irc. org. Available at: http://www.unicef-irc.org/publications/forthcoming/ [Accessed 25 Jun. 2014].

[306] Women and the Economics of Equality," *Harvard Business Review*, April 2013. p.30-31

[307] Heymann, op. cit.

[308] Comments at USAID CECA/CPC Network panel discussion, June 15, 2015.

[309] Easterly, op. cit.

"In a hearing before the U.S. Senate Committee on Foreign Relations in May 2004, Jeffrey Winters, a professor at Northwestern University, argued that the World Bank had participated in the corruption of roughly $100 billion of its loan funds intended for development."

Dambisa Moyo, *Wall Street Journal*, March 21, 2009, "Why Foreign Aid Is Hurting Africa" http://online.wsj.com/article/SB123758895999200083.html. Dambisa Moyo, a former economist at Goldman Sachs, is the author of *Dead Aid: Why Aid Is Not Working and How There Is a Better Way for Africa*.

A. Alesina and B. Weder (1999) National Bureau of Economic Research, "Do Corrupt Governments Receive Less Foreign Aid?" (NBER Working Paper No. 7108),"The United States...stands out for giving more aid to more corrupt governments, other things equal." Available at http://www.nber.org/digest/nov99/w7108.html

Ben Quinn, The Guardian, November 21, 2011, "UK aid programme open to corruption and fraud, report warns" "Aid to fragile but corrupt countries should be conditional, a committee of MPs has said, amid concerns that taxpayers' money is being U.S.ed to prop-up corrupt regimes. The International Development Committee said countries that flout agreements or refuse to become accountable should have their aid withdrawn. The warning comes as the Department for International Development (DFiD) prepare to spend 30% of their budget on projects in fragile states."

[310] Foundation, T. (2014). [online] Trust.org. Available at: http://www.trust.org/alertnet/blogs/technotalk/will-twitter-put-the-un-out-of-the-disaster-business/ [Accessed 25 Jun. 2014].

[311] "Humanitarian Aid and Social Media: Possibilities and Considerations" European Interagency Security Forum. May 16, 2012. S. (2014). *Humanitarian Aid and Social Media: Possibilities and Considerations | Alerts | EISF.* [online] Eisf.eu. Available at: http://www.eisf.eu/alerts/item.asp?n=15275 [Accessed 25 Jun. 2014].

[312] The author once had the occasion to visit an orphanage in Saigon sponsored by an international NGO to which he was then contributing. A picture taken with his "sponsee" was a prized possession, proof of "making a difference." Forty-four years later, it is impossible to know, except by taking it on faith, that a difference was really made. The Hunger Site, (2014). *Click every day to give food for the hungry..* [online] Available at: http://www.thehungersite.com [Accessed 25 Jun. 2014].

[313] J. Shiffman, S. Smith. 2007. Generation of political priority for global health initiatives: a framework and case study of maternal mortality. *Lancet* 370: 1370-79. C. Heath and D. Heath, (2007) Made *to Stick, Why Some Ideas Survive and Others Die*, Random House, New York.

[314] Yet responses to these spotlights can still be very narrow in impact. One U.S. official pointed to a one-time congressional appropriation restricted to Rwanda and the child soldiers issue as the only serious congressional response to the advocacy triggered by the Kony video.

[315] In the following chapter we discuss more positive developments on recent appropriations and presidential requests for foreign assistance changes.

[316] Endslaveryandtrafficking.org, (2014). *TVPRA Funding Success: The Child Protection Compact Act | ATEST.* [online] Available at: http://www.endslaveryandtrafficking.org/tvpra-funding-success-child-protection-compact-act#sthash.LLaPd42B.dpuf [Accessed 25 Jun. 2014].

[317] Speculation about former Secretary Clinton's future efforts after leaving the State Department has included a continuing role in girls and women's programs, which could give added impetus to that approach to priority-setting and coordination.

[318] These funds peaked at $240 million in the 2000 campaign, dropping to $139 million in the 2008 campaign when both candidates refused the funding.

CHAPTER NINE

[319] D. Rieff, (2002) *A Bed for the Night*, Simon and Schuster, New York. 235-6 Rieff's provocative book is about humanitarian assistance, but is focused primarily upon its impact in war zones, rather than in broader terms; it does not discuss child protection as such.

[320] "USAID Policy on Gender Equality and Female Empowerment," March 2012.

[321] These include The Secretary-General's appointment of a Special Rapporteur on violence against women and the issuance in August 2009 of the Secretary-General's Report to the General Assembly on "The Girl Child."

[322] Fifth Annual Report to Congress on Public Law 109-95, USAID, 2012. The Fifth Annual Report to Congress explains the definitional issue as follows: "Though the term "vulnerability" can be defined in many ways, the methodology merges various. Pre-existing vulnerability indicators into a single index, creating a rating scale that makes it easier to understand the magnitude of vulnerability in a given location and compare it to other geographical areas."

[323] Ibid, 35, 36.

[324] R. Clay, et al. "A call for coordinated and evidence-based action to protect children outside of family care, *Lancet*, Published Online December 12, 2011 DOI:10.1016/S0140-6736(11)61821-7.

[325] Children in Adversity Updates, (2014). *U.S. Government Assistance for Children in Adversity Updates*. [online] Available at: http://content.govdelivery.com/bulletins/gd/USAIDHVC-3f19aa [Accessed 25 Jun. 2014].

[326] D. Zakheim, (2011) *A Vulcan's Tale*, The Brookings Institution, Washington, D.C.

[327] http://www.oecd.org/dac/stats/

[328] Michael Hiltzik, "More than charity needed," *Los Angeles Times*, March 30, 2014, B1, citing a study by Indiana University.

[329] S. Greenhouse and J, Yardley, "Despite Safety Vows, Walmart is seen as Obstacle," *New York Times*, December 29, 2012. While this article deals with overall safety standards in foreign factories, it refers to standards that include child labor issues.

[330] Kaiser Family Foundation Global Health (2013). Available at http://globalhealth.kff.org/

[331] F. Kaplan, (2013) *The Insurgents*, Simon and Schuster. New York.

[332] Modernizeaid.net, (2014). *Modernizing Foreign Assistance Network*. [online] Available at: http://www.modernizeaid.net/ [Accessed 25 Jun. 2014].

[333] For context, the UK contribution was $332 million; Japan's was $321 million, and Sweden's was $248. These were the top four nations in contributions to UNICEF.

[334] The three "principal objectives" are Build strong beginnings, Put family care first, and Protect children; the three "supporting objectives" are Strengthen systems, Promote evidence-based programs, and Integrate within the U.S. government.

[335] Fifth Annual Report to Congress on Public Law 109-95, USAID, 2012. These include the President's Global Development Policy; the Quadrennial Diplomacy and Development Review; the National Action Plan on Women, Peace and Security; the U.S. Strategy to Prevent and Respond to Gender-Based Violence Globally; USAID's Education Strategy and its Counter Trafficking in Persons Policy; the State Department's Youth Policy; and the forthcoming USAID Policy on Youth In Development. *Action Plan*, 21

[336] USAID Annual Report to Congress "The US Government Action Plan on Children in Adversity," October 2014. P. 9

[337] These staffing allocations are supplemented in part by interns available from local universities.

[338] http://www.globalallianceforchildren.org/challenges/

[339] R. Marcus. et al., (2011*) Progress in Child Well-being: Building on What Works*. Overseas Development Institute, London, U.K.

CHAPTER TEN

[340] Ibid., 108. Citing S. Lilley et al. (2011) *Too little, too late: child protection funding in emergencies*. Global Protection cluster on child protection funding in emergencies.

[341] The U.S. remains the only nation that has not ratified the Convention on the Rights of the Child; it has signed protocols associated with the Convention, but has not ratified the Convention itself. Advocates for child rights view this as a major handicap affecting U.S.-based efforts to advocate for improved child protection systems in other nations.

[342] M. Robinson, as quoted in Kristoff and WuDunn, op.cit p. 229.

[343] S. Bissell, et al. "UNICEF's approach to preventing violence at home," in *Hidden Violence: Protecting Young Children at Home, Early Childhood Matters*, June 2011, Bernard van Leer Foundation, The Hague, The Netherlands.

[344] *Child Rights and Governance Roundtable: Report and Conclusions*, (2011) UNICEF, London. iii.

[345] T. Smedley, "Shifting sands: the changing landscape for international NGOs" *The Guardian*, March 28, 2014.
   http://www.theguardian.com/global-development-professionals-network/2014/mar/28/internaitonal-ngos-funding-network

[346] Ibid.

[347] http://degrees.fhi360.org/2014/02/is-there-a-future-for-international-ngos-in-the-21ˢᵗ-century

[348] http://www.fsg.org/downloads?file=7121&nid=5476&cmpn=7017000000129q2AAA

[349] "The Global Conversation Begins," United Nations Development Group, 2012.

[350] Unicef.org, (2014). | *UNICEF*. [online] http://www.unicef.org/about/execboard/files/u nicef-executive-director-statement-4feb2014.pdf

[351] J. Sachs, "The End of Poverty, Soon," New *York Times* September 24, 2013.

APPENDIX

[352] This section has been prepared in part by Selia Wang, a student who graduated from SIAS University in China in June 2013, and who participated in the research for this book, including translation of materials from sources in China.

[353] Loc.gov, (2014). *Children's Rights: China | Law Library of Congress*. [online] Available at: http://www.loc.gov/law/help/child-rights/china.php [Accessed 25 Jun. 2014].

[354] China.or.co (2014). *Child Welfare needs legislative backup.* Available at http://www.china.org.cn/china/2010-12/06/content_21489516.htm

[355] Wenku.baidu.com, (2014). [online] Available at: http://wenku.baidu.com/view/a0f1bd6c011ca300a6c390cd.html [Accessed 25 Jun. 2014]. (translated)

[356] Crin.org, (2011). *International Criminal Court (ICC) | CRIN*. [online] Available at: http://www.crin.org/resources/infoDetail.asp?ID=18048&flag=report [Accessed 25 Jun. 2014].

[357] UNICEF (2014). *China*. Available at: http://www.unicefchina.org/en/index.php?m=content&c=index&a=lists&catid=33

[358] Kirsten Di Martino, child rights chief of UNICEF in China at Forum on Child Welfare and Child Protection at One Foundation Philanthropy Research Institute, Beijing Normal University. Available at http://www.china.org.cn/china/2010-12/06/content_21489516.htm

[359] This section has been prepared in part by Selia Wang, a student who graduated from SIAS University in China in June 2013, and who participated in the research for this book, including translation of materials from sources in China.

[360] Zhonglin Chen. (2011). "The Development and Reflection of Child Protection in China," Available at http://www.socialwork.hku.hk/eventfiles/201106/29/download.htm (translated)

[361] Womenofchina.cn, (2014). *Sexual Abuse of Left-behind Children Arouse Attention - All China Women's Federation*. [online] Available at: http://www.womenofchina.cn/html/womenofchina/report/142923-1.htm [Accessed 25 Jun. 2014].

362 Michael P. Dunne, Jing Qi Chen and Wan Yuen Choo. (2008). *Asia Pacific Journal of Public Health*[8] "The Evolving Evidence Base for Child Protection in Chinese Societies," Available at http://aph.sagepub.com/content/20/4/

363 D. (2014). *Child sexual abuse 'disturbingly common' in India | Asia | DW.DE | 13.02.2013.* [online] DW.DE. Available at: http://www.dw.de/child-sexual-abuse-disturbingly-common-in-india/a-16596565 [Accessed 25 Jun. 2014].

364 A perspective by CHILDLINE India Foundation, (2009). Available at www.childlineindia.org

365 Childlineindia.org.in, (2014). *Child Rights in India. Child in India Statistics and Children in India.* [online] Available at: http://www.childlineindia.org.in/child-in-india.htm [Accessed 25 Jun. 2014].

366 Wcd.nic.in, (2014). *Ministry of Women & Child Development, Govt. of India.* [online] Available at: http://wcd.nic.in/ [Accessed 25 Jun. 2014].

   http://wcd.nic.in/childact/ReportChildMarriage.pdf

367 Report of the Working Group on Child Rights, 2012. Available at http://wcd.nic.in/

368 Ministry of Women and Child Development, Government of India, "Integrated Child Protection Scheme."

369 The National Policy for Children, Available at http://wcd.nic.in/

370 Gender Budgeting, Available at http://wcd.nic.in/

371 Unicef.org, (2014). *UNICEF India - Child protection - Child Protection.* [online] Available at: http://www.unicef.org/india/child_protection.html [Accessed 25 Jun. 2014].

372 H. Timmons, "Child Sexual Abuse Rampant and Untreated in India, Report Says," *New York Times*, February 7, 2013.

373 Shiree@work, (2010). *Dowry and Poverty are two sides of a coin- by Saidur Rahman.* [online] Available at: http://shiree-blog.org/2010/03/30/dowry-and-poverty-are-two-sides-of-a-coin-by-saidur-rahman/ [Accessed 25 Jun. 2014].

374 CEDAW Initial Report: India. United Nations. Available at http://www.womenchangemakers.net/resources/governance/316-initial-status-report-on-cedaw-by-india

375 A. Sen, "India's Women: The Mixed Truth." *New York Review of Books*, October 10, 2013. p.26.

376 Working Group, op.cit 27.

377 S. Deb, "Child Protection: Scenario in India," in H. Dubovitz, J. Merrick, (2010) *International Aspects of Child Abuse and Neglect,* Nova Science Publishing, New York. 11-23.

www.ingramcontent.com/pod-product-compliance
Lightning Source LLC
Chambersburg PA
CBHW020732180526
45163CB00001B/208